Passports to
College Success

Passports to College Success

R. Scott Baldwin
Elinore Kress Schatz
Arlene Soffer Weiss

University of Miami

Kendall/Hunt
Publishing Company
Dubuque, Iowa

Printed in the United States of America

Contents

Passports to
College Success

1
How to Use *Passports*

Now that you are in college you may feel bombarded by masses of classes, hordes of reading materials, and swarms of writing assignments. *Passports to College Success* will show you how to cut your way through this confusion. It will help you to:

- Read faster
- Improve your notetaking
- Tune-in to your instructors
- Conquer your textbooks
- Understand difficult words
- Improve your reading comprehension
- Recognize when you are being manipulated with words
- Raise your test scores
- Locate and use the resources of your college library

What's First?

Probably the first thing you did when you bought this book—after checking the price—was turn to the page you are now reading. That was a mistake! There are a few things you should do before starting to read the first chapter of this book, or any book. First, look at the title, *Passports to College Success*. What does this title bring to mind? Perhaps you would like to know what a passport has to do with being successful in college. Think of two other questions the title of this book brings to mind and write them here.

1. _____

2. _____

Now turn to the "title page" at the very front of the book. You see that this book has three authors. Therefore, the book represents the combined efforts of three individuals. Notice the publication date of 1985. If you are not aware of a book's copyright, you might find yourself reading a book that is badly out-of-date. In the sciences, for example, the copyright date of a book is very important because new scientific breakthroughs occur so rapidly.

Next, turn to the back of the book. Notice that the book has a *glossary* on page 187, an *index* on page 191, and several *appendices* that begin on page 149. A special feature of this book is that it has its own mini–dictionary. You may be wondering why this book contains a dictionary. The answer is in Chapter 5.

Now turn to the "Table of Contents" on page v for an overview of *Passports*. Notice the various topics that are covered. Place a checkmark in front of the topics which you feel will be most helpful. Then spend a few moments thumbing through those chapters. In the space provided below write three thoughts that come to mind as you look through the book.

1. _____

2. _____

3. _____

Now turn to Chapter 3, "How to Take Good Notes," which begins on page 25. As you can see, the chapter opens with thought-provoking statements with which you are asked to agree or disagree. This is called an *anticipation guide*. You will find one at the beginning of each chapter. The purpose of the *anticipation guide* is to get you thinking about the topic at hand.

On page 31 of Chapter 3 we have highlighted important research facts about listening and note-taking. The information in *Passports* isn't just a reflection of our professional judgment; it is also based on the most current research findings. Look for the highlighted research boxes in the other chapters as well.

One of the major purposes of this book is to give you strategies for coping with the demands of the college classroom. The notetaking strategy on pages 26–28 of Chapter 3 is an example of this.

Passports includes many selections taken directly from college textbooks like the ones you are probably using in other courses right now. Some of the selections will be easy to read; others will be more difficult. In any event, the materials have been included because they are typical of college reading.

Throughout the text we have included activities that are designed to help you take the information in this book and apply it in the dorm, library, and lecture hall. We call this a *content-area* approach to reading. Content-area reading skills are those that help you to learn more effectively in subject-area classes.

We have "walked through" *Passports* to give you an overview of the text and to familiarize you with some of its features. Your next step is to dive right into the information and strategies that should make your college career more successful.

2
How to Increase Your Reading Rate

What Do You Believe about Speed Reading?

Directions: Read each of the statements below. Place a checkmark on the line in front of each statement you believe is true.

1. _____ It is not possible to read 5000 words per minute.

2. _____ A good reader almost always reads at the same high rate of speed.

3. _____ A speed reader can read lines of print just by looking down the middle of the page.

4. _____ You can learn to read faster by having your eye movements trained.

5. _____ If you increase your reading rate from 200 words per minute to 300 words per minute, you will lose half of your comprehension.

Speed reading is an exciting topic. Everyone wants to know just what is and what is not possible in speed reading. This chapter will give you that information and will also show you how you can improve your own reading speed and efficiency.

> "I took a course in speed reading and read *War and Peace* in two minutes. It's about Russia."
>
> Woody Allen

How Fast Do You Read?

How fast do you read—250, 350, 2000 words per minute? If you think you have an answer to that question, let us ask you one more. Would you read an article in *Sports Illustrated,* a Spiderman comic book, a stock market report, and a textbook on computer programming all at the same rate?

Yes _____

No _____

If your answer to this question was yes, then you are probably an inefficient reader because you do not adjust your speed to suit the difficulty and importance of what you read. On the other hand, if you do adjust your rate, it should be obvious that our original question doesn't make much sense. How fast you read should depend upon what you are reading and why you are reading it.

There are four types of reading:

1. *Careful Reading.* This is the slowest kind of reading, ranging from 50 to 350 words per minute. Careful reading normally is used to master difficult material and to solve problems. You generally use this style of reading when you are going to be tested on material you are reading.

2. *Rapid Reading.* This style is used when the material is not too difficult or when you don't have to remember large amounts of information from the text. The rate ranges from 300 to 600 words per minute.

3. *Skimming.* This kind of reading allows you to read very fast by sacrificing detail. In other words, when you skim, you skip some of the material. The purpose of skimming is to gain the general idea of the material or to review something which you have read before. With practice you can learn to skim efficiently at rates as high as 1500 words per minute.

5

4. *Scanning.* This the fastest type of reading, but it also provides the least amount of information about the material read. Scanning is what we do when we search for specific information such as numbers, dates, or names in a telephone book. People can learn to scan 3000 words per minute.

Speed Reading: Rip Through or Rip Off?

LEARN TO READ 3, 5, 10 TIMES FASTER!
SEE HOW YOU CAN READ AS FAST AS
YOU CAN TURN PAGES, AND WITH
BETTER COMPREHENSION!!!
REDUCE YOUR STUDY TIME BY 50%!
COME TO OUR FREE INTRODUCTORY LESSON
INCREASE YOUR READING RATE BY 100%
TODAY!!

Sounds fantastic, doesn't it? And because it does appear so attractive, many people often wind up paying as much as $1000 for speed reading courses.

As an unlucky undergraduate, one of the authors of this book enrolled in a speed reading course. The advertisement for the course stated that all of the speed reading instructors were certified teachers. In this case, the instructor was a high school football coach who had never taken a college course in reading. As the course progressed it became somewhat questionable as to whether or not the coach could read.

The class was given a pep talk and simple reading materials. Instruction consisted of timed drills. As the class read, the coach charged around the room beating a stick against the walls and shouting to read faster and faster. Each time the coach struck a blow for reading improvement, the students were supposed to have reached the end of a line of print. This forced-paced drill seemed rational until we were told to begin reading more than one line of print at a time, first forwards, then backwards! By the end of the course, the entire class could "read" left to right and then right to left, five lines at a clip.

This kind of nonsense is standard procedure for commercial speed reading outfits. To give you an idea of what it is like to read five lines of print backwards at the same time, read the following passage. You have one second to complete the task, and you must read all of the lines at the same time from left to right.

,output productive his from returns maximize To
point the find to has manager business a
between difference the which at curve revenue his on
,labor, capital of costs total and revenue total
.greatest is factors productive other and

Fisk, G. *Marketing Systems: An Introductory Analysis.* New
York: Harper and Row, 1967.

Well, how did you do? Not very well, we imagine. The passage will make some sense to you if you read it from right to left and one line at a time.

It might interest you to know that if you read the passage above in one second, you read at a rate of about 2000 words per minute. There is one major drawback to reading more than one line at a time and with reading right to left. The problem is that English is a word-order language. It isn't enough to see words in print; words must also be processed in order, left to right. This is clearly impossible if lines of print are processed in reverse; under those conditions, the result can only be a profound garbling of grammar and thought. For the same reason, the authors' intended meanings will also escape your understanding if you attempt to read more than one line of print at a time. Furthermore, the physical limitations of the human eye make it quite impossible to focus on five lines of words at one time and still see the words clearly enough to read them.

The final examination in the speed reading course required the students to read an entire novel in fifteen minutes and with good comprehension. To accomplish this silly task, the class was forced to read more than 2000 words per minute. With great difficulty and some frustration, most of the people in the class fumbled through to the end of the book in the time allowed and scored well on the ten-question multiple-choice comprehension test which followed. Unfortunately, the test was phony.

Before reading the novel the class was told to carefully read the description on the inside cover. The book was a paperback western written at a fourth-grade reading level. The comprehension questions were so general that the description on the book's jacket and a quick peek at the cover were enough to answer most of the questions. For example, the picture on the front cover was of a cowboy riding a horse across a prairie. Question number one on the comprehension test was:

Where did the story take place?
(a) The Antarctic
(b) France
(c) China
(d) The American West

The other questions were equally mindless and insulting. Yet there were people who, after paying $300 for the course, believed they had learned to read thousands of words a minute. In reality, a group of people paid a lot of money for some very poor skimming and scanning instruction.

On another occasion one of the authors took two college students to a different speed reading academy for a free mini lesson. Each took a book along. The books included an advanced linguistics text, a novel by James Joyce, and an introductory text on matrix algebra. The representative of the speed reading academy informed the class that each person could learn to read the books they had brought at more than a thousand words per minute and with excellent comprehension. If you know anything about matrix algebra, linguistics, or stream-of-consciousness writing, you also know that the representative was either stupid or lying through his teeth.

We wish we could tell you that there exists some trick, secret formula, or an incantation that could quickly and painlessly turn you into a super reader. We can't. Learning to read rapidly (300 to 600 words per minute) comes from regular practice, and promises to the contrary are only attempts to take your money.

We have obviously been describing the dark side of adult reading programs. Happily, there is also a bright side. Thousands of reputable reading improvement programs do exist. Normally, they are associated with a university, college, or public school system. Their promises regarding how fast they can teach people to read are more realistic than the claims of most commercial speed reading enterprises. Generally, their fees are smaller and they will emphasize comprehension, study skills, and vocabulary development as well as reading rate. Most importantly, these honest adult programs are directed by trained professionals in the field of reading.

Two Things to Keep in Mind about Reading Rate

1. *It is not wrong to skip material.* Most people leave high school believing that it is wrong, even sinful, to skip anything during reading. This misconception is so deeply ingrained in most people that they experience pangs of guilt if they do not read each and every word of a reading assignment. Clearly, skimming, scanning, and, to some extent, rapid reading demand that the reader ignore certain words, sentences, paragraphs, and even bigger chunks of text when they are irrelevant to the comprehension task at hand.

2. *Comprehension can improve along with rate.* One of the greatest fears people experience when they enter a program for increasing reading rate is that a faster reading rate will automatically result in poorer comprehension. This is untrue; most people are capable of increasing their "careful" and "rapid" reading rates by 50% to 100% without suffering a loss of comprehension.

What Research Has to Say about Reading Rate

1. The average college student's rapid reading rate is only about 200 to 250 words per minute (wpm).
2. Without skipping words and sentences, the theoretical upper limit on reading rate is 800 wpm.
3. Anyone who appears to read faster than 800 wpm is either skimming or scanning.
4. Irregular eye movements are a symptom rather than a cause of slow reading.
5. Reading rate should depend upon the reader's purpose.

How to Calculate Your Reading Rate

The two types of reading rate which you must learn to compute are *raw rate* in words per minute and *rate of comprehension*. The first of these is a matter of simple math and will vary a lot depending upon what you are reading. Rate of comprehension, on other other hand, requires good judgment rather than a calculator. Reading improvement courses usually estimate comprehension with tests which follow each reading passage. Such tests do give the reader some feedback, but they have limitations.

In the real world there are no multiple-choice comprehension tests. You must judge the quality of your comprehension in your everyday reading taks. Do you gather the necessary information? Do you get the information as quickly as possible? If the answer to both questions is yes, then your rate of comprehension is satisfactory. If the answer to either question is no, then you need to adjust your raw reading rate.

Calculating your raw reading rate takes two bits of information: (1) the number of words you read or covered, and (2) the number of minutes you spent reading. For example, if a passage is 1000 words long and you read it in five minutes, your raw rate in words per minute will be:

$$\frac{1000 \text{ words}}{5 \text{ minutes}} = 200 \text{ words per minute (wpm)}$$

Unfortunately, people don't always complete a reading selection in a whole number of minutes, and the words-per-minute formula can get complicated when fractions of minutes are employed in the computation. To simplify matters, the formula can be transformed so that seconds, rather than minutes, are used in the denominator. This is easily accomplished by multiplying the number of words (the numerator) by 60 and then dividing by the number of seconds required to read the selection. Given the previous example, the following computations can be made:

$$\frac{1000 \text{ words}}{5 \text{ minutes}} = 200 \text{ wpm}$$

is transformed to

$$\frac{1000 \text{ words} \times 60}{5 \text{ minutes} \times 60} = \frac{60,000}{300} = 200 \text{ wpm}$$

Scanning

Scanning is a rapid search procedure for locating specific information in print. Before you begin to scan, develop a mind set for the information you seek. Fix clearly in your mind's eye a picture or description of what you are seeking, such as names, dates, addresses, or words that are underlined, *italicized,* or CAPITALIZED. If the rows of print are narrow, as in a newspaper column, allow your eyes to float down the center of the column. If the lines are long, as in most books, your eyes should move in a rapid zigzag pattern across and down the page. The prime directive for scanning is to fine-tune your selective attention; block out everything *except* the specific information you seek. Concentrate on the words or facts that you want, and you will find that they seem to "pop out at you" from the printed page.

From pp. 78–108 in EFFECTIVE READING TECHNIQUES: Business and Personal Applications by John N. Mangieri and R. Scott Baldwin. Copyright © 1978 by John N. Mangieri and R. Scott Baldwin. By permission of Harper & Row, Publishers, Inc.

Scan 1: As quickly as you can, draw a line through every *e* in the following sentence.

Would you be offended if Donald Duck wanted to marry Mickey Mouse?

There were six *e*'s in the sentence. If you were truly scanning, you did not read the sentence as you searched for the *e*'s. Remember—close your mind to everything but the stated objective. To do otherwise only impedes your speed and efficiency.

From this point on, you will need to time yourself on each exercise. A stopwatch is best for this, but any watch with a second hand will work.

Scan 2: You have five seconds to locate and recall the specific occupations mentioned in the following paragraph.

It is extremely unlikely that you have lived long enough to be reading this book without having known a doctor, a lawyer, a banker, many teachers, and the proprietors of local businesses, such as a clothing store or a gasoline station or a dry cleaning establishment. There is a good chance, too, that you know someone who owns or manages or works in a factory or industrial plant of some kind—someone who is in the business of making something for sale.[1]

Number of words = <u>82</u>

Elapsed time   = _____ seconds

Scanning rate $\dfrac{82 \times 60}{\text{seconds}} = \dfrac{4920}{\text{seconds}} =$ _____ wpm

Occupations recalled: _____

_____

_____

Scan 3: Find out how many Americans are killed each year as a result of home accidents with consumer products. Scan as quickly as possible.

Americans—20 million of them—are injured each year in the home as a result of incidents connected with consumer products. Of the total, 100,000 are permanently disabled and 30,000 are killed. A significant number could have been spared if more attention had been paid to hazard reduction. The annual cost to the Nation of product-related injuries may exceed $5.5 billion.[2]

Number of words = <u>78</u>

Elapsed time   = _____ seconds

Scanning rate $\dfrac{4680}{(\text{seconds})} =$ _____ wpm

Number killed: _____

You have now completed three scanning exercises. We could include an infinite number of exercises, but we do not know what specific kind of information you may need to scan for. We suggest that you attempt to integrate scanning into your daily reading routine, regardless of the subject area. In any case, you need practice. If you conscientiously exercise your scanning skills, they will automatically improve. On the other hand, a hundred scanning exercises in this book would be useless unless you made scanning part of your reading routine. Learning to scan isn't at all like learning to ride a bike—you can forget how to do it very easily.

1. B. Ryan, Jr. *So You Want to Go into Advertising,* New York: Harper and Brothers. 1961.
2. National Commission on Product Safety. "Perspective on Product Safety." In Ralph M. Gaedeke and Warren W. Etcheson eds., *Consumerism: Viewpoints from Business, Government, and the Public Interest.* New York: Harper and Row. 1972.

Rapid Reading

Rapid reading is just a faster version of the slow reading you probably do most of the time. It is continuous, left-to-right, line-by-line reading. Of course, this does not mean that you can't skip words, sentences, or even paragraphs if they seem unimportant or redundant. But, for the most part, rapid reading requires that you read almost all of the words in a given passage.

The key to successful rapid reading is your desire to read faster. You will have to give yourself a sales pitch and say something like, "Hey!! You up there in my head, go faster!" Desire and practice are the only efficient means of increasing your reading rate to 400 to 600 wpm. If you have the persistence to master rapid reading on your own, you will be far ahead of those who substitute $500 for personal drive and go two nights a week to a place where someone stands in front of them and forces them to do what they might have done for themselves.

The exercises that follow are designed to get you started on a self-directed program of rapid reading development. Pit yourself against the clock.

Rapid 1: The following passage is taken from Marvin Grosswirth's fascinating book, *The Art of Growing a Beard*. Read the passage as rapidly as possible, but be prepared to answer a few questions.

The Superlative Beard

If a youth begins shaving at the age of 15, he is likely to dispose of some nine yards of whiskers in his lifetime and expend about 3,350 hours—the equivalent of approximately 139 days—at the task.

Among those who considered such labors as wasteful was Hans Steininger, distinguished burgomaster of Braunau, Austria, whose beard was over eight feet long. In 1567, Herr Steininger, doubtlessly preoccupied with the cares of office, tripped over his beard, plummeted down a flight of stairs, and met his untimely end.

The *Guiness Book of World Records* (New York: 1971 Revised Edition: Sterling Publishing Co., Inc.) informs that the longest beard ever recorded belonged to Hans Langreth. Born in Norway in 1846, Langreth emigrated to the United States where he died in 1927, leaving behind a beard measuring 17½ feet. In 1967, the beard was presented to the Smithsonian Institution in Washington. I have no idea where, how, or by whom it was cared for in the intervening years.

Despite the vagaries of custom and the vicissitudes of history, one fact stands out with diamondlike clarity: the beard has always been a symbol of manhood and virility. The artist, the poet, the sculptor— and woman—have all paid tribute to beards through the ages; and though transient, fickle fashion may dictate the temporary discontinuance of facial growth, beards always return, for it is only natural that they should do so.

If God had wanted you to have a hairless chin, He would have given you one.[3]

Determine your rate of reading for Rapid 1; plot it on the graph on page 21.

Number of words = <u>255</u>

Elapsed time   = _____ seconds

Rapid Rate $\dfrac{15,300}{(\text{seconds})}$ = _____ wpm

Now, as a check on your comprehension, try to answer the following questions:

1. What was the general topic under discussion? _____

2. How did Hans Steininger die? _____

3. How long was the world's longest beard? _____

3. Marvin Grosswirth, *The Art of Growing a Beard.* New York: Harper and Row, 1975.

4. Where is the world's longest beard now? _____

_____

5. What does Grosswirth believe to be the future of the beard?

_____

(Answers are on page 22.)

You will now encounter three more rapid reading exercises, which vary in length and difficulty. Your objectives in each case are the same—to read as rapidly as possible while maintaining a grip on main ideas and pertinent facts. Continue to plot your reading rate. If your rate and comprehension fluctuate on these exercises, do not be alarmed. Simply perform to the best of your abilities.

Rapid 2: The following passage is an informative extract from Peter F. Drucker's book, *Technology, Management, and Society,* (New York: Harper and Row, 1970).

Communication Is Perception

An old riddle asked by the mystics of many religions—the Zen Buddhists, the Sufis of Islam, or the rabbis of the Talmud—asks: "Is there a sound in the forest if a tree crashes down and no one is around to hear it?" We now know that the right answer to this is "no." There are sound waves. But there is no sound unless someone perceives it. Sound is created by perception. Sound is communication.

This may seem trite; after all, the mystics of old already knew this, for they, too, always answered that there is no sound unless someone can hear it. Yet the implications of this rather trite statement are great indeed.

(a) First, it means that it is the recipient who communicates. The so-called communicator, that is, the person who emits the communication, does not communicate. He utters. Unless there is someone who hears, there is no communication. There is only noise. The communicator speaks or writes or sings—but he does not communicate. Indeed, he cannot communicate. He can only make it possible, or impossible, for a recipient—or rather, percipient—to perceive.

(b) Perception, we know, is not logic. It is experience. This means, in the first place, that one always perceives a configuration. One cannot perceive single specifics. They are always part of a total picture. "The silent language" (as Edward T. Hall called it in the title of his pioneering work ten years ago)—that is, the gestures, the tone of voice, the environment all together, not to mention the cultural and social referents—cannot be dissociated from the spoken language. In fact, without them, the spoken word has no meaning and cannot communicate. It is not only that the same words, e.g., "I enjoyed meeting you," will be heard as having a wide variety of meanings. Whether they are heard as warm or as icy cold, as endearment or as rejection, depends on their setting in the silent language, such as the tone of voice or the occasion. More important is that by themselves, that is, without being part of the total configuration of occasion, value, silent language, and so on, the phrase has no meaning at all. By itself it cannot make possible communication. It cannot be understood. Indeed, it cannot be heard. To paraphrase an old proverb of the Human Relations school: "One cannot communicate a word; the whole man always comes with it."

(c) But we know about perception also that one can only perceive what one is capable of perceiving. Just as the human ear does not hear sounds above a certain pitch, so does human perception all together not perceive what is beyond its range of perception. It may, of course, hear physically, or see visually, but it cannot accept. The stimulus cannot become communication.

This is a very fancy way of stating something the teachers of rhetoric have known for a very long time—though the practitioners of communication tend to forget it again and again. In Plato's *Phaedrus,* which, among other things, is also the earliest extant treatise on rhetoric, Socrates points out that one has to talk to people in terms of their own experience, that is, that one has to use a carpenter's metaphors when talking to carpenters, and so on. One can only communicate in the recipient's language or altogether in his terms. And the terms have to be experience-based. It, therefore, does very little good to try to explain terms to people. They will not be able to receive them if the terms are not of their own experience. They simply exceed their perception capacity.

The connection between experience, perception, and concept formation, that is, cognition, is, we now know, infinitely subtler and richer than any earlier philosopher imagined. But one fact is proven and comes out strongly in the most disparate work, e.g., that of Piaget in Switzerland, that of B. F. Skinner of Harvard, or that of Jerome Bruner (also of Harvard). Percept and concept in the learner, whether child or adult, are not separate. We cannot perceive unless we also conceive. But we also cannot form concepts unless we can perceive. To communicate a concept is impossible unless the recipient can perceive it, that is, unless it is within his perception.

There is a very old saying among writers: "Difficulties with a sentence always mean confused thinking. It is not the sentence that needs straightening out, it is the thought behind it." In writing, we attempt, of course, to communicate with ourselves. An unclear sentence is one that exceeds our own capacity for perception. Working on the sentence, that is, working on what is normally called communications, cannot solve the problem. We have to work on our own concepts first to be able to understand what we are trying to say—and only then can we write the sentence.

In communicating, whatever the medium, the first question has to be, "Is this communication within the recipient's range of perception? Can he receive it?"

The "range of perception" is, of course, physiological and largely (though not entirely) set by physical limitations of man's animal body. When we speak of communications, however, the most important limitations on perception are usually cultural and emotional rather than physical. That fanatics are not being convinced by rational arguments, we have known for thousands of years. Now we are beginning to understand that it is not "argument" that is lacking. Fanatics do not have the ability to perceive a communication which goes beyond their range of emotions. Before this is possible, their emotions would have to be altered. In other words, no one is really "in touch with reality," if by that we mean complete openness to evidence. The distinction between sanity and paranoia is not in the ability to perceive, but in the ability to learn, that is, in the ability to change one's emotions on the basis of experience.

That perception is conditioned by what we are capable of perceiving was realized forty years ago by the most quoted but probably least heeded of all students of organization, Mary Parker Follet, especially in her collected essays, *Dynamic Administration* (New York, Harper's, 1941). Follett taught that a disagreement or a conflict is likely not to be about the answers, or, indeed, about anything ostensible. It is, in most cases, the result of incongruity in perceptions. What A sees so vividly, B does not see at all. And, therefore, what A argues has no pertinence to B's concerns, and vice versa. Both, Follet argued, are likely to see reality. But each is likely to see a different aspect thereof. The world, and not only the material world, is multidimensional. Yet one can only see one dimension at a time. One rarely realizes that there could be other dimensions, and that something that is so obvious to us and so clearly validated by our emotional experience has other dimensions, a back and sides, which are entirely different and which, therefore, lead to entirely different perception. The old story about the blind men and the elephant in which every one of them, upon encountering this strange beast, feels one of the elephant's parts, his leg, his trunk, his hide, and reports an entirely different conclusion, each held tenaciously, is simply a story of the human condition. And there is no possibility of communication until this is understood and until he who has felt the hide of the elephant goes over to him who has felt the leg and feels the leg himself. There is no possibility of communications, in other words, unless we first know what the recipient, the true communicator, can see and why.

Determine your rate of reading for Rapid 2; plot it on the graph on page 21.

Number of words = <u>1284</u>

Elapsed time   = ____ seconds

Rapid rate $= \dfrac{77{,}040}{\text{(seconds)}} =$ ____ wpm

Comprehension questions:

1. In Drucker's opinion, is there a sound in the forest if a tree crashes down and no one is around to hear it? _____

2. Can you recall the title of the book by Edward T. Hall which deals with the relationship between cultural referents and communication? _____

_____

3. Do you think Drucker would agree with the following statement: The medium is the message?

_____

4. What did Follett claim was the major reason for disagreement or conflict among human beings?

_____

5. What do you think is the most important point that Drucker is trying to get across to the reader in this passage? _____

_____

(Answers are on page 22).

Rapid 3: This passage is the introduction to Paul Zindel's compelling novel, *My Darling, My Hamburger*, (New York: Harper and Row, 1969). Read it as rapidly as you can.

"It was Marie Kazinski who asked how to stop a boy if he wants to go all the way," Maggie whispered.

Liz dragged her trig book along the wall tiles so it clicked at every crack.

"I'll bet she didn't ask it like that," Liz said.

" 'Sexually stimulated' was how she said it, if you must know the sordid details."

"Go on."

"She simply raised her hand," Maggie said, "and asked Miss Fanuzzi in front of the whole class."

"What'd she say?"

"Who?"

"Miss Fanuzzi."

Maggie shifted her books from one arm to the other. "Oh, something dumb. Miss Fanuzi knows a lot about puberty and mitosis, but I think she needs a little more experience with men."

They moved down the center aisle of the auditorium. Maggie watched Liz scan the crowd. How she envied the way Liz was so conscious of everything that was going on! She could walk into a party and instantly know who was doing what to whom and what they were wearing. Maggie had to look at one thing at a time, and it was always something minuscule, like fingers. She always looked at people's fingers.

"Come to order. I want it quiet in the auditorium!" Mr. Zamborsky, the grade advisor, called out as Maggie took a seat. She jumped when he blew his loud, shrill whistle, Wrrrrrrrrrr! Liz calmly unwrapped a piece of bubble gum and stuffed it in her mouth. She was still looking over the gathering of seniors that continued to churn and buzz while she lowered herself into the seat next to Maggie.

Wrrrrrrrrrr! "We have many important decisions to make at this meeting: Senior Day, the prom, and graduation in June," Mr. Zamborsky started.

"Yahooooooooooo!" everyone yelled.

"Quiet! I want it quiet!" Mr. Zamborsky screamed.

Liz passed the bubble-gum wrapper to Maggie and watched her read the joke on it: "At school she was voted the girl with whom you are most likely to succeed."

Mr. Zamborsky fumbled with a batch of papers, then cleared his throat. "Now I'll turn the meeting over to the class president, Pierre Jefferson."

A young man walked up to the podium. He straightened his tie and smoothed down his hair. "God, Pierre loves himself," Maggie whispered. Liz had slumped down in her seat to read an astrology magazine.

"A big brownie," Liz said.

"I think he's cute," Maggie said.

"The first item on the agenda," Pierre started, "is whether we want the prom formal or semiformal."

Maggie suddenly felt depressed. She knew it wouldn't matter if everyone were going nude to the senior prom because nobody was going to ask her.

"You think my hair looks OK today?" Maggie asked.

"It looks like thin fungus."

"At least my eyebrows are better, aren't they?"

Liz sat up and turned Maggie's face toward her. "They're cockeyed." She slumped back down.

Maggie sat quietly for a minute. "You're always telling me I need more confidence, and then you tell me I've got cockeyed eyebrows."

"They *are* cockeyed."

Maggie took a hand mirror out of her pocketbook. Liz was right. Everything Maggie did to make herself look better never worked. "Oh, Liz," she wailed, "why didn't you tell me my hair was so messed?"

"I told you it looked like fungus."

"It didn't look bad before I was a wheelbarrow."

"A what?"

"A wheelbarrow. In gym." Maggie stared at herself in the mirror. "Don't you do wheelbarrows?"

"No."

"We've got that new instructor—the sadistic-looking one. Every day she's got half of us lying on the floor, and a squad-mate picks up our legs. We have to walk around on our hands."

Liz yawned and closed the astrology magazine. "She sounds demented." She leaned on the back of the seat in front of her and surveyed the auditorium again.

"Is Sean here?" Maggie asked.

"Front row."

"Where?"

"*There!*"

The class president's voice intruded. "The principal suggested we spend Senior Day at Bear Mountain, as opposed to the customary practice of taking over the school for the day. There were complaints about beer drinking and ungentlemanly behavior . . ."

"What a schnook," Liz sighed.

"Who is that sitting next to Sean? He's with him a lot lately." Maggie sat forward.

"Dennis Holowitz."

"Oh."

Liz smiled strangely. "Sean and I decided we're going to get him to ask you out."

"Oh, Liz, I thought you were my friend! I wouldn't go anywhere with him. He looks weird." He actually was weird-looking, Maggie thought, studying him closely. How skinny! A face like an under-nourished zucchini. She chuckled to herself. And always wearing the same baggy green sweater. He must love that sweater. Any time she ever passed him in the halls, there it was, baggy as ever. He wouldn't ask her out anyway.

Liz lowered herself again. She opened her loose-leaf notebook and started reading a love comic hidden inside.

"Miss Fanuzzi said we're going to discuss masturbation tomorrow," Maggie put the mirror back in her pocketbook.

"That's nice." Liz waited a moment, then asked, "What advice did she give for stopping a guy on the make?"

"Who?"

"Miss Fanuzzi," Liz snapped.

"You mean about what to do when things get out of control?" Maggie could tell when Liz Carstensen really wanted to know something because she would start tapping her fingers.

"Yes, stupid."

"Well"—Maggie lowered her voice—"Miss Fanuzzi's advice was that you're supposed to suggest going to get a hamburger."

Determine your rate of reading for Rapid 3; plot it on the graph on page 000.

Number of words = <u>900</u>

Elapsed time   = _____ seconds

Rapid rate   = $\dfrac{54,000}{\text{(seconds)}}$ = _____ wpm

Comprehension questions:

1. In what grade are the main characters? _____

2. Who is Miss Fanuzzi? _____

3. Do you remember what Liz said Maggie's hair looked like? _____

(Answers on page 22)

Rapid 4: The following passage is from The *Sound Pattern of English* by Noam Chomsky and Morris M. Halle, (New York: Harper and Row, 1968). Read it as rapidly as you can, but again, we will ask you a few questions when you have finished it.

Appendix: Formalism

In this Appendix we shall restate succinctly the formalism used for presenting phonological rules and the schemata that represent them, the interpretation of this formalism, and the system of evaluation that we have proposed. Our general assumption is that the phonology consists of a linearly ordered sequence of rules that apply to a surface structure in accordance with the principle of the transformational cycle, within the phonological phrase. Certain of these rules, the rules of word phonology, apply only when the level of a word (as defined in Section 6.2) is reached in the cycle. Under formal conditions of a highly abstract sort, the relation of disjunctive ordering is assigned to certain pairs of rules. The sequence of rules is represented by a minimal scheme that assigns a value to this sequence and also determines the relationship of disjunctive ordering. As we have noted, it is a significant fact that the same formal notions are involved in the very different functions of determining an evaluation measure and assigning disjunctive ordering.

Determine your rate of reading for Rapid 4; plot it on the graph on page 21.

Number of words = <u>213</u>

Elapsed time = ____ seconds

Rapid rate $= \dfrac{12,780}{\text{(seconds)}} =$ ____ wpm

Comprehension questions:

1. What kinds of rules does the phonology have? _____

_____

2. What is the relationship between evaluation measures and disjunctive ordering? ____

_____

3. Do you have any idea what the main idea of the passage is?

_____

(Answers on page 22)

You have just completed reading four very different types of passages, and your reading rates and levels of comprehension should have varied accordingly. Our best guess is that your rate was highest on exercises one and three, with two next, and four way behind in last place. You probably felt that your comprehension followed a similar pattern. What this should have clearly demonstrated to you is that there is no single appropriate reading rate. There will always be a trade-off between raw speed and the difficulty of the material you read.

In our opinion, you now have all of the information necessary to construct and conduct your own program of rapid reading improvement. Follow these directions:

1. Select a book you think will be pleasurable and fairly easy to read.
2. Mark off the book in sections of five or ten pages, depending upon how much you intend to read in one sitting. Each section should be the same length.
3. Figure the average number of words per section. This can be done in a number of ways. One way is to count the words on a page that is representative of the text. Multiplying that number by the number of pages per section will yield a close approximation.
4. Select a specific time of day when you will practice rapid reading—directly after supper, right before bedtime, or whenever. The time you choose is irrelevant. What is important is that you practice on a regular basis.
5. Read at least one section a day under speed pressure. You can use the practice passages in Appendix A. Time yourself, and compute your rate using the wpm formula. Then plot your day-by-day progress in rapid reading on the chart on page 21. If you read 250 wpm on day one, shoot for 275 wpm on day two. Constantly raise your expectations. Plot your reading rate; and honestly judge your comprehension. In a few short weeks, with a few minutes' practice each day, you will find that you are reading comfortably at rates 50 to 150 percent faster than your present rate.

One final word about rapid reading. Trying to keep your comprehension up along with your reading rate will be difficult and a little uncomfortable. When this occurs, do not resort to drastic measures or, worse yet, enroll in a speed reading course! Instead, keep forcing yourself to go faster. Your comprehension will eventually catch up as your mind and eyes adjust to the higher rate of speed.

Skimming

Skimming is a combination of rapid reading and scanning. It allows you to read large numbers of words per minute while still allowing you to get main ideas and some detail. Skimming is useful for reviewing material and for helping you decide whether to read something carefully or to skip it. To skim:

1. Read all titles and subheadings.
2. Read the first and last paragraphs if they are short, or if the passage is more than a few pages long.
3. Read the first sentence in each paragraph.
4. Scan the insides of each paragraph for lead information such as names, dates, numbers, or other bits of information which may suggest the need for further reading.
5. If there is a summary at the end of the selection, read that too.

The following exercise will introduce you to skimming. Remember, try to beat the clock.

Skim 1: Skim the following passage, an article by Ralph M. Gaedeke. Rapidly read *only* the underlined portions of the text. Attempt to complete the skimming in one minute or less. Time yourself.

The Muckraking Era[4]

The consumer protection movement is not new, although the extent of its fervor and the source of its strength may be. The author points out that the early efforts at consumer protection (some federal consumer protection legislation is a century old) did not enjoy today's favor and were generally branded as muckraking. The movement for consumer protection began to crystallize as early as the late nineteenth century. This was reflected in the formation of various local and regional consumer groups, in muckraking, and by concerted federal legislation.

---

4. R. M. Gaedeke, "The Muckraking Era." In Ralph M. Gaedeke and Warren W. Etcheson eds. *Consumerism: Viewpoints from Business, Government, and the Public Interest.* New York: Harper and Row, pp. 57–59, 1972.

In 1872, the first consumer protection law was passed, making it a federal crime to defraud through the use of mails. The law revised, consolidated, and amended the statutes relating to the Post Office Department. Section 149 of the 1872 Act stated:

It shall not be lawful to convey by mail, nor to deposit in a post office to be sent by mail, any letters or circulars concerning illegal lotteries, so-called gift concerts, or other similar enterprises offering prizes, or concerning schemes devised and intended to deceive and defraud the public for the purpose of obtaining money under false pretenses, and a penalty of not more than five hundred dollars nor less than one hundred dollars, with cost of prosecution, is hereby imposed upon conviction, in any federal court of the violation of this section.

In 1883 the importation of unwholesome tea was prohibited, and in 1890 an act was passed preventing the importation of adulterated food and drink. These and certain other federal consumer protection laws were, however, merely piecemeal and were not aimed at the broad issues of general government regulation of the quality of products sold.

Between 1879 and 1905, more than 100 bills were introduced in Congress to regulate interstate production and sale of foods and drugs. But the Congress and public were largely apathetic, business opposition was strong, and no action was taken on any of the proposed measures.

Exposés of business corruption and avarice—e.g., muckraking—finally marked a substantive turning point in the movement for consumer protection. With Upton Sinclair's publication, *The Jungle,* Congress was at last jarred to action. The book focused on conditions in the Chicago meat-packing industry which made the need for consumer protection apparent. It helped assure passage of the *Food and Drug Act of 1906* which provided for "preventing the manufacture, sale, or transportation of adulterated or misbranded or poisonous or deleterious foods, drugs, medicines, and liquors, and for regulating traffic therein."

Passage of the Food and Drug Act of 1906 was a substantial victory for consumers. It showed that consumer interests finally counted, at least in politics, and it "did a great deal to dissolve the old nineteenth-century American habit of viewing political issues solely from the standpoint of the producer." It also demonstrated that the era of muckraking made the public and Congress more conscious of the need for consumer protection. Finally, it served as a stimulus for the formation of numerous private committees, clubs, and leagues which were organized to push for further protection of the consumer.

While these victories were indeed great achievements at the time, they were largely failures when viewed from a longer perspective. They were failures because the wave of strong pro-consumer public sentiment rapidly abated after 1906 and, with it, the political interest in consumer protection. Passage of the Act also failed to change the negative and indifferent posture of the business community toward consumer protection. CAVEAT EMPTOR was very much the rule of the day.

In the years preceding and following World War I, consumer organizations became largely concerned with sanitary conditions in food stores and retail prices which were considered excessive. Informal boycotts were arranged against merchants while housewives' leagues sold eggs (and later apples) at prices below those prevailing in retail stores. These activities, which were sporadic and confined to few cities—notably Chicago and Philadelphia—were generally inconsequential, having no measurable impact on retail prices.

The Food and Drug Act itself proved to have a number of serious weaknesses. It failed to eliminate practices which made the legislation necessary because the Act did not authorize inspection of food-processing plants. In addition, the Act was merely piecemeal legislation since it exempted foods sold under proprietary names and the sale of cosmetics and therapeutic devices, as well as the advertising thereof. The effectiveness of the Act was further weakened because it was administered by a small staff which had difficulty in obtaining convictions. Weaknesses inherent in the law provided, on the other hand, new exposes for consumer crusaders.

A new drive for consumer protection began to develop in the late 1920s and early 1930s with the publication of several popular books on the abuses of advertising and the sale of adulterated products. When Stuart Chase and F. J. Schlink published *Your Money's Worth* in 1927, it became an immediate best-seller. It pictures the consumer as an "Alice in Wonderland" of conflicting product claims and bright promises and pleaded for impartial product-testing agencies.

Your Money's Worth was the first publication since *The Jungle* to arouse the public once again. This and subsequent protest literature helped crystallize a vaguely felt but widespread discontent among consumers, and succeeded in acquainting the public with the need for more protection than was provided by the Food and Drug Act of 1906. A period thus emerged which saw the rise of an articulate consumer consciousness, generally labeled as the "consumer movement."

Number of words = 921

Elapsed time = ____ seconds

Skimming rate = $\dfrac{55,260}{\text{(seconds)}}$ = ____ wpm

Comprehension questions:

1. When was the first consumer protection law passed?
   (a) 1765   (b) 1906   (c) 1872   (d) 1894

2. The law referred to in question one involved:
   (a) mail   (b) drugs   (c) food   (d) imports

3. What is *muckraking*?
   (a) The process of exploiting consumer behavior
   (b) Exposés of business corruption and avarice
   (c) Legalistic intimidation by corporations
   (d) *Caveat emptor,* "let the buyer beware"

4. When was the Food and Drug Act passed?
   (a) 1903   (b) 1905   (c) 1906   (d) 1907

5. True or False. According to Gaedeke, the rise of an articulate consumer consciousness was brought about by the Food and Drug Act.

(Answers on page 22.)

Skim 2: Following is an extract from *Marketing Systems: An Introductory Analysis* by George Fisk, (New York: Harper and Row, 1967). In this selection, there will be no underlined parts to guide your reading. You must do this yourself. Remember, you are skimming the passage, *not* studying it. Attempt to complete your skimming in one minute or less.

Goals of Organizations with a Single Center of Control

The common goals of business organizations in marketing may be easily distinguished: survival, short-term market share, long-term growth, profits, power, and prestige. These six major goals are further identified below.

Survival

To grow, to enjoy profits, prestige, or power, an organization must first adopt forms of behavior which will enable it to survive. Wroe Alderson has postulated a number of survival theorems which purport to explain how an organization can survive under competitive conditions. European family-dominated firms are more likely to seek survival as a central long-run purpose than are American corporations guided by professional managers.

Short-Term Market Share

This goal, sometimes called *market standing,* is reflected in the adage "nothing succeeds like success." A strong current of demand is viewed as evidence of ability to discern and meet the wants of buyers. A firm that is able to attain its market-share objective is usually able to plan effectively. Conversely, a declining market share is an indication that forces within the control of management are not being properly administered. Market share is considered a goal because it indicates the efficiency of management performance.

A firm that gains an excessive market share frequently operates at relatively low rates of profit because the cost of each additional sale is greater than the additional income generated by that sale. On the other hand, a firm whose market share is below the most economic marketing and production level cannot attain the selling production economies needed to generate profits commensurate with the opportunities afforded by the prevailing level of demand.

Long-Term Growth

Many firms seek increasing long-run gross sales in order to enhance their market position, even at the expense of profits or ability to survive serious reverses. Growth is preferred because if the company does grow, it achieves other goals at the same time. In particular, growth is expected to lead to larger profits than long-run stability.

Profits

Most administrators in privately owned organizations are employed to produce profits for the owners of the firm. It is assumed that profits can be earned only by producing goods and services which yield satisfaction in use. Profits are often a consequence of growth or of increasing market share so that these become complementary and not mutually exclusive ends. Because, unless qualified, the word *profit* is ambiguous, care is ordinarily taken to indicate both the time period and the elements of profit sought. If the time is so short that the supply of goods is fixed, the profit on a fixed stock of goods is called *market-period profit*. Short-run profit is the goal when profit is sought for a period in which the output capacity of the plant is fixed but additions to existing stocks can be made within capacity limits. Conversely, if profit is sought over a period sufficiently long to permit variations in plant capacity, the "long-run supergoal is the maximization of the present value of an ownership interest."

The elements of profit must also be specified. In practice it is difficult to distinguish between pure interest on capital, profit as a risk-taker's surplus, and payment to management for its labor. Probability theory and utility theory have in recent years made possible increasingly fine distinctions. Profits associated with "successful" marketing programs are in fact a reward for entrepreneurial risk, but elements of interest on capital and wages to management are also present. Marketing risks are much greater than other types of economic risks because of uncontrollable influences on marketing decisions. Consequently, the rewards for success in marketing tend to be greater than for lending money to the Federal government or for other "interest-bearing" riskless investments.

Power

Individuals and groups seek power either because of the status and privileges it may confer, or because they get satisfaction through its exercise. Although power to control one's own corporate destiny in the market is often a prerequisite for survival, many business leaders enjoy the exercise of power simply "for the fun of the game."

With the transition from the nineteenth-century small business to the corporate form of organization in the present century, power to preserve one's position has become more important in explaining managerial behavior than profit-seeking. Most professional managers in big firms find it easier to avert risks or take smaller risks than they would as proprietors of small independent establishments. Under conditions of oligopolitic competition between a few giant firms in an industry, profit-seeking has to stay within limits prescribed by government and public sanction, but only a handful of stockholders are wealthy enough to dislodge an entrenched management seeking to retail its power to control a corporation.

Prestige

Good public relations, corporate image, product image, store image, and brand image enhance the prestige of a firm and its members. A firm often seeks to make an impression upon the various publics it serves because it needs the good will of the groups and organizations with which it comes in contact. Its prospective customers must be able to find satisfaction in the use of its products, its suppliers must not come to regard it as a difficult company to deal with, the community in which its plants or stores are located must welcome it, its stockholders must view its management with confidence, and so on. In order to enjoy satisfactory profits, retain power to act, increase its market share, and attain other goals, a good image is a positive asset for a firm.

Suboptimization

However many goals an organization seeks, its managers are ordinarily forced to choose from among several combinations offering less than the maximum attainment of any one goal in order to secure a satisfactory degree of attainment of others. Known as *suboptimization,* this procedure permits organizations to resolve their goal conflicts. Without it, organizations linked together in marketing channels would have great difficulty in achieving their common goals. Suboptimization must also be practiced by individuals within organizations in order to maintain effective cooperation among departmental work groups. In fact, suboptimization is a device used consciously or unconsciously by everyone in all formal organizations requiring conforming behavior.

Suboptimization requires that each individual perform the "office" assigned to him sufficiently well to enable the organization to move toward its purposes without an undue amount of conflict. Different persons are assigned different offices or areas of specialization. The individual's ability to perform is determined by how well he plays his social role within the firm. Viewed in this light, marketing channels are intersections of the role performances of individuals in successive agencies engaged in complementary specialization of the related activities required to move goods from producer to user.

Number of words $= \underline{1500}$

Elapsed time $= \underline{\hphantom{xxx}}$ seconds

Skimming rate $= \dfrac{90,000}{\text{(seconds)}} = \underline{\hphantom{xxx}}$ wpm

Comprehension: Close your eyes and think about the information which you have just processed. Can you recall some detail as well as the major thrust of the passage? On the basis of what you have learned by skimming, could you determine whether or not the passage required further consideration? If your answers to these questions are yes, and if you completed your skimming in approximately one minute, then you are well on your way to developing efficient skimming skills. The only thing left for you to do is to instill it into your daily reading routine.

If your answers were no, then we urge you to re-read our comments on skimming. After doing this, try the techniques again on the excerpt from Fisk's book or on some similar material.

Personal Style and Reading Techniques

It is just about impossible to say exactly what material should be scanned, skimmed, read rapidly, or read carefully. Your purpose for reading and your knowledge of the subject matter should determine which type of reading is best at any given time. For example, a professor of business administration might find a text on financial administration simple enough to justify only skimming; this is far less likely to be true of the professor's students.

In addition, your reading should seldom involve only one type of reading. One moment you may be skimming, the next moment reading rapidly, and the next moment reading carefully or rereading. No two people will read a given passage in exactly the same manner; this is a matter of personal style.

You now have the knowledge to vastly improve your rate of reading and your efficiency in comprehending, so read, practice, and read some more. Force yourself. If you have the ambition and can stick to a practice schedule, you can learn to read faster and better without spending a cent.

Reading Rate Chart

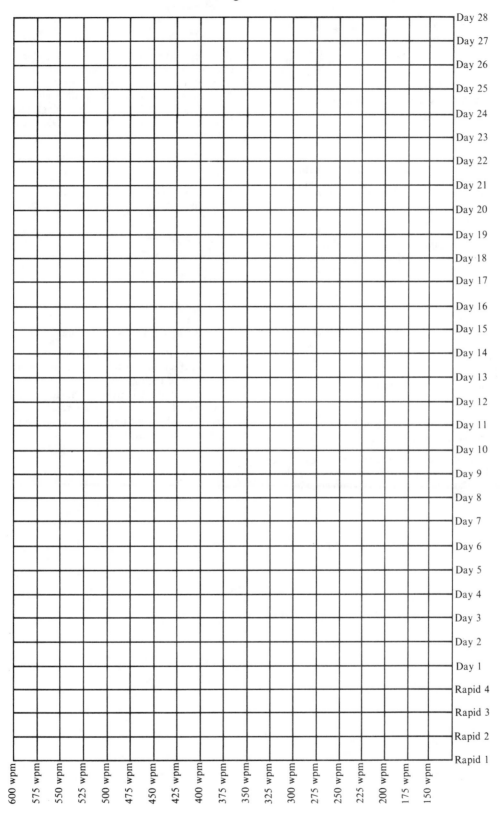

ANSWERS

Scan 2. Answers: doctor; lawyer; banker; teacher; proprietor of clothing store, gasoline station, dry cleaning establishment; factory owner, worker, manager.

Comment: There were ten possible answers. If you finished in five seconds, you were scanning at 1000 wpm. Five or more occupations recalled? Excellent! If not, keep concentrating. Your ability to quickly extract and recall appropriate information will improve with practice.

Scan 3. Answer: 30,000

Rapid 1. Answers:
1. Beards, long beards, and/or the destiny of beards
2. He tripped over his beard and fell down the stairs.
3. 17 1/2 feet
4. The Smithsonian Institution
5. Beards are here to stay

Comments: If you were able to answer most of the questions, you probably read "The Superlative Beard" with suitable comprehension. If not, go back and read Chapter 2!

Rapid 2. Answers:
1. No (see first paragraph)
2. *The Silent Language*
3. Probably not. The medium may be sounds, words, or gestures; but "the message" is a message only if the perceptions of the listener or reader allow communication to take place.
4. The fact that people perceive things in different and conflicting ways
5. In order to communicate with people, it is essential that you do so in terms which will match their perceptions and background experiences.

Comments: Answers three and five reflect the authors' interpretations of the text. You are, of course, free to disagree with us. After you have honestly graded your comprehension, move on to Rapid 3.

Rapid 3. Answers:
1. Seniors, grade 12
2. A biology teacher
3. Fungus

Comments: It would, of course, be possible to ask you many questions about this passage. Most of them, by themselves, would be trivial. The important thing to do in reading a novel is to comprehend sufficient detail in plot, setting, and characterization to make the story meaningful without having to labor over each and every word. Only you can determine whether you succeed in this respect.

Rapid 4. Answers: Don't worry about them; we are 99 percent certain that this passage is irrelevant to you.

Comments: Return to the text that follows Rapid 4. By the way, this is one of the books we were told people could learn to SPEED READ!

Skim 1. Answers:
1. (c)
2. (a)
3. (b)
4. (c)
5. False. Gaedeke does not say this. In fact he implies that it was protest literature years after the Food and Drug Act which caused the "consumer movement."

Comments: If you followed our directions and read only the underlined portions of the passage, you actually "read" only 40 percent of the total text. Obviously, the other 60 percent contained additional information. However, you should have absorbed sufficient detail to comprehend the nature of the article—enough to decide whether or not you needed to read the remaining 60 percent.

3
How to Take Good Notes

What Do You Believe about Notetaking?

Directions: Read each of the statements below. Place a checkmark on the line in front of each statement you believe is true.

1. _____ You should take notes neatly and in outline form.

2. _____ If you don't review your notes, they are worthless.

3. _____ Notes should always be written in pencil.

4. _____ Notetaking is a waste of time.

5. _____ Notetaking can interfere with listening.

We hope these statements have created in your own mind some questions about listening and notetaking. You should find the answers as you read and work your way through the chapter ahead.

Taking lecture notes is part of college life. Taking good notes can mean the difference between passing and failing a rough course. The reason for this is simple. At the college level enormous amounts of new information are presented through lectures and class discussions, and examinations usually include test items which are based on lectures as well as reading assignments. If you don't bother to take notes at all or if your notes are sloppy, sparse, and disorganized, your grades will suffer. Part of surviving to graduation is learning how to take, revise, and review notes from class lectures. The following dramatization uses stereotypes to illustrate the basic do's and don'ts of notetaking.

The Lecture

A Short Dramatization
By Ellie

The Characters:

PROFESSOR SMIRNOFF: A slightly absent-minded, but brilliant old biology professor who thinks all of his students love biology the way he does.
ANXIOUS ALICE: A somewhat nervous, overenthusiastic freshman. Anxiety level: Mount Everest.
COOL CAL: A good-looking, jock type who is "mellowed out." He tries to adopt the casual "I've done this many times before" approach. Anxiety level: nonexistent.
TOM TOGETHER: A "most likely to succeed" type. Anxiety level: low to moderate.

Scene One: Day of the First Lecture
PROFESSOR SMIRNOFF: Today we will be discussing the theory that ontogeny recapitulates phylogeny. . . . (*The old boy continues with a highly technical and somewhat rambling lecture.*)
ALICE: Gosh, I've done my reading for today but I'm so nervous. I want to take down everything he says but I can't seem to listen and write at the same time. He talks so fast! Darn, my pen ran out of ink! (*As she reaches for another pen her notebook goes crashing to the floor.*)
COOL CAL: (*Obviously lost at the opening remark.*) Maybe I'm in the wrong class. Sounds like Greek to me. This guy isn't speaking English. Oh well, as long as my notebook is open let's see if I can sketch out a few new plays for football practice tonight.
TOM: Boy, am I glad I read the text assignment for today! That concept about ontogeny recapitulating phylogeny makes some sense now. Whatever I don't get in my notes, I know I'll find in the textbook.

Scene Two: That Night

ALICE: (*On the phone to Tom Together.*) Tom, are you busy?

TOM: As a matter of fact, I'm revising the notes from Professor Smirnoff's class. Even though he spoke a mile a minute I was able to get the major concepts. Right now I'm organizing my notes and comparing them with the text assignment. Soon they'll be in perfect form to use as a review for the midterm.

ALICE: (*By now utterly impressed and totally in love.*) Would you show me how you take notes so that maybe I can fill in the tremendous gaps in my notes? Otherwise, I just know I won't be able to use them to review.

TOM: Sure! Come on over. (*He had noticed Alice when her books crashed to the floor, and he liked what he saw.*)

Scene Three: Cool Cal's Room the Day before the Midterm

COOL CAL: Well, I'll just whip open my notes and see what I have. . . . Gee, a lot of doodles and scribbles but nothing much to study from. Guess I'll just have to count on my memory. Now, what was the name of that course?

Moral: Learn from Tom Together to be prepared to take good notes *and then use them*. Learn from Anxious Alice to ask for help when you need it. Above all, avoid the Cool Cal Syndrome.

Good Notes Are Tough to Take

Imagine that you are in class. The professor is presenting new information like an auctioneer, students are asking questions, and you're trying to write all this down even though you have a million other things on your mind. What makes this situation difficult is that you don't have enough "attention" to monitor all of these activities at the same time. In fact, research has shown that human beings have the capacity to attend to only one demanding task at a time. If you are doing two or more things at the same time, all but one of these tasks must be done automatically. Psychologists refer to this as *capacity limitation*.

Remember how difficult it was to drive a car at first. Every time you turned a corner you found yourself fumbling to move your foot from the brake to the gas pedal; and when someone tried to talk to you, you were just as likely as not to take a detour through someone's front yard. This is because each aspect of driving required your active attention; you had to think about everything before you could do it. The experienced driver turns, signals, brakes, adjusts speed, and reads signs automatically.

The college classroom presents similar problems for the student. If you focus too much attention on taking and organizing neat notes, you will miss important lecture information. On the other hand, if you don't take notes, you won't have anything to study from. This nasty little "catch–22" exists because people have trouble listening and writing at the same time. However, the PARR system of notetaking will help you to avoid this dilemma.

The PARR System

The *Prepare-Abbreviate-Revise-Review* notetaking system is based on sound educational research. Mastering the system will require some practice on your part, but it will be time well spent.

Prepare. The first step in taking good notes is to be prepared for the lecture. Most class lectures are related to outside reading assignments. Too many students fall into the trap of postponing reading assignments until after the class lectures which pertain to them. This is a grave error since it leads to confusion during the lecture. If you haven't read the text assignment you cannot know which lecture facts and ideas are unique and which ones are also presented in the text. This seriously interferes with your ability to take meaningful notes.

Prepare yourself psychologically by sitting as close to the front of the room as possible. This makes eye contact with the professor easier and you will listen better. Sitting up front also makes a positive impression on many instructors since the "sleepers" and "talkers" tend to migrate to the back of the room.

Plan to be a selective listener. Remember, the world's greatest notetaking system is worthless to you if you don't know what notes to take. You may be tempted to write down everything you hear the professor say. In most cases this is an impossible task as well as a waste of time. Your strategy should be to listen for important information. Don't expect the professor to give you information in nice, neat outline form. Professors are human too, and their lectures are often disorganized or vague to the audience. Search for main ideas in the lecture and try to figure out where the professor is heading. Listen for clues such as "remember this," "there are three causes of," "above all," "let me repeat that," "first of all," "the most significant," "Wouldn't that make a nice exam question?" and so on. In general, write down information which falls into the following categories:

1. Main ideas (important generalizations or facts)
2. Important details and examples of main ideas
3. Unfamiliar technical terms

In Chapter 6 we will discuss ways of identifying main ideas. The thing to keep in mind now is the idea of including in your notes only *important* information.

Finally, prepare to take notes in the proper format. How you organize your notes can be as important as what you write down. To begin with, you should leave lots of space around your notes so that you will have room to revise. Write on every other line and leave generous margins on all sides. Be especially careful to leave several inches at the bottom so that you can write in additional information later. You may feel a little strange at first leaving so much blank space in your notes. You may even feel guilty or foolish about wasting paper. Don't! If you commit yourself to revising and reviewing your notes, the space will save you hours of effort. You couldn't make a better investment.

Always date your notes so that you will be able to make quick comparisons with other students. Starting each major topic on a new sheet of paper will also help to organize your notes.

Taking notes in the form of a perfect, detailed outline is probably impossible for two reasons: (1) it requires so much attention that it detracts from listening, and (2) lectures are seldom delivered in a perfectly organized manner. However, it is possible to make your notes reflect the major organization of the lecture through a simple outlining procedure.

Most lectures consist of main ideas or principles followed by examples or important supporting details. Try to capture this organization by indenting, numbering, or lettering using a system something like the one below:

          Topic
1 Main Idea or General Principle
    A Example or Important Detail
    B Example or Important Detail
2 Main Idea or General Principle
    A Example or Important Detail
    B Example or Important Detail

Abbreviate. The second step in taking good notes is to abbreviate. Writing speed is a major consideration. Each fact or principle you record should take up as little time and space as possible. Forget about neatness and precision at this point. Once you've made the decision to take a note don't dwell on what you're writing; concentrate your full attention on the speaker. Here are some specific recommendations.

1. Create your own abbreviations for terms that will be used frequently in a course, for example:
   psy   = psychology
   neg   = negative
   lx   = linguistics
   soc   = sociology

2. Use symbols and abbreviations for common words, for example:

    & = and
    imp = important
    grp = group
    cp = compare
    / = and/or
    ex = example
    w/ = with
    def = definition

3. Don't dot *i*'s, punctuate, or capitalize unnecessarily.
4. Omit unimportant words such as *a* and *the*.
5. Omit suffixes such as *-ed* and *-ing* whenever possible.

To see how the abbreviation process works, read the mini lecture below and the abbreviated notes which follow it.

Harry and Margaret Harlow investigated the behavior of rhesus monkeys reared in isolation. In the experiment monkeys were isolated for periods of three, six, or twelve months. All of the monkeys, regardless of the period of their isolation, demonstrated fear when exposed to strange monkeys for the first time. Monkeys that had been isolated for three months recovered quickly and were indistinguishable from nonisolated monkeys after a month. Monkeys isolated for six months adapted poorly to their new environment with other monkeys. Their play activities consisted mainly of amusing themselves with toys. The small amount of social activity that did occur was with other isolates, monkeys that had also been in isolation. These monkeys accepted abuse without defending themselves. Monkeys that had been isolated for twelve months displayed no social behavior or aggression. They crouched in terror, meekly accepting the attacks of other monkeys.

Two years later the monkeys that had been isolated for six and twelve months began to attack other monkeys viciously. Even though they were terrified by strange monkeys, they engaged in uncontrolled aggression. Suicidal attacks against large, adult male monkeys and attacks upon baby monkeys were common. These behaviors are almost never displayed by normal monkeys their age. It appeared that the antisocial behavior of these monkeys reared in isolation increased with the passage of time.

The abbreviated notes illustrated in Figure 1 consist of only about twenty-five percent of the professor's words, and those words have been shortened considerably. Abbreviating in this way can help you to spend less time writing and more time listening. By developing your own personal system of abbreviation you can become even more efficient.

Revise/Review. Your abbreviated notes are easy to read because you are familiar with the content. This is, however, a temporary state of affairs. As time passes those same notes will become harder and harder to read until they are practically useless. Many students have opened their notebooks the night before an important examination only to discover that their notes look like upside-down Egyptian hieroglyphics. For this reason, *it is essential that abbreviated notes be revised within 24 hours.* How much revising you have to do will depend upon the lecture, that is, how well organized the lecture is and how much information you have to "jam" onto the paper in a short space of time. The following kinds of revisions are illustrated in red in Figure 2:

1. Abbreviations are expanded so that they will make sense later.
2. New or unknown terms are circled and defined.
3. Important phrases are expanded into whole sentences.
4. Stars are placed next to information that is considered "most critical."
5. Questions for the professor are written into the margins.
6. New information is added based on comparisons with other students' notes, and memory of the lecture.
7. Mistakes are corrected based on comparisons with other students' notes, and contradictions with the textbook.

Harlow   inv   rs   monk

fear   new   monk

3   m
recov   1m

6   m
soc   act
other   isol
accept   abuse
12   m
no soc behav
accept abuse
3 yrs later - 6 + 12 m
uncontr   aggress
suicid   attacks
attack   baby

Figure 1. Abbreviated notes for the Harlow experiment.

It is usually possible to transform sloppy, abbreviated notes into a readable study guide without recopying everything. Sadly, however, there are some professors whose lectures are so disorganized that students wind up with notes that don't follow any sensible pattern. Under these conditions it is probably best to completely reorganize your notes on a clean sheet of paper. In either case, your notes will have been sufficiently revised when you are able to read them easily and with good comprehension.

Once you have revised your notes, it is essential that you do something with them. Research indicates that the act of taking notes is not very valuable by itself. Lecture notes are worth little if they aren't reviewed. Spending a few minutes a week reviewing your notes will save hours of frustration at exam time.

One of the best ways to review is through questioning. Ask yourself questions or study with a classmate who also needs the review. Try to identify the most important generalizations as well as facts which your instructor has emphasized in class. Imagine yourself behind the professor's podium and try to guess what questions will be asked on the exam. It is a very comfortable feeling when your questions start showing up on their tests!

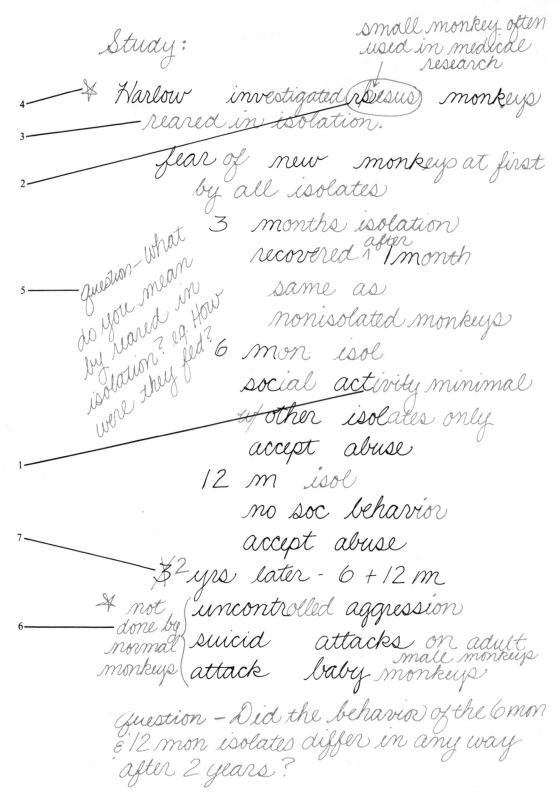

Study:

small monkey often
used in medical
research

4 — * Harlow investigated (Resus) monkeys

3 — reared in isolation.

2 — fear of new monkeys at first
by all isolates

3 months isolation
recovered after 1 month

5 — question—what do you mean by reared in isolation? eg. How were they fed?

same as
nonisolated monkeys

6 mon isol
social activity minimal
with other isolates only
accept abuse

12 m isol
no soc behavior
accept abuse

7 — *2 yrs later - 6 + 12 m

* not done by normal monkeys (uncontrolled aggression
6 — suicid attacks on adult male monkeys
attack baby monkeys

question — Did the behavior of the 6 mon
& 12 mon isolates differ in any way
after 2 years?

Figure 2. Revised notes for the Harlow experiment.

Research-Based Hints for Better Notetaking

---

1. If the professor writes it on the board, put it in your notes.
2. If the professor repeats it, put it in your notes.
3. Don't try to write down every word. Writing too much interferes with learning from lectures.
4. If you don't review notes, you forget up to 75% of the lecture material within eight weeks. Review regularly.
5. You will learn more from taking your own notes than from copying someone else's notes. So go to class!

"Think It Through" Review

Decide how you would handle each of the following situations. If you aren't sure, the page numbers in parentheses should provide a clue.

1. The lecture contains many technical terms which take a long time to write out. You're falling behind. (27–28)

   _____

2. The lecturer is talking too fast. (27–28)

   _____

3. A "friend" offers to take notes for you for a small fee. (31)

   _____

4. Your professor is extremely boring and you find yourself daydreaming in class. (26)

   _____

5. Your notes seem meaningful when you first take them, but when you review them just before the big test, they no longer make sense. (28–30)

   _____

6. You've missed some of the main points of a big lecture. (27–28)

   _____

7. Your professor's lectures are filled with technical terminology that you aren't familiar with. (28)

   _____

8. You look at your notes and find that important facts don't stand out. (27)

   _____

9. Five minutes into a psychology lecture you develop severe finger cramps in your writing hand. (27–28)

   _____

10. The professor shocks your class with a miserable, disorganized lecture. As a result your notes are a total mess. (26, 28)

   _____

4
How to Study from Textbooks?

What Do You Believe about Studying from Textbooks?

Directions: Read each of the statements below. Place a checkmark on the line in front of each statement you believe is true.

1. _____ When you review textbook assignments, the reviews should be short and sweet.

2. _____ The best study questions are the ones that students ask themselves.

3. _____ The more you highlight your textbooks the better.

4. _____ It is a good idea to ask yourself questions while you read.

5. _____ Textbooks are worth less once you have written in them.

We hope these statements have made you curious about studying from textbooks. Perhaps you have some questions now that you didn't have before. You may be asking, "Should I write in my textbooks? If so, should I underline or highlight? How much?" Look for answers to your questions as you read and work your way through this chapter.

PQMR: Reading for a Reason

How do you behave when you are given a long reading assignment? If you are like many college students, you first count the number of pages to see just how bad the situation is. Then you yawn through one or two pages and count those remaining. You keep hoping that counting the pages will make some of them go away, not that you can't do the heavy subtraction. Unfortunately, there is no happy ending if your sole objective is to stagger through to the end of the assignment so that you can raise your hand in class and swear by all that's holy that you *really did* read the assignment (even if you didn't understand a darned thing). Having read the assignment might keep you out of trouble in high school, but it won't get you the grades you need in college. The bottom line in college is what you can *learn*, and that means changing your reason for reading.

FROM: Getting to the end of the reading assignment

TO: Getting as much as possible from your textbook.

Study strategies are designed to help you make this critical transition.

A study strategy is a series of activities which will help you to

1. develop the right purpose for reading,
2. focus your attention on important information,
3. keep your mind from wandering,
4. improve your reading comprehension, and
5. prepare for examinations.

Over the years many different study strategies have been developed to accomplish the five objectives listed above. The study strategy we recommend is called *PQMR*, which stands for *P*review, *Q*uestion, *M*ark, and *R*eview. It is a powerful educational tool which we believe can improve your life in college.

PQMR is based on the most recent research in educational psychology and our current understanding of how the reading process works. Here, in brief, is what research has to say about reading and study strategies:

1. Any study strategy is better than none at all.
2. Looking over an assignment before reading it enhances comprehension.
3. Asking questions during reading promotes comprehension.
4. It is a good idea to underline or highlight, but not too much.
5. Reviewing within 24 hours after reading an assignment will drastically reduce forgetting.
6. Short, frequent review sessions are more effective than long review sessions and "all-nighters" before exams.

Most study strategies are composed of separate stages which follow one after the other; first you do this, then you do that, etc. PQMR is different. We believe that the elements of a study strategy should be *interactive*. What this means is that the various steps in the procedure do not take place in any special order. Also these steps are continuous. The acts of previewing, asking questions, marking the text, and reviewing should be ongoing events whenever you are reading a textbook assignment.

Previewing the Text

Previewing is an important reading technique for increasing your comprehension and retention of textbook reading assignments. Previewing tells you in advance what to expect in a reading assignment. This information does two things for you: (1) it gives you a purpose for reading, and (2) it organizes your thinking so that you can better understand and remember new information. Previewing only takes three or four minutes, but it can save you the extra hours it takes to plod through purposeless reading assignments. Here are the steps of successful previewing:

1. Read the title and the first paragraph to determine the purpose and scope of the reading assignment.
2. Read the closing paragraph (or chapter summary) to find out what information the author considers most important.
3. Skim the assignment by reading all headings and the first sentence that comes directly after each heading.
4. As you skim the assignment, focus your attention on italicized and boldfaced words, pictures, graphs, charts, or anything else that "jumps out at you" and might provide quick, important information.

Questioning the Text

Questioning is also an important part of PQMR and should take place in all stages of the study strategy. For example, when previewing a chapter from one of your textbooks, you should constantly ask yourself the following questions:

What do I already know about this?
What do I need to find out?

As you begin to read the chapter in depth, old questions will be answered and new ones will come to mind. Write them down, remember them, and make sure that they get answered. As a college student you have a right to ask questions and expect answers. When the textbooks don't have the answers to your questions, ask your instructors for help. It's part of their job.

Marking the Text

A textbook is a tool for learning, just as a circular saw is a tool for cutting wood. If the tool is used improperly or casually the result is a poor job. Absolutely the worst thing you can do when reading is allow your mind to wander. If you turn your mind on automatic pilot you will surely begin to think about other things: your bowling average, something that's stuck in your teeth, or the hot date you've got lined up for Friday night. This lackadaisical approach will work fine for the Sunday funnies or the sports page, but the results are devastating with accounting, chemistry, or early European history.

To help keep yourself from tuning out and losing comprehension, we recommend a system of underlining, highlighting, circling, starring, numbering, and written comments for marking in your text. When you are actively responding to the text by deciding what to mark, your comprehension will be much greater than if you are just moving your eyeballs passively toward a rendezvous with the end of the assignment. In addition to better comprehension, a textbook marking system provides a handy guide in which key points and new concepts are identified, explained, and ready for instant review. Here are the elements of the marking system:

_____	Underline or highlight main ideas and important details.
[ ]	Use brackets to mark particularly important paragraphs or parts of paragraphs.
(phoneme)	Circle new technical terms you think you will need to remember.
(1) (2) (3)	Number important steps, causes, or reasons that are buried in the text. Look for signal phrases such as *three steps* or *several methods*.
* ! ?	Use the asterisk or exclamation point to indicate EXTREME IMPORTANCE. Use the question mark to show confusion or disagreement.
Great! Bingo! Garbage Rot Yes No I doubt it.	Jot down personal comments in the margins to respond to what the author is saying. A negative comment is better than no comment at all.

Students generally make one of two mistakes when they begin marking their texts. Either they mark nothing or they go berserk and mark almost everything. These extremes are equally inefficient in promoting comprehension and recall. A middle-of-the-road approach in which only main ideas and significant facts are marked is more effective. In general, you should mark about one sentence per paragraph or about 10–15% of the text. Be as selective as you can. Try to mark major points, possible exam questions, and points that you need to ask about in class.

Another marking strategy is summarizing. After reading the material under each subheading, it is a good idea to write a sentence or two summarizing the material you have just read. One way to do this is to say to yourself: "If there is only one thing I'm going to remember about this material, it's _____ ." Write your brief summary in the text margin or in some strategic location in your notebook. This procedure will help you to organize your thinking. It will also help you to find and remember important generalizations in your reading assignments. It isn't always easy to tell what is important and what isn't. However, just *trying* to find the important information will eventually enable you to do so.

You should probably apply the marking strategy to all regular textbooks that belong to you. *Do not* mark in library books, magazines, or journals. If you need a marked copy of something from the library, make a photocopy first, and then mark on the copy.

Reviewing the Text

One of the most important devices for remembering is review. Your initial review should begin no more than 24 hours after reading the assignment. This will prevent you from forgetting most of the material. Between this initial review and examination time you should schedule frequent, brief review sessions. Research indicates that such study periods are more effective than giant cramming sessions before exams.

Believe it or not, review actually begins while you are reading. It begins with the marks you make in the text and the comments you write in the margins or in your notebook. These things will make your review sessions rapid and effective.

As you review specific reading assignments, check any class notes which refer to the same material. Class notes often will help to clarify fuzzy textbook concepts. It works the other way too. Sometimes the textbook fills in the blanks in class lecture notes.

Check to see if your class notes agree with the text. If they don't agree, ask your instructor to settle the disagreement. One thing that really impresses a professor is a question that shows a student honestly cares about understanding a reading assignment.

Try to set up review sessions with another student in your class. Seek out a serious student who attends class regularly. If you study with people who are successful in college, the chances are better that you will be successful too. Avoid "mellowed-out" types, parasites, and academic losers. Their bad attitudes and habits will rub off on you if you aren't careful.

As you review, try to second guess the instructor. There is nothing wrong with doing this. It amounts to trying to focus on what the professor thinks is important. If you are studying with classmates, it may even be beneficial to write practice exams for each other.

Regardless of how you review, the following formula will hold true:

$$N \times T = G$$

The *N*umber of review sessions times the amount of *T*ime you spend in review equals improved *G*rades in college courses.

Observing the PQMR Strategy

You are now ready to observe the PQMR strategy. What follows is the first half of a typical textbook chapter. The PQMR strategy has already been used so that you can see exactly what to do.

1. Material that should be previewed has been shaded in gray.
2. Underlining and other important marks have been included.
3. Important questions, comments, and summary statements have been written into the text for you.

Begin this practice session by previewing the shaded material. Then, as you read the selection, pay close attention to the marks, questions, and comments which have been written into the text. Also, prepare yourself to answer a few questions when you are finished.

CAREER PLANNING:
Assessment—Exploration—Placement

How can I decide what career is for me?

Is "Career Planning" just another name for "Job Hunting"? The past two decades have taught us a lot about careers. The following words are part of our vocabulary and need no definitions: Overeducated . . . Underemployed . . . Pink Slip . . . RIF . . . SUB . . . Displaced Worker . . . Affirmative Action . . . Protected Class . . . Out-placement . . . Baby Boom . . . Enrollment Decline . . . Supply/Demand . . . Foreign Competition . . . Glut of Engineers . . . Riots.

Is "Career Planning" just a new name for "Job Hunting"? The wealth of a nation is not just its natural resources; it is also its people. The world is not only changing; it is moving in "future shock" proportions. The trends suggest that basic career truths cannot be ignored any longer. People cannot always be shuffled into and out of jobs. The situation calls for much forethought.

CAREER PLANNING

Career planning is an individual activity. In a free society, no giant bureaucratic government dares chart courses for individuals to follow. Individuals cannot survive happily for very long unless they take responsibility for the directions and courses of their lives. The declining lifespan of many jobs (and even whole career fields) demands a personal planning posture. The short job life cycles may force individuals to make rolling decisions annually in order to regenerate new career plans.

Career planning is not just a new name for job hunting. Career planning is conceptually and practically different. Job hunting is only one component of career planning. The future is likely to prove that formal education is not solely for the 6 to 22-year-old. The future may see formal education (university, trade, OJT, etc.) as a renewing component planned in a person's working life and an event which is part of a formal retraining process. *Where do I start?*

Planning Ahead

Exciting productivity advancements imply that more work will be done with the human mind than with physical skills. Automation is common in manufacturing, mining, and finance. Automation is spreading to service industries. The jobs of today may not be the jobs of tomorrow.

The starting point for tomorrow's careers are the specific jobs of today. Tomorrow's skills will likely build upon those required in today's jobs. Career field progress may move at a differing pace in different fields. Today's career plan may not be tomorrow's career plan, so one must look upon career planning as a process that changes over time. Job hunting is no longer career planning. Nonetheless, millions will cling to the

Career planning is an individual activity that is renewed throughout one's lifetime job hunting is part of career planning.

From PLANNING YOUR CAREER by C. Randall Powell, copyright © 1981 by C. Randall Powell. Reprinted by permission of Kendall/Hunt Publishing Company.

old ways and roll from job to job, never achieving their ultimate potential.

Career planning is a bold, exciting, new approach. It will enrich lives of young and old alike. Planning implies more work, but the returns throughout life will pay excellent dividends.

"AND ANOTHER THING L'IL PAL...IT'S NEVER TOO EARLY TO CONSIDER A CAREER IN MEDICINE."

The Work Setting

The future . . . what will it hold? The world of work holds open a massive array of work possibilities. The future . . . will I be happy? Work is a significant part of your life.

Work is not a person's whole reason for being, but it has historically provided a major influence on how our society views the success of an individual. Success

is often defined in terms of significant work achievements. Newspaper obituaries cite these past achievements daily.

From about the time a person turns 20 until he reaches about age 60, the American value system places great importance upon his work. Work is frequently defined as the process through which one earns the resources that allow him or her to live in a manner to which he or she is accustomed. The great philosopher Voltaire once said that work "spares us from three great evils: boredom, vice, and need."

How work is defined and for what period of life it is most significant is not really all that important. Some people start work very early in life and never stop. Others view work as a necessary evil. *really?* The premise of this book is that work can be enjoyable. A person's satisfactions and happiness come about in many various ways and from many different things, but the proper work activity and work environment can be sources of much satisfaction and happiness in life.

Life Decisions

Three of the most important decisions people make in life relate to buying an automobile, investing in a home, and choosing a marriage partner. Hours, days, weeks, and months are spent making these decisions. Every aspect is usually analyzed very thoroughly. Those decisions usually have long-term impacts on happiness.

Deciding what to do tonight and the decision about where to go next Saturday night are important to most people. Many hours go into making "Saturday night" types of decisions. Short-term decisions, when placed in a series, form the basis of long-term happiness.

All of this is leading up to illustrating the extent of personal involvement in planning and analyzing before you make a decision in your personal life. Many

things can motivate this planning, but the desired end product is happiness.

This book is about work. You need to spend more time thinking about it. Work is too important to leave to chance. Thousands of people, nonetheless, let their lives haphazardly fall into work activities, and allow important decisions to be made for them by others and by happenstance. Some get lucky. Others pay too high a price for many years.

Why not spend some time planning for a lifetime of work activity? Is that not just as important as the decision about which car, stereo, or house to purchase? Why do most people spend so much time on the minor decisions in life and so little time on decisions that can mean so much? A person's quality of life is greatly enhanced by work—a job—which is right for him or her.

Significance of Planning

This book is directed toward those individuals who are seeking careers in managerial, technical, or professional fields. Although applicable to a very wide age range, the most directly affected age category is the 20 to 40 age range. Most positions in the fields we will deal with in this book currently pay salaries in the $12—40,000 range, depending upon the required education level and experience, the type of position, supply/demand, etc. Assuming a starting salary of $15,000 annually at age 22, and a 10% increase per year until retirement at age 65, a person would earn well over one million dollars in his lifetime.

Career decisions are significant decisions! Perhaps no other decision that an individual makes has such a major impact on economic well-being. Not everyone will earn that large sum in a lifetime of work, but many will earn an even greater amount.

Career planning is hard work. It is not fun for everyone. It can be boring. It can be exciting. It is

important. Everyone, including you, should prepare a plan. Plans can be modified as new information arrives.

Many people do not bother with career planning. They prefer to roll with the punches . . . and they sometimes get knocked out of the real meaning of life before they get started. Satisfaction comes from knowing that you recognized the challenge and then took a deliberate course of action to achieve your career, life, and personal goals. The work setting has a major impact on a person's longer-term view of life and self.

Work Planning

Planning work events over a long time span is career planning. A person may carry out several unrelated work roles over time. Why can't one be a business executive, a doctor, and an architect in his or her lifetime? The logic comes through a rational decision-making process. Career planning then becomes life planning.

Planning involves setting goals that can be realistically achieved. Goals motivate us, and striving to satisfy goals can be fun. A person may have a few major goals and hundreds of subgoals that serve as building blocks for his or her future.

The basis of life planning is setting achievable personal objectives. Career planning is a major element of life planning. For some work-oriented people, life planning is career planning. The two are always interrelated. This book zeroes in on the career aspect of life planning.

Career Jargon *Look up*

Career planning professionals throw a fair share of jargon at people they counsel. There are several words which when taken out of context have multiple meanings.

Job. A work situation taken for the purpose of earning wages for completing a task, a series of tasks,

★ Career planning is a major element of life planning.

WHAT ARE YOU DOING, RALPH?

I'M TRYING TO THINK OF A CREATIVE WAY TO ASK DAD FOR SOME MONEY.

WHY DON'T YOU TRY WORKING INSTEAD?

I AM WORKING! THIS IS HARDER THAN IT LOOKS.

or a definitive piece of work. A job frequently is temporary in nature and the word seldom implies a long-term commitment to a given type of work. A job rarely requires a long training period for mastery of the work assigned. Exceptions to this can exist in skilled trades and crafts, however.

Career. A work or vocational experience that an individual elects to pursue during a significant period of time in life. A career involves a relatively long-term commitment to a given work activity. A career requires a significant level of formal education, training, and background for satisfactorily performing in the work area.

Planning. Planning means devising a scheme for doing, making, or arranging a project, program, or schedule. Planning is a process that occurs over time and one that adjusts itself when new information becomes available. Planning involves charting a course of action and then adjusting the course as the situation changes from the orginally hypothesized projection.

Applying the PQMR Strategy

You are now ready to apply the PQMR strategy. What follows is the second part of the chapter on career planning. *You* will use the PQMR strategy with this material to prove to yourself that PQMR works. The following summary outline should help you to apply the strategy efficiently:

A. To preview
1. Read the title and the first paragraph.
2. Read the closing paragraph (or chapter summary).
3. Skim the assignment by reading all headings and the first sentence that comes directly after each heading.
4. As you skim, focus your attention on italicized words, pictures, graphs, and charts.

B. To Question
Write down at least five questions which you have about the subject matter.

C. To Mark

_____	Underline or highlight main ideas and important details.
[ ]	Use brackets to mark important paragraphs.
Jargon	Circle new technical terms.
(1) (2) (3)	Number important steps, causes, or reasons.
* ! ?	Use the asterisk or exclamation point to indicate EXTREME IMPORTANCE. Use the question mark to show confusion or disagreement.
Super! Barf! True	Jot down personal comments and summarize each major subheading.

WHAT IS CAREER PLANNING?

Career planning is an activity that occurs throughout a person's working lifetime. It is futuristic. Career planning is distinct from life planning in that it does not initially attempt to integrate a broader array of planning variables such as early childhood, family, religion, values, leisure, retirement, etc. Career planning is indeed a sub-component of life planning that draws upon many of the same background variables, but it focuses attention on the work activity and work envi-

CAREER PLANNING PROCESS

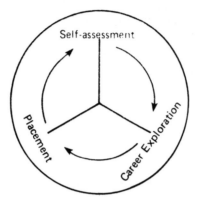

Figure 1.1

ronment. There are many instances in which career and life planning cannot be completely separated.

Career planning is a process that draws upon three major planning activities: self-assessment, career exploration, and job placement. Career planning reverts to solely job hunting unless these three activities are addressed individually and in concert. Assessment, exploration, and placement form the framework of sound career planning. The concept builds a method of appraising career potential, exploring various alternatives, and implementing an action plan designed to achieve a predetermined set of career goals.

Self-Assessment

The purpose of career decision making is to aid the person in obtaining career position consistent with his or her academic training, past work and life experiences, personality, abilities, aptitudes, values, interests, etc. A thorough understanding of all one's characteristics is thus necessary. Socrates referred to this understanding with the term "know thyself," and in this book we refer to the process through which a person comes to know himself better as self-assessment.

The collecting, analyzing, and evaluating of information about the self creates a much higher level of awareness about all aspects of self, especially about life goals. Although this process is essentially one of personal choice, one approach to the task enlists the aid of advisors, friends, and numerous publications.

A framework organizes thoughts in a meaningful way and permits a much more detailed specification of background characteristics. Exercises, projects, tests, and other instruments aid in the drawing out of these variables in a way that they can be organized and meaningfully related to career options.

Career Exploration

The number of potential career options is staggering. The self-assessment helps narrow the field by discarding obviously conflicting options. Developing an array of information about specific career alternatives requires an intense detective-minded approach. For every career cluster with its related positions, a wealth of data exists. No single career information source can cover every occupation.

Career exploration involves digging into a mass of information with the objective of narrowing the scope of career alternatives. Thousands of alternatives may be discarded on the basis of job title alone. The key question is: what pertinent facts might influence my decision?

Career exploration analyzes information about the world of work. The process may be an in-depth analysis of a given career option, or it may be a cursory view of occupations clustered in a broad career field. Career exploration thus begins with a specification of need for breadth or depth in analysis. Once depth is in order, the next task is to identify the variables which are most likely to be crucial in acceptance or rejection of various career alternatives.

Given your personally defined array of factors and criteria which are important in the selection of a career field (or specific job), the role of career exploration is to add selected pieces of data that may impact upon important career decisions.

"YOU DON'T MIND IF I PICK UP SOME TIPS DO YOU?.. I'M THINKING OF A MEDICAL CAREER MYSELF."

Placement

This phase of career planning activity takes on meaning only after some tentative career choice decisions emerge. Placement begins the final phase of career planning. Placement is a reality test of tentative decisions.

Placement is marketing, and it progresses from self-assessment and career exploration.

In spite of its "ring of finality," the placement process continues to add new, real-world information into the assessment-exploration-placement triangle. Bridges are not burned, but bridges do wear out. Placement provides the road map and serves as a feedback loop that reinforces (or changes) earlier career decisions.

Placement includes resume preparation, cover letter introductions, contact development, search strategy, job interviewing, all facets of employment communications, and job decision making.

Placement success depends upon matching career goals (tentatively decided upon after assessment and exploration) with job requirements. The placement decision, in effect, forecasts a realistic career path. In reality, a perfect match between assessment and exploration rarely occurs.

42

Finally, the placement process is time and decision oriented. Success depends upon career goals matching job requirements. Without compromise, the match may never occur. Employment calls for a firm decision at a given point in time.

Time pressures force career choices. Time places pressure on the need for compromise. A preplanned time and decision framework permits a rational placement process based upon a realistic evaluation of the current work environment.

Placement must be viewed in the total framework of the career planning process. A run-away placement strategy is for fools only. It connotes getting a job at any cost and taking whatever is available.

Jumping into the placement function without the prior assessment and exploration phases of career plan-

ning is like entering the "Indy 500" with a passenger car. The race may be completed, but the well-designed and well-engineered race cars with experienced drivers will finish far sooner and far better.

INTEGRATED CONCEPTS

Each of the three major career planning process components may be completed initially as an independent project. But the career planning process cannot be optimally successful without viewing each activity as part of an integrated system. Important feedback loops in each component tend to reinforce or modify earlier preliminary decisions. There is a continuous recycling of information and thus adjustment and modification of earlier decisions.

Compromise

As the career planning process continues, compromises occur. Your self-assessment leads to a much more accurate view of yourself, and the picture becomes more and more clearly defined as new information is added from your career exploration activity.

The placement or job search activity feeds real world career information into the model. As a result, specification and clarification, adjusted by necessary compromises, begin to firm up an overall career plan.

Feedback Loops

The initial phase of career planning is completed upon acceptance of a career-related assignment with a specific employer. Another phase sets in as you replay the process as work-related experiences add new information to the process. Re-evaluation phases continue throughout life. The new information continually is fed back into the career planning model and you make appropriate adjustments.

Process

Career planning can be viewed as a logical, patterned, sequential approach to the task of assessing, analyzing, and deciding how you want to perform in a work setting. Career planning is a series of events that recur over and over through a planned pattern controlled by you. Sound career planning is designed to renew itself continually over time.

CAREER INFORMATION PROCESS

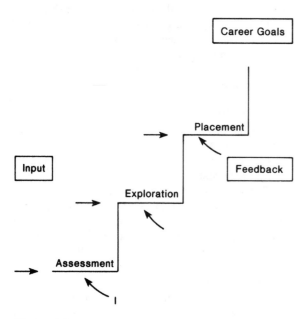

Figure 1.2

Individual Activity

Career planning is an individual exercise. You are the center. You possess a unique set of values, philosophy, personality, interests, intelligence level, education, and work experience background. A major role of a career counselor is to assist an individual in drawing out all of these characteristics and understanding the nature of these characteristics and career alternatives.

Work-Centered

Career planning is more than an understanding of self. It is also an understanding of the world of work. Only by understanding occupational options are you in a position to objectively correlate personal characteristics with employment realities.

Career planning is a way of thinking about the future. It is not simply a sterile academic exercise of matching personal characteristics and job possibilities in order to ascertain your ideal niche.

The implementation of a career plan involves actual employment in a work setting. Career planning goes beyond the placement function. There are continual evaluation and feedback loops that clarify the adequacy of the employment decision or suggest a reassessment of the entire career planning process. This dynamic process continues throughout life.

Decision-Oriented

What am I going to do with my life? That is a heavy question for a career search handbook, but it is a relevant question. People tend to postpone the most critical decisions they must face. Procrastination is a way of life.

Career planning is decision-oriented, and decision making is a skill that can be mastered. Like all decisions, career decisions require information. Information is available, but it must be requested and then processed in proper fashions.

People procrastinate because they do not see a way to get a handle on a problem. People want to make career decisions, but the magnitude of the decisions is often overwhelming. What if I make the wrong decision? Is no decision better than a bad decision? Why do I have to make any decision?

There are no perfectly bad or perfectly good decisions in choosing a career. The situation is never black or white. There are thousands of shades of grey. Most people convince themselves that the decisions they made were good ones, and they usually are. That is the case because most people after making a decision tend to mobilize their resources and make subsequent decisions which assure that the first decision was right.

"WOULD YOU RATE YOUR CAREER AS Ⓐ... EXTREMELY REWARDING... Ⓑ MILDLY REWARDING.... Ⓒ MODERATELY REWARDING...OR Ⓓ..A BUMMER?"

44

Decision making takes career planning to an action-oriented level. Decision-makers take career planning out of an academic exercise and into a practical, necessary activity. In its most elementary form, decision making is a six-step process:

1. Define the problem
2. Develop alternative solutions
3. Establish evaluative criteria
4. Evaluate alternatives
5. Make a decision
6. Evaluate decision

There is a closed loop which connects the evaluation, the decision, and the review of the original problem in light of the information gathered. This rolling process can be used on the smallest sub-component of the problem area as well as on the largest element of the total decision. The key point is that a decision must be made at designated points in time. Even procrastination becomes a decision after a certain amount of time.

Career decision making involves compromises. The compromise solution impacts upon other people, personal preferences, and hypothetical concepts. In any decision, there are elements of positioning, negotiating, flexibility, and defining between self-concepts and/or other people. There rarely is a perfect solution. This systematic, analytical process of decision making molds a realistic and acceptable match between the world of work and personal goals.

Career Planning Summary

Career planning seeks answers to four questions:

1. What do I want to do?
2. What can I do?
3. What needs to be done?
4. How can I get the job I want?

If one could always provide definitive answers to these basic questions, career planning would always be optimally achieved. Career planning boils down to some very simple ideas. The complexity of life creates difficult answers to those questions. If a marketing expert were dealing with a specific product, some basic marketing fundamentals would be quickly applied by answering three questions:

1. What do you have to offer?
2. Who needs it?
3. How do you make them want it?

Human lives and marketing principles may be miles apart, however. Career decisions require a much more complex approach. Yet every approach must begin with a first step. The first step is often the hardest, but the longest journey starts with that one first step. Career planning must be approached one step at a time, and the first step is the hardest.

You can get a handle on complex career decisions. Career planning offers a logical, structured, and sequential method in career decision making. This method builds upon a theory-based framework proposed by leading career theorists. The largest laboratory in the world is the job market. Consequently, the approach of this book is not some "pie in the sky" academic theory, but an approach which has stood the test of time in a real world setting. It works.

This career planning model offers a fresh look at career decisions. There is much interrelatedness within a complex set of variables. Conceptually, the model focuses attention on the three concepts of self-assessment, career exploration, and placement. Information is fed into one or all of these components. Based upon a process of integration, compromise, work settings, and goal specification, career decisions are reached, assessed, and reassessed over time. Figure 1.1 gives an overview of this model.

The following pages contain our own version of the selection you just marked. We want you to make comparisons, but we don't want you to think that your version should look just like ours. Marking in texts is a highly personal activity, so there should be individual differences. You may have missed a few things, but you may also have noted something important that we missed. Therefore, use the following marked text only as a *guide*. Also note that for purposes of illustration we have placed parentheses around material which we think you should have previewed.

CAREER PLANNING PROCESS

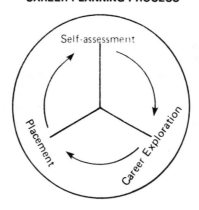

Figure 1.1

Why should I start now?

(**WHAT IS CAREER PLANNING?**

Career planning is an activity that occurs through-out a person's working lifetime. It is futuristic. Career) planning is distinct from (life planning) in that it does not initially attempt to integrate a broader array of planning variables such as early childhood, family, religion, values, leisure, retirement, etc. (Career planning) is indeed a sub-component of life planning that draws upon many of the same background variables, but it focuses attention on the work activity and work environment. There are many instances in which career and life planning cannot be completely separated.

Career planning is a process that draws upon three major planning activities: self-assessment, career ex-

ploration, and job placement. Career planning reverts to solely job hunting unless these three activities are addressed individually and in concert. Assessment, exploration, and placement form the framework of sound career planning. The concept builds a method of appraising career potential, exploring various alternatives, and implementing an action plan designed to achieve a predetermined set of career goals.

(**Self-Assessment**

The purpose of career decision making is to aid the person in obtaining career position consistent with)

Career planning is a process that uses 1) self assessment, 2) career exploration, and 3) job placement information to set career goals.

46

his or her academic training, past work and life experiences, personality, abilities, aptitudes, values, interests, etc. A thorough understanding of all one's characteristics is thus necessary. Socrates referred to this understanding with the term "know thyself," and in this book we refer to the process through which a person comes to know himself better as self-assessment.

Do this necessary?

The collecting, analyzing, and evaluating of information about the self creates a much higher level of awareness about all aspects of self, especially about life goals. Although this process is essentially one of personal choice, one approach to the task enlists the aid of advisors, friends, and numerous publications.

A framework organizes thoughts in a meaningful way and permits a much more detailed specification of background characteristics. Exercises, projects, tests, and other instruments aid in the drawing out of these variables in a way that they can be organized and meaningfully related to career options.

"YOU DON'T MIND IF I PICK UP SOME TIPS DO YOU?.. I'M THINKING OF A MEDICAL CAREER MYSELF."

Career Exploration

O.K.

The number of potential career options is staggering. The self-assessment helps narrow the field by discarding obviously conflicting options. Developing an array of information about specific career alternatives requires an intense detective-minded approach. For every career cluster with its related positions, a wealth of data exists. No single career information source can cover every occupation.

Career exploration involves digging into a mass of information with the objective of narrowing the scope of career alternatives. Thousands of alternatives may be discarded on the basis of job title alone. The key question is: what pertinent facts might influence my decision?

Career exploration analyzes information about the world of work. The process may be an in-depth analysis of a given career option, or it may be a cursory view of occupations clustered in a broad career field. Career exploration thus begins with a specification of need for breadth or depth in analysis. Once depth is in order, the next task is to identify the variables which are most likely to be crucial in acceptance or rejection of various career alternatives.

hasty

Given your personally defined array of factors and criteria which are important in the selection of a career field (or specific job), the role of career exploration is to add selected pieces of data that may impact upon important career decisions.

→ *this paragraph doesn't mean anything to me. what is an array of factors?*

Once I'm placed in a job does career exploration stop?

Placement

This phase of career planning activity takes on meaning only after some tentative career choice decisions emerge. Placement begins the final phase of career planning. Placement is a reality test of tentative decisions.

Placement is marketing, and it progresses from self-assessment and career exploration.

In spite of its "ring of finality," the placement process continues to add new, real-world information into the assessment-exploration-placement triangle. Bridges are not burned, but bridges do wear out. Placement provides the road map and serves as a feedback loop that reinforces (or changes) earlier career decisions.

?

Placement includes resume preparation, cover letter introductions, contact development, search strategy, job interviewing, all facets of employment communications, and job decision making.

Placement success depends upon matching career goals (tentatively decided upon after assessment and exploration) with job requirements. The placement decision, in effect, forecasts a realistic career path. In reality, a perfect match between assessment and exploration rarely occurs.

Where do I go for placement help?

47

ning is like entering the "Indy 500" with a passenger car. The race may be completed, but the well-designed and well-engineered race cars with experienced drivers will finish far sooner and far better.

INTEGRATED CONCEPTS

Each of the three major career planning process components may be completed initially as an independent project. But the career planning process cannot be optimally successful without viewing each activity as part of an integrated system. Important feedback loops in each component tend to reinforce or modify earlier preliminary decisions. There is a continuous re-cycling of information and thus adjustment and modification of earlier decisions.

change
?

Compromise

As the career planning process continues, compromises occur. Your self-assessment leads to a much more accurate view of yourself, and the picture becomes more and more clearly defined as new information is added from your career exploration activity.

The placement or job search activity feeds real world career information into the model. As a result, specification and clarification, adjusted by necessary compromises, begin to firm up an overall career plan.

Feedback Loops

The initial phase of career planning is completed upon acceptance of a career-related assignment with a specific employer. Another phase sets in as you replay the process as work-related experiences add new information to the process. Re-evaluation phases continue throughout life. The new information continually is fed back into the career planning model and you make appropriate adjustments.

Finally, the placement process is time and decision oriented. Success depends upon career goals matching job requirements. Without compromise, the match may never occur. Employment calls for a firm decision at a given point in time.

Time pressures force career choices. Time places pressure on the need for compromise. A preplanned time and decision framework permits a rational placement process based upon a realistic evaluation of the current work environment. *!!!*

Placement must be viewed in the total framework of the career planning process. A run-away placement strategy is for fools only. It connotes getting a job at any cost and taking whatever is available.

Jumping into the placement function without the prior assessment and exploration phases of career plan-

Be realistic and willing to compromise.

48

Process

Career planning can be viewed as a logical, patterned, sequential approach to the task of assessing, analyzing, and deciding how you want to perform in a work setting. Career planning is a series of events that recur over and over through a planned pattern controlled by you. Sound career planning is designed to renew itself continually over time.

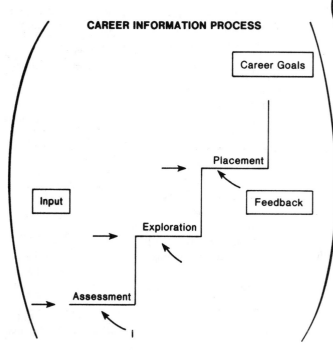

CAREER INFORMATION PROCESS

Career Goals

Placement

Feedback

Input

Exploration

Assessment

Figure 1.2

← carrying out

The implementation of a career plan involves actual employment in a work setting. Career planning goes beyond the placement function. There are continual evaluation and feedback loops that clarify the adequacy of the employment decision or suggest a reassessment of the entire career planning process. This dynamic process continues throughout life.

What if I decide on the wrong job?

Decision-Oriented

What am I going to do with my life? That is a heavy question for a career search handbook, but it is a relevant question. People tend to postpone the most critical decisions they must face. Procrastination is a way of life.

Career planning is decision-oriented, and decision making is a skill that can be mastered. Like all decisions, career decisions require information. Information is available, but it must be requested and then processed in proper fashions.

People procrastinate because they do not see a way to get a handle on a problem. People want to make career decisions, but the magnitude of the decisions is often overwhelming. What if I make the wrong decision? Is no decision better than a bad decision? Why do I have to make any decision?

There are no perfectly bad or perfectly good decisions in choosing a career. The situation is never black or white. There are thousands of shades of grey. Most people convince themselves that the decisions they made were good ones, and they usually are. That is the case because most people after making a decision tend to mobilize their resources and make subsequent decisions which assure that the first decision was right.

Individual Activity

Career planning is an individual exercise. You are the center. You possess a unique set of values, philosophy, personality, interests, intelligence level, education, and work experience background. A major role of a career counselor is to assist an individual in drawing out all of these characteristics and understanding the nature of these characteristics and career alternatives.

Work-Centered

Career planning is more than an understanding of self. It is also an understanding of the world of work. Only by understanding occupational options are you in a position to objectively correlate personal characteristics with employment realities. *relate*

Career planning is a way of thinking about the future. It is not simply a sterile academic exercise of matching personal characteristics and job possibilities in order to ascertain your ideal niche.

"WOULD YOU RATE YOUR CAREER AS Ⓐ... EXTREMELY REWARDING... Ⓑ MILDLY REWARDING... Ⓒ MODERATELY REWARDING... OR Ⓓ .. A BUMMER?"

Decision making takes career planning to an action-oriented level. Decision-makers take career planning out of an academic exercise and into a practical, necessary activity. In its most elementary form, decision making is a six-step process:

1. Define the problem
2. Develop alternative solutions
3. Establish evaluative criteria
4. Evaluate alternatives
5. Make a decision
6. Evaluate decision

know these!

There is a closed loop which connects the evaluation, the decision, and the review of the original problem in light of the information gathered. This rolling process can be used on the smallest sub-component of the problem area as well as on the largest element of the total decision. The key point is that a decision must be made at designated points in time. Even procrastination becomes a decision after a certain amount of time.

Career decision making involves compromises. The compromise solution impacts upon other people, personal preferences, and hypothetical concepts. In any decision, there are elements of positioning, negotiating, flexibility, and defining between self-concepts and/or other people. There rarely is a perfect solution. This systematic, analytical process of decision making molds a realistic and acceptable match between the world of work and personal goals.

ask instructor!

Career Planning Summary

Career planning seeks answers to four questions:

1. What do I want to do?
2. What can I do?
3. What needs to be done?
4. How can I get the job I want?

If one could always provide definitive answers to these basic questions, career planning would always be optimally achieved. Career planning boils down to some very simple ideas. The complexity of life creates difficult answers to those questions. If a marketing expert were dealing with a specific product, some basic marketing fundamentals would be quickly applied by answering three questions:

1. What do you have to offer?
2. Who needs it?
3. How do you make them want it?

Human lives and marketing principles may be miles apart, however. Career decisions require a much more complex approach. Yet every approach must begin with a first step. The first step is often the hardest, but the longest journey starts with that one first step. Career planning must be approached one step at a time, and the first step is the hardest.

You can get a handle on complex career decisions. Career planning offers a logical, structured, and sequential method in career decision making. This method builds upon a theory-based framework proposed by leading career theorists. The largest laboratory in the world is the job market. Consequently, the approach of this book is not some "pie in the sky" academic theory, but an approach which has stood the test of time in a real world setting. It works.

This career planning model offers a fresh look at career decisions. There is much interrelatedness within a complex set of variables. Conceptually, the model focuses attention on the three concepts of self-assessment, career exploration, and placement. Information is fed into one or all of these components. Based upon a process of integration, compromise, work settings, and goal specification, career decisions are reached, assessed, and reassessed over time. Figure 1.1 gives an overview of this model.

Reviewing the Assignment

Now that you have applied the PQMR strategy, you are ready to review and take a test over the material. That's the normal course of events! If you have used the marking strategy properly, you should be able to review the material with great efficiency. Give yourself three minutes to review and find the answers to the following questions from the second part of the chapter on career planning. Refer to your own marked version of the chapter. (The answers to this quiz are on page 54):

1. Name one placement activity. _____

2. What is the fourth step in the six-step decision making process? _____

3. What are the three major planning activities of the career planning process?

    _____

    _____

    _____

4. Define the term *career exploration.* _____

    _____

5. What two factors must be matched in order to insure placement success?

    _____

    _____

Study Sense and Classroom Manners

Study sense is common sense applied to study habits. It is important because all of the speed reading and study techniques in the world are of limited value unless they are applied in a consistent and intelligent fashion. Complete the following questionnaire to find out how good your study sense is. After you have answered all of the questions, total your points.

Study Sense Questionnaire

1. When you are given a reading assignment in a textbook, do you finish the reading assignment on time?

    (a) Always _____ (5 points)

    (b) Usually _____ (3 points)

    (c) Sometimes _____ (1 point)

    (d) Almost never _____ (0 points)

2. How often do you take your textbooks to class with you?

    (a) Always _____ (5 points)

    (b) Usually _____ (3 points)

    (c) Sometimes _____ (1 point)

    (d) Almost never _____ (0 points)

3. Do you take notes in your classes?

    (a) Always _____ (5 points)

    (b) Usually _____ (3 points)

    (c) Sometimes _____ (1 point)

    (d) Almost never _____ (0 points)

4. Do you participate in class discussions?

    (a) Always _____ (5 points)

    (b) Usually _____ (3 points)

    (c) Sometimes _____ (1 point)

    (d) Almost never _____ (0 points)

5. Where do you sit in most of your classes?

    (a) At the front or in the middle of the room _____ (5 points)

    (b) Along the sides in the front or middle _____ (2 points)

    (c) At the back _____ (0 points)

6. How many times have you been late to this class so far this semester or quarter?

    (a) None _____ (5 points)

    (b) Once _____ (4 points)

    (c) Twice _____ (1 point)

    (d) More than two times _____ (0 points)

7. How many times have you missed this class so far this semester or quarter?

    (a) None _____ (10 points)

    (b) Once _____ (7 points)

    (c) Twice _____ (2 points)

    (d) Three or more times _____ (0 points)

8. How many written assignments have you failed to turn in on time this semester or quarter for all of your classes combined?

    (a) None _____ (10 points)

    (b) One _____ (5 points)

    (c) Two _____ (1 point)

    (d) Three or more _____ (0 points)

POSSIBLE POINTS = 50

YOUR SCORE = _____

Interpretation

40–50 points: *Excellent.* We predict a bright future for you. You have the study sense that leads to success in college.

30–39 points: *Good.* You will probably make it through college. Your study sense is above average.

20–29 points: *Fair.* You are a borderline case. There is a lot of room for improvement in your study sense.

10–19 points: *Poor.* College is going to be a rocky road for you. Unless you change your attitudes, failure is probable.

0–9 points: *Disastrous.* Our prediction is that you are soon going to flunk out of college. Change your attitudes or be prepared to ship out.

We are convinced that your attitude is as important as your IQ in determining your success as a college student. Your mental attitude is also something which is totally within your control. In other words, you *can* make it in college if you are willing to develop your study sense. Here are the *Passport* rules for good study sense and classroom manners:

1. *Develop a weekly schedule.* On page 55 you will find a blank schedule which you can photocopy. Plan your time for each week. Plan for the following things:
   Classes
   Study Time
   Free Time
   Meals
   Exercise
   Work

2. *Make study regular.* Set up regular, daily hours for study even if nothing is due. Many students mistakenly assume that study is something they should do just before exams and when papers are due. This attitude leads to cramming, poor test scores, and inferior papers. You should probably set aside three hours a week for study for each course you are taking. For some classes you may need a lot more.

3. *Find a good place to study.* We have seen a good many student schedules over the last ten years. One frequent, major mistake is to block out five hours an evening for study, but then locate that study in a dorm filled with loud music, friends, and a hundred other distractions. The result is usually five hours of either goofing off or frustration instead of five hours of study. We recommend the library or some other quiet place. One hour of honest concentrated study in a quiet location is worth more than five hours of constant interruption and noise.

4. *Never cut classes.* The more classes you cut the lower your grades are going to be. Don't fool yourself into thinking you will get the notes from someone else. It doesn't work.

5. *Get to class on time.* Getting to class late makes it look like you don't care. It is also rude to the class and instructor, and you miss assignments and other important information.

6. *Sit at the front or in the center of the classroom.* You will hear everything. You will stay more alert. You will learn more. Your scores on tests will be higher.

7. *Turn in assignments on time.* There is often a penalty for late work.

8. *Take notes.* No one has a perfect memory. Good notes lead to higher test scores.

9. *Always take your textbooks to class.* You never know when your instructor will refer you to the text in class. In addition, your marked text will contain the questions and insights you have formulated by using PQMR. They can be your contribution to the class.

Follow these rules for classroom manners and study sense, and you will be well on your way to a college diploma.

Think It Through Review

1. You are trying to study in your dorm room, but there is noise coming at you from all sides. What should you do? _____

   _____

2. Your buddies always sit in the back of the class where they sleep or make funny noises. What should you do? _____

   _____

3. You have an opportunity to buy a textbook which is already underlined. What should you do? ___

   _____

4. Two acquaintances from your chemistry class ask you if you would like to review with them two nights a week for 30 minutes each night. What should you do? _____

   _____

Answers to the Career Planning Quiz on page 51:
1. Any one of the following:
   resumé preparation
   cover letter introductions
   search strategies
   job interviewing
   employment communications
   job decision making
2. Evaluate alternatives
3. a. self-assessment
   b. career exploration
   c. placement
4. Career exploration means looking closely at all of your career options to find out which one suits you best.
5. Placement success depends upon matching career goals with job requirements.

Weekly Schedule

Schedule for Week of _____

	Sunday	Monday	Tuesday	Wednesday	Thursday	Friday	Saturday
6 AM							
7 AM							
8 AM							
9							
10							
11							
12							
1 PM							
2							
3							
4							
5							
6							
7							
8							
9							
10							
11							
12							

Cop·a·ce·tic ^{Def.}(Very Satisfactory.)

5
How to Improve Your Subject Area Vocabulary

What Do You Believe about Vocabulary?

Directions: Read each of the statements below. Place a checkmark on the line in front of each statement you believe is true.

1. _____ Usually, the meanings of difficult words can be discovered by looking at the context in which the words occur.

2. _____ Nothing predicts IQ better than the size of a person's vocabulary.

3. _____ The best place to find the meanings of technical words is the dictionary.

4. _____ A book's glossary tells you the page on which a particular topic begins.

5. _____ The average adult learns about 1,000 new words each year.

We hope these statements have made you curious about words and the value of vocabulary development. Perhaps you have developed a few questions of your own, such as, "How much should I use the dictionary when I'm reading? or How can I develop a bigger and better vocabulary?" Look for the answers to your questions as you read and work your way through this chapter.

Double Double Talk Talk

"Our paper is two days late this week," writes a Nebraska editor, "owing to an accident to our press. When we started to run the press Wednesday night, as usual, one of the guy ropes gave away, allowing the forward glider fluke to fall and break as it struck the flunker flopper. This, of course, as anyone who knows anything about a press will readily understand, left the gang-plank with only the flip-flap to support it, which also dropped and broke off the wooper-chock. This loosened the flunking from between the ramrod and the flipper-snatcher, which also caused trouble. The report that the delay was caused by the overindulgence in stimulants by ourselves, is a tissue of falsehoods, the peeled appearance of our right eye being caught by our going into the hatchway of the press in our anxiety to start it, and pulling the coupling pin after the slap-bang was broken, which caused the dingus to rise up and welt us in the optic. We expect a brand-new glider fluke on this afternoon's train."

From *Treasury of American Folk Humor* by James M. Tidwell. Crown Publishers, from *American Wit and Humor*, George W. Jacobs & Co., Philadelphia, from *The Joy of Words* J. G. Ferguson Publishing Company, Chicago, 1960.

Aside from its obvious humor, the passage you just read provides a good example of how comprehension is impaired by the use of unfamiliar words. In this case words like *dingus, slap-bang,* and *glider-fluke* are purposely used to confuse the issue. You will also encounter strange new words in college textbooks. They won't often be as silly as *wooper-chock,* but they can be just as confusing. The purposes of this chapter are: (1) to explain why vocabulary development is an important part of your overall study strategy, and (2) to show you how you can improve your vocabulary.

Vocabulary Facts of Life

The average child of six learns several thousand words during a single year; yet the average adult of 30 learns as few as ten. Why is there such a great difference? You might imagine that it is because the adult already knows most of the English words so that there are only a few left to master. This would be a worthy guess but a wrong one. English has more than 400,000 words, and the average adult knows only about fifteen percent of them. There is plenty of room for vocabulary growth. A better explanation is that young children are driven to learn new words by their natural desire to communicate more efficiently. This desire seems to disappear once the average person's vocabulary becomes large enough to meet everyday needs.

But, you are *not* average, and neither is your need to communicate. You are in college. This means that you must cope with difficult textbooks, tough lectures, and many new concepts. In order to communicate effectively with authors, instructors, and future employers, you need to be able to use more words than the average person. The larger your vocabulary, the better you will read, write, and speak; and the better you read, write, and speak the more successful you are likely to be in your chosen profession.

The research on personal vocabulary development is very clear. Here are some of the findings.

---

1. People who are successful in business have larger vocabularies than people who are less successful.
2. The larger your vocabulary, the better you will comprehend what you read.
3. Size of vocabulary is the single best predictor of IQ.
4. Developing a larger vocabulary improves all communications skills.
5. People with larger vocabularies get better grades in school.
6. It is possible to improve your vocabulary.

Insiders-Outsiders

Read the following passage. Circle each word or phrase that is unfamiliar to you, then summarize the passage in the space provided.

> Sometimes a mob might "grift" all day without "turning them over," but this is unlikely except in the case of a "jug mob" which takes a limited number of "pokes." Any pick-pocket who has on his person more than one wallet is something of a hazard both to himself and to the mob, for each wallet can count as a separate offense if he should be caught. Therefore, it is safer to have cash only. "Class mobs" usually count the money each time they "skin the pokes," one "stall" commonly is responsible for all of it, and an accounting in full is made at the end of the day. When there is a woman with the mob, she usually carries the "knock up." (Maurer, D. W. Whiz mob. *Publication of the American Dialect Society,* 1955, No. 24, p. 194.)

_____

_____

_____

_____

_____ .

All groups of people, whether they be pickpockets, construction workers, or college professors, share a special vocabulary which identifies the group. Insiders use this vocabulary freely to find out what the group knows and to receive the benefits of membership. Likewise, outsiders are identified by their inability to speak the language of the group and are not allowed to belong.

In order to survive in college you must to make yourself an insider in every course you take. History, mathematics, or mortuary science, they're all the same in at least one way. They each have a special vocabulary that you must master if you are to succeed in that course.

The passage you just read probably left you feeling a bit uneasy; you probably got the idea but didn't quite comprehend everything. This is often the way college students feel after reading a textbook chapter. The reason is also often the same, too many unknown words in the passage. Study the following list of words. Then read the pickpocket passage again. You will see how much easier it is to understand.

Pickpocket Vocabulary

<u>Mob</u>: Three to five pickpockets who work together
<u>Grift</u>: To steal through cunning or skill; usually does not involve violence as in "mugging"
<u>Turning them over</u>: Successful theft of wallets or purses
<u>Jug Mob</u>: A third-rate gang of pickpockets
<u>Pokes</u>: Another name for wallets
<u>Class mobs</u>: A first-rate group of pickpockets
<u>Skin the pokes</u>: To take the money from stolen wallets or purses
<u>Stall</u>: The person who distracts the victims, sometimes by bumping into them, so that another pickpocket can lift the wallet without being detected
<u>Knock-up</u>: The mob's cash.

Technical and General Vocabulary

General vocabulary words are those which might be used in many different kinds of textbooks, for example, *horrendous, clandestine,* and *specify.* In contrast, **technical** words are usually associated with a particular field of study such as physics, environmental engineering, or psychology. Knowing the meanings of technical words such as *proton, biodegradable,* and *ego* is frequently the key to comprehension and success in college classes. For example, the pickpocket passage should have been much more meaningful the second time around because you understood its technical vocabulary. The same will be true with your textbooks.

Both general and technical vocabulary are crucial. If you build both kinds of vocabulary, your comprehension of textbooks and everything else you read will improve. It will work in your psychology text just as it did in the pickpocket passage.

Razzle Dazzle vs. Subject Area Vocabulary Programs

There are two basic approaches to building vocabulary. The usual approach is the Razzle Dazzle Crash Vocabulary Program. In this approach you spend one semester trying to cram thousands of new words into your vocabulary. While it is possible to improve your vocabulary this way, the crash method has two major limitations: (1) it does not deal with the technical vocabulary which students must face in nearly every college course, and (2) the crash program is almost always based on the memorization of lists of words and definitions. Students are not given sufficient opportunity to read, write, and speak the words, so most of them are soon forgotten.

The second method of building vocabulary is a Content-Area Approach. This method assumes that the best words to learn are those which are being introduced in classrooms and textbooks. It also assumes that building a good vocabulary is a long-term process. It is not possible for someone with a poor vocabulary to become a word wizard in a few short weeks. Therefore, the rest of this chapter will be devoted to showing you how to identify, define, and remember important words that are a part of your regular college classes.

Word Radar

In order to develop a larger vocabulary you first have to make yourself aware of new words when you encounter them. This means you must ask yourself questions as you read: "Hey, what's that word mean?" "Have I ever seen this word before?" "Is this word messing up my comprehension?" Develop the habit of marking *every* unfamiliar word or phrase in every reading assignment. As you will see, it takes very little time to do this.

Use your word radar in the following exercise. Circle every word whose meaning is unclear to you. This includes those words you have seen before but cannot define or use properly. Remember, your goal is to circle every unknown word.

Amniocentesis is a technique used by fetologists when the parents are known or suspected to carry one of several types of genetic diseases or when the woman is over age 40. Older women are more likely to have a fetus with Down's syndrome. The diseases specifically tested for are caused by having an extra or missing chromosome, a chromosome which has been broken, or a metabolic disease such as phenylketonuria. A hypodermic needle is inserted through the abdomen of the pregnant woman and into the amnion. A small amount of amniotic fluid, containing fetal cells, is drawn into the syringe. These cells are then cultured (grown) for a period of time; when enough culture cells are available, they can be tested for many metabolic defects. Cells can also be specially stained and prepared so that the chromosomes can be seen under a microscope. A total of 140 congenital diseases can now be detected by amniocentesis, and that figure is expected to increase to 500 by the year 1980.

The passage is printed again below, and we have circled the words which are most likely to baffle college students. Compare your word radar with ours.

Amniocentesis is a technique used by fetologists when the parents are known or suspected to carry one of several types of genetic disease or when the woman is over age 40. Older women are more likely to have a fetus with Down's syndrome. The diseases specifically tested for are caused by having an extra or missing chromosome, a chromosome which has been broken, or a metabolic disease such as phenylketonuria. A hypodermic needle is inserted through the abdomen of the pregnant woman and into the amnion. A small amount of amniotic fluid, containing fetal cells, is drawn into the syringe. These cells are then cultured (grown) for a period of time; when enough culture cells are available, they can be tested for many metabolic defects. Cells can also be specially stained and prepared so that the chromosomes can be seen under a microscope. A total of 140 congenital diseases can now be detected by amniocentesis, and that figure is expected to increase to 500 by the year 1980. (Brum, G. D. et al. *Biology and Man.* Dubuque, Iowa: Kendall/Hunt Publishing Company, 1978, p. 105.)

Strategies for Finding Word Meanings

The quickest and easiest way to handle unknown words is to skip them. Or, if it bothers you to skip a word altogether, you can mumble the word *wheelbarrow* each time you encounter an unfamiliar set of letters. Of course, this is silly. Unfortunately, many students are in the habit of ignoring difficult words. From our point of view, that's not much better than saying *wheelbarrow*. To give you an idea of the consequences of skipping unknown words, we have taken the following passage and replaced some of the words with blanks. Read the passage without trying to figure out which word belongs in each blank.

Food Fads

It is true that many people have recently become _____ by nutrition. The "health food" industry is booming; _____ grown products command very high prices; lectures, and _____ on health are very popular; and special pills, pellets, and food supplements _____ with popular diets and health programs are consumed in great quantities. How accurate is all this information on nutrition that is passed out _____ ? Should we pay more for "health food" and _____ products? How safe are all of the pills and _____ products associated with _____ diets? (Adapted from Brum, G. D. et al. *Biology and Man.* Dubuque, Iowa: Kendall/Hunt Publishing Company, 1978, p. 203.)

If you are like most people, this passage seems vague to you. The topic may seem clear enough, but it just doesn't hang together. And that's the real trouble. When you skip words you may feel as though you are understanding, but in the end your comprehension just isn't good enough. Comprehension disaster can strike even when you do know 95% to 97% of the words in your text.

To see the impact that just a few words can have, read the passage again, this time with the omitted words included and their definitions written in above them.

Food Fads

refers to crops grown without chemicals

hypnotized

conversations

free

weird

various

associated or connected

It is true that many people have recently become mesmerized by nutrition. The "health food" industry is booming; organically grown products command very high prices; lectures and confabulations on health are very popular; and special pills, pellets, and food supplements allied with popular diets and health programs are consumed in great quantities. How accurate is all this information on nutrition that is passed out gratis? Should we pay more for "health food" and organic products? How safe are all of the pills and exotic products associated with sundry diets?

We hope this illustrates the importance of finding the meanings of unknown words. Now, the question is: "What is the best way to go about discovering the meanings of unknown words?"

Context-Structure Strategies

Context-structure strategies are ways of figuring out the meanings of unknown words by looking at the words in their contexts. There are two basic strategies: (1) context clues, and (2) structural analysis (word parts).

Context Clues. Sometimes you will be able to figure out the meaning of an unfamiliar word by using context clues. Most college textbooks provide context clues when introducing new concepts. Generally, these new words are *italicized,* underlined, or written in **bold face print** to call attention to the fact that a new word is being introduced.

There are three main types of context clues:

A. Definition . . . The word is defined, usually in the same sentence. For example:
   1. *Linguistics* is the scientific study of language.
   2. Uxoricide, which means to murder one's wife, is the ultimate form of marital abuse.

B. Description . . . The word is described by the context in such a way that you can take a good guess at its meaning. For example:
   1. Because his approach to teaching seemed so **atavistic,** Jed's students were always joking that their teacher must have been trained in a dungeon during the Middle Ages.
   2. Their *vociferous* chatter made me wish I had ear plugs.

C. Contrast . . . The word is compared with some other word or concept, often an opposite. For example:
   1. Mike was loquacious while Susan said very little.
   2. The popular girl was **comely** while the unpopular girl was homely.

In these examples, clues to the meanings of the underlined word are given by definition, description, or contrast. You should recognize, however, that reliance on contextual clues does have some limitations. Usually, context provides very little information about a word's meaning. Sometimes the context can even cause you to guess incorrectly. For example, see if you can use context successfully to figure out the meanings of the underlined words in the following passage. (The definitions are given in the box on page 75.)

The convivial ambiance of college life offers the incoming freshman myriad distractions. Thus, the tyro can easily capitulate to temptation, with devastating results. The prescient student will be circumspect when setting priorities, scholastic and otherwise.

Your guess for convivial: _____

_____

Your guess for ambiance: _____

_____

Your guess for myriad: _____

_____

Your guess for tyro: _____

_____

Your guess for capitulate: _____

_____

Your guess for devastating: _____

_____

Your guess for prescient: _____

_____

Your guess for circumspect: _____

_____

Your guess for scholastic: _____

_____

Check your answers on page 75.

Now evaluate your performance using the following scale:

0	Right . . .	Better go buy a good dictionary!
1	Right . . .	Not so hot. Context doesn't help much, does it?
2–3	Right . . .	Pretty good!
4–5	Right . . .	Super vocabulary!
6–7	Right . . .	You should be writing dictionaries.
8	Right . . .	You will be president of Harvard in two years.

In our opinion this passage shows how much help you can usually expect from context in figuring out unknown words. You should make use of context clues that textbook authors provide, of course, but you should also know that most of the time context isn't much help.

Structural Analysis. Knowing the meanings of common roots, prefixes, and suffixes can help you to figure out word meanings. For example, knowing that *meter* means "measure" and *chron* means "time" could help you to figure out that the word *chronometer* has to do with measuring time, as with a watch perhaps. In addition, these same word parts could help you to figure out the meanings of related words such as *chronograph, micrometer,* and *altimeter.*

An even more dramatic example of how word parts can be combined to discover a definition is the longest word in English: *pneumonoultramicroscopicsilicovolcanoconiosis*. Do not be intimidated by its length. The whole of the word is rather easy to figure out if you know the meanings of its parts.

pneumono = lungs
ultra = very
microscopic = small
silico = hard stone, flint, quartz
volcano = something to do with a volcano
coni = dust
osis = abnormal or diseased condition

Just by adding the meanings of these word parts you should have been able to figure out that "the big word" is a lung disease caused by inhaling very small pieces of volcanic rock dust.

Studies have shown that about 80% of all English words are based on Latin or Greek words. Because of this, some textbooks recommend the intensive study of Latin and Greek word parts. For example, studying the following list of 15 common prefixes and 10 roots should, in theory, enable readers to figure out the meanings of over 10,000 words.

Common Prefixes

Prefix	Examples
dis (appart, not)	disengage, disarm
en, em (in)	embrace, enjoy, endanger
ex (out)	exterminate, export
in, im (not)	incorrect, impure
pre, pro (before, in front of)	prepare, predict, project
re (back)	refer, remodel
post (behind)	postoperative
super (over, above)	superior, supervisor
trans (across)	transcontinental
sub (under)	submarine, subject
un (not)	unarmed, unbroken
ab (from)	abnormal, abuse
be (by)	beside, behind, behead
con, com, col (with)	conduct, commercial, collect

Common Latin Roots

Root	Examples
sta, stat (to stand)	stationary, static
spect, spic (to look, see)	inspection, conspicuous
par (to get ready)	prepare, repair
port (to carry)	export, import
pos, pon (to place, put)	opponent, position
fer (bear, carry)	fertile, ferry, infer
mis, mit (to send)	submit, admission
tend, tens (to stretch)	tender, tension, extend
vid, vis (to see)	vision, provide
mov, mot (to move)	motive, motion

Go ahead and memorize these lists if you like. However, we think they are of limited value. Listed below are several words from the lists above. Also listed are the definitions we came up with when we combined the meanings of their prefixes and roots.

Word	Prefix	Root	Combined Meaning
infer	in	fer	not carry
submit	sub	mit	under send
disarm	dis	arm	not arm (leg?)
repair	re	par	back get ready
export	ex	port	out carry

Below are five sentences which use the meanings we arrived at through structural analysis. Write the word that belongs in each sentence in the space provided.

1. I not carry from your letter that you are quitting your job.

   _____

2. After capturing Thidwick the Thug, the police not armed him.

   _____

3. I am going to under send my resignation.

   _____

4. Why can't we out carry computer chips to Russia?

   _____

5. The TV is acting up again. Call the TV back get ready man.

   _____

The awkwardness of these sentences should illustrate the major limitation of studying word parts as a method of deciphering unknown words. YOU WILL ALMOST NEVER GET ACCURATE DEFINITIONS JUST BY ADDING TOGETHER THE MEANINGS OF WORD PARTS. These Latin and Greek words became a part of English hundreds of years ago, and their meanings have changed since then.

The study of word parts is interesting, and it may help you to remember the meanings of words which you are trying to learn. However, it offers very little assistance when you are reading along and come to an unknown word for which you need an accurate definition. For example, knowing that *egregious* comes from the Latin *gregis* meaning "herd" or "flock" will not help you to figure out that *egregious* means outstandingly bad. For that we suggest a good dictionary.

Reference Strategies

When you come to a word you don't know, context clues and roots and affixes usually will not be enough. In most cases, references outside the passage must be used to learn the meanings of unknown words. The three most important references are the textbook glossary, the index and the dictionary.

A *glossary* is an alphabetized list of the words used in a book. After each word in the list is the definition of the word as it is used in the book. Turn to page 187 and look at this textbook's glossary. Not all textbooks have glossaries, but those that do usually place it at the back of the book. Sometimes authors put the glossary at the oeginning or end of each chapter in the text.

When a book does not contain a glossary, the *index* can help you find word meanings. An index is an alphabetized list of important terms and topics included in the book, and it is always located at the back of the book. Turn to page 191 to find the index for this book. The index lists the page numbers in the text where information pertaining to each topic can be found. Usually, the word you are hunting for will be defined in context on one of those pages.

The word *amniocentesis* is a technical word that was used earlier in this chapter. It is defined in the glossary at the back of this book (see page 187). *Chromosome* is another technical word used in this chapter. However, it is not included in the glossary. Locate *chromosome* in the index (page 191). Then find the word and its definition on the page indicated in the index.

Use the glossary or index in this book to find the meanings of the following words. Write brief definitions in the spaces provided.

1. amniocentesis . . . _____

_____

2. Fetus . . . _____

_____

3. Context . . . _____

_____

4. metabolic . . . _____

_____

5. mortuary science . . . _____

_____

The Dictionary. When you need to find the meaning of a nontechnical word, use a dictionary. If you don't own a good dictionary, go and buy one. Keep the dictionary with you when you are reading, and dont' be too lazy to use it. It is a great evil for dictionaries to remain unopened.

At the back of this book on page 172 is a mini-dictionary. It contains most of the difficult nontechnical words used in *Passports*. Below is a page from the Scott-Foresman *Advanced Dictionary*. Please note that the dictionary contains more than just the spellings and meanings of words. Read about the different kinds of information that the dictionary has to offer. Then look at the keyed dictionary page to see exactly where this information is found.

1. The *entry,* the word you are looking up, is usually in **bold print.** The entry itself is commonly broken up into syllables.
2. The *pronunciation* of the word follows the entry in parentheses (   ).
3. A *pronunciation guide* is usually found at the bottom or top corner of each page. The symbols for various sounds are illustrated with common words so that you can determine how to pronounce an unknown word.
4. The *part of speech* (noun, verb, adjective, etc.) usually follows the pronunciation.
5. The *etymology* is the history of the word. Usually this tells the meanings of the various roots and affixes in the word. Sometimes the etymology tells an interesting story. For example, the word *berserk* comes from the name of a fierce Viking warrior named Bear Shirt. The etymology is usually found after the part of speech and is enclosed in brackets, [   ].
6. *Multiple meanings* are listed under the same entry if they are related. However, when a word is used in a totally different way (see *grouse*), the dictionary will usually give each word its own entry. When more than one meaning is listed for an entry, you must make sure that the definition you choose makes sense in context. This will help you to determine the appropriate definition. For example, the word *passage* is a noun which can mean: (a) a hall between parts of a building, (b) a movement, (c) a portion of a literary work or musical composition, (d) a voyage. All these definitions are in the dictionary. Now, which one best fits the context below?

Dud ley (dud′lē), *n.* **Robert.** See Leicester.

Entry ——→ **due** (dü, dyü), *adj.* **1** owed as a debt; to be paid as a right: *The money due him for his work was paid today.* **2** proper; suitable; rightful: *due reward for good work.* **3** as much as needed; enough: *Use due care in crossing streets.* **4** promised to come or be ready; looked for; expected: *The train is due at noon. Your report is due tomorrow.* **5** (of notes, bills, etc.) becoming payable; having reached maturity; mature. **6 due to, a** caused by: *The accident was due to careless driving.* **b** INFORMAL. because of; on account of: *The game was called off due to rain.* **7 fall due,** be required to be paid. —*n.* **1** what is owed to a person; a person's right: *I am asking no more than my due.* **2 dues,** *pl.* amount of money owed or to be paid to a club, etc., by a member; fee or tax for some purpose. **3 give a person his due,** be fair to a person. —*adv.* straight; directly; exactly: *travel due west.* [< Old French *deü,* past participle of *devoir* owe < Latin *debere*]

hat, āge, fär; let, ēqual, tèrm;
it, īce; hot, ōpen, ôrder;
oil, out; cup, pút, rüle;
ch, child; ng, long; sh, she;
th, thin; ᴛʜ, then; zh, measure;

ə represents *a* in about, *e* in taken,
i in pencil, *o* in lemon, *u* in circus.

< = from, derived from, taken from.

← Pronunciation guide

ducking stool

du el (dü′əl, dyü′əl), *n., v.,* **-eled, -el ing** or **-elled, -el ling.** —*n.* **1** a formal fight between two persons armed with pistols or swords. Duels, intended to settle quarrels, avenge insults, etc., are fought in the presence of attendants called seconds. **2** any fight or contest between two opponents: *The two debate teams fought a duel of wits.* —*v.i.* fight a duel. [< Latin *duellum,* early form of *bellum* war] —**du′el er,** *n.*

Pronunciation ——→ **du el ist** (dü′ə list, dyü′ə list), *n.* person who fights a duel or duels.

du en na (dü en′ə, dyü en′ə), *n.* **1** an elderly woman who is the governess and chaperon of young girls in a Spanish or Portuguese family. **2** governess or chaperon. [< earlier Spanish, married woman < Latin *domina* mistress]

Parts of speech ——→ **du et** (dü et′, dyü et′), *n.* **1** piece of music for two voices or instruments. **2** two singers or players performing together. [< Italian *duetto,* diminutive of *duo*]

duff (duf), *n.* a flour pudding boiled in a cloth bag. [variant of *dough*]

duf fel (duf′əl), *n.* **1** a coarse, woolen cloth with a thick nap. **2** camping equipment. [< Dutch < *Duffel,* town near Antwerp, Belgium]

duffel bag, a large canvas sack used by soldiers, campers, etc., for carrying clothing and other belongings.

Informal ——→ **duff er** (duf′ər), *n.* INFORMAL. a clumsy, stupid, or incompetent person.

Person ——→ **Du fy** (dʏ fē′), *n.* **Raoul,** 1877-1953, French painter.

Multiple meanings ——→ **dug¹** (dug), *v.* pt. and pp. of **dig.**
dug² (dug), *n.* nipple; teat. [probably < Scandinavian (Danish) *dægge* suckle]

du gong (dü′gong), *n.* a large herbivorous sea mammal of the coastal waters of southern Asia and Australia, with flipperlike forelimbs and a forked tail; sea cow. It is of

the same order as the manatee. [< Malay]

dug out (dug′out′), *n.* **1** a rough shelter or cave dug into the side of a hill, trench, etc., and often reinforced with logs, used for protection against bullets and bombs. **2** a small shelter at the side of a baseball field, used by players who are not at bat or not in the game. **3** a crude boat made by hollowing out a large log.

dui ker (dī′kər), *n.* any of various small South African antelopes. [< Afrikaans *duiker (bok)* diver (buck)] ←—— Etymology

Duis burg (dʏs′bùrk), *n.* city in W West Germany, at the point where the Ruhr and Rhine rivers meet. 458,000. ←—— Place

duke (dük, dyük), *n.* **1** nobleman of the highest title, ranking next below a prince and next above a marquis. **2** prince who rules a duchy. **3 dukes,** *pl.* SLANG. hands or fists. [< Old French *duc* < Latin *ducem* leader. Doublet of DOGE, DUCE.] ←—— Slang

duke dom (dük′dəm, dyük′dəm), *n.* **1** duchy. **2** title or rank of a duke.

dul cet (dul′sit), *adj.* soothing, especially to the ear; sweet or pleasing. [< Latin *dulcis*]

dulcimer

dul ci mer (dul′sə mər), *n.* a musical instrument with metal strings, played by striking the strings with two hammers. [< Old French *doulcemer, doulcemele* < Latin *dulcis* sweet + *melos* song]

dull (dul), *adj.* **1** not sharp or pointed; blunt: *a dull knife.* See synonym study below. **2** not bright or clear; lacking in vividness or intensity: *dull eyes, a dull day.* **3** slow in understanding; stupid: *a dull mind.* See **stupid** for synonym study. **4** having little feeling; insensitive. **5** not felt sharply; vague: *a dull pain.* **6** not interesting; tiresome; boring: *a dull book.* **7** having little life, energy, or spirit; not active: *The fur coat business is usually dull in the summer.* **8** lacking zest; depressed. —*v.t., v.i.* make or become dull. [Middle English *dul*] —**dull′ness, dul′ness,** *n.*
Syn. *adj.* **1 Dull, blunt** mean without a sharp edge or point. **Dull** suggests that the object described has lost the sharpness it had or is not as sharp as it should be: *This knife is dull.* **Blunt** suggests that the edge or point is not intended to be sharp or keen: *The blunt side of a knife will not cut meat.*

dull ard (dul′ərd), *n.* person who is stupid and learns very slowly.

After paying the toll, passage through the tunnel was granted.

Answer: _____

7. *Slang* is made up of colorful words, such as *crud, grungy,* and *rip-off,* which are considered improper. Slang should be used only in friendly conversation or writing that is very informal, such as letters to friends. You should not use slang at all in your college assignments.

8. *Informalisms* are like slang words except that they are a little more acceptable in conversation and daily writing assignments. However, to play it safe, avoid informalisms in English compositions. Many dictionaries refer to these as colloquialisms.

9. Important persons and places are included for easy reference.

Every dictionary contains an introduction or user's guide which explains how to use the dictionary. Turn to the *Passports* dictionary user's guide on page 171 and read it before going on to the next exercise.

Dictionary Quiz

Directions: Use the *Passports* mini-dictionary to answer the following questions. See if you can finish in less than five minutes.

1. *epitome* rhymes with
   a. metronome
   b. soliloquy
   c. matinee
   d. pizza

2. *colonel* refers to
   a. a military officer
   b. a style of furniture
   c. a family of insects
   d. the American Revolution

3. An enclosure for horses is a
   a. coral
   b. carol
   c. corral
   d. corale

4. Which meaning of *respite* best applies to the following sentence: His vacation was a welcome respite from long days at the office.

   _____

5. Where is Afghanistan?

   _____

6. Why would you choose not to use the word *dump* in your term paper to describe an old building?

   _____

7. What is the past tense of *bring*?

   _____

Word Strategy for Textbooks

When you encounter an unknown word, you should use the following steps:

1. Decide whether the word is technical or general. When in doubt, assume the word is technical.
2. If the word is technical
   a. try the glossary first;
   b. then try the index;
   c. then try the dictionary.
3. If the word is general
   a. try the dictionary first;
   b. then try the glossary;
   c. then try the index.
4. After you have found a meaning for the word, check the meaning in the context of the sentence to make sure that the definition fits. This is particularly important when you use a dictionary.

Word Strategy Practice Exercise

Below is a passage on heredity taken from a college textbook. Words which might be unfamiliar to you have been circled. On page 69 is a list of the circled words. Do these things for each circled word:

1. Indicate the source in which you found the word.
2. Cram a brief definition near the word in the passage. Be sure that the definition you select is one which fits the context.

Myriad diseases doctors confront today are genetically inherited aberrations. Research has shown that defective genes are the cause of many diseases such as sickle cell anemia and cystic fibrosis. If normal genes could be isolated from normal persons, or synthesized and then placed into individuals with inherited diseases, it might be possible to cure their illnesses. What a boon this would be to the world. Normal or synthesized genes could also be injected into fertilized eggs or embryos after fertilization in the test-tube and before implantation. Perfecting such techniques would rocket medicine into a new age of genetic therapy and possibly rid humanity of many diseases that have plagued it for thousands of years.

Applying Strategies for Finding Word Meanings

You are now ready to apply your word strategies to a real college text. To do so, use the PQMR strategy on the following excerpt, which is about frustration. Pay particular attention to vocabulary. One final comment: *when in doubt about a word, mark it, and check it out.* It's all too easy to fool yourself into thinking that you know and understand the word just because you've heard it before. The following summary outline is provided as a review of the PQMR strategy.

A. To preview: (Underline previewed material for this exercise.)
   1. Read the title and the first paragraph.
   2. Read the closing paragraph (or chapter summary).
   3. Skim the assignment by reading all headings and the first sentence that follows each heading.
   4. As you skim, focus your attention on italicized words, pictures, graphs, and charts.
B. To Question: Write down at least five questions you have about the subject matter.

Word	Source of Definition					
	Already Known	Context Clues	Word Parts	Glossary	Index	Dictionary
myriad				X		
genetically						
aberrations						
defective						
sickle cell anemia						
cystic fibrosis						
synthesized						
boon						
genetic therapy						
plagued						

C. To Mark:

———	Underline or highlight main ideas and important details.
[ ]	Use brackets to mark important paragraphs.
Jargon	Circle new technical terms.
(1) (2) (3)	Number important steps, causes, or reasons.
* ! ?	Use the asterisk or exclamation point to indicate EXTREME IMPORTANCE. Use the question mark to show confusion or disagreement.
Super! Yuk! True	Use personal comments and summarize each major subheading.

D. Now read!

Immediate Consequences of Frustration

Frustration has both immediate and remote consequences. When blocked in his goal-seeking, the individual may react immediately or may develop attitudes toward uncertainty or risk-taking that have more enduring consequences. We shall first turn to a consideration of some of the immediate consequences of frustration. These consequences might equally well be called *symptoms* or *signs* of frustration.

An experiment on the effects of frustration in young children illustrates several of its immediate consequences. The subjects were 30 young children, ages two to five—that is, of nursery school and kindergarten age. The experiment will be described in the present tense, as though we were observing it.

The children come one at a time into a room which contains several toys, parts of which are missing—a chair without a table, an ironing board but no iron, a telephone receiver without a transmitter, a boat and other water toys but no water. There are also papers and crayons. Some of the children set about playing eagerly and happily. They make up for the missing parts imaginatively. They use paper as water in which to sail a boat or they substitute their fist for the telephone transmitter.

Another group of children behave quite differently. Although they appear to be in the same general physical condition as the first group, and their clothes show that they come from similar social and economic backgrounds, something is the matter. They seem unable to play constructively, unable to fit the toys into meaningful and satisfying activities. They play roughly with the toys, occasionally jumping on one and breaking it. If they draw with the crayons, they scribble like younger children. They whine and nag at the adult present. One of them lies on the floor, stares at the ceiling, and recites nursery rhymes, paying no attention to anyone else.

What accounts for the differences in behavior of these two sets of youngsters? Is the second group suffering from some sort of emotional disturbance? Have some of these children been mistreated at home? Actually, the children in this second group are the same as those in the first group; they are simply in a

later stage of the experiment. They are showing the symptoms of frustration—frustration that has been deliberately created in the following way.

After playing happily with the half-toys, as described earlier, the children had been given an added experience. An opaque screen had been removed, allowing them to see that they were in a larger room containing not only the half-toys but other toys much more elaborate and attractive. This part of the room has a table for the chair, a dial and bell for the telephone, a pond of real water for the boat. When we see the children so unhappy, in this later stage of the experiment, a chicken-wire screen has been placed between them and their happy hunting ground. They are denied the "whole" toys; they can use only the "part" ones. They are frustrated (Barker, Dembo, and Lewin, 1941).

Why was the half-toy situation satisfying the first time and frustrating the second? The answer is easy to find. Goal-seeking behavior was satisfied the first time, as the children played happily with the available toys; in the second stage they knew of the existence of the more attractive and satisfying toys, and so a new goal had been set up. The first day the goal was attainable; the second day, it was not. To play now with the half-toys is to be stopped short of a richer possible experience, and hence is frustrating.

This experiment illustrates a number of the immediate consequences of frustration. In discussing some of these consequences, we shall make reference to additional details of the experiment and draw further illustrations from related experiments and from the frustrating experiences of everyday life.

Restlessness and tension

In the toy experiment, one of the first evidences of frustration shown by the children was an excess of movement: fidgeting about and generally restless behavior. Drawings took the form of scribbling, because the muscles were tense and movements were thus jerky. This restlessness was associated with many actions indicating unhappiness: whimpering, sighing, complaining. Unhappy actions were recorded

Abridged from INTRODUCTION TO PSYCHOLOGY, Third Edition by Ernest R. Hilgard, copyright © 1962 by Harcourt Brace Jovanovich, Inc. Reprinted by permission of the publisher.

for only 7 of the 30 children in the free-play situation but for 22 of the same 30 in the frustrating situation.

An increase in tension and in the level of excitement also occurs when adults are blocked and thwarted. They blush or tremble or clench their fists. Children under tension fall back upon thumb sucking and nail biting; adults also turn to nail biting, as well as to smoking and gum chewing, as outlets for their restlessness.

Destructiveness

Closely related to increased tension and restless movements are the rage states that lead to destructiveness and hostile attacks. In the frustration experiment, kicking, knocking, breaking, and destroying were greatly increased following frustration. Only 5 children did any kicking or knocking in the original free-play situation, but 18 did so in frustration.

Direct Aggression. Frustration often leads to aggression against the individual or object that is the source of the frustration. In the experiment just described, direct attack on the barrier was not uncommon. In ordinary play situations, when one small child takes a toy from another child, the second is likely to attack the first in an attempt to regain the toy. The victim of a slighting remark usually replies in kind—though for many adults the aggression may be verbal rather than physical. The anger engendered when one is blocked tends to find expression in some kind of direct attack. Because the obstacle or barrier was the source of the blocking in the experiment, the children's first attempt at problem-solving was to get by the barrier or remove it. Aggression of this kind need not be hostile; it may be a learned way of solving a problem. When the obstacle is another person, the first tendency is to attack that person, treating him as a barrier. But this may not be the only form in which frustration is met through aggression.

Displaced Aggression. Frequently the frustrated individual cannot satisfactorily express his aggression against the source of the frustration. Sometimes the source is vague and intangible. Then he does not know what to attack and yet feels angry and seeks *something* to attack. At other times the person responsible for the frustration is so powerful that to attack him would be dangerous. When circumstances block direct attack on the cause of frustration, the result is what we call "displaced aggression." Displaced aggression is an aggressive action against an innocent person or object rather than against the actual or intangible cause of the frustration. The man who is bawled out by his boss may come home and take out his unexpressed resentment on his wife or children. The tongue-lashing Bill gives his quiet freshman roommate may be related to the poor grade Bill received in the midterm quiz. The child who is not getting along well with his playmates may come home and pull the kitten's tail.

Displaced aggression can be demonstrated experimentally. One rat is taught to strike another by being rewarded for such aggression. An electric current gradually builds up in the grid on which he stands. When he strikes the other rat, the electricity is turned off and he escapes the shock. This rewards the aggressive behavior. When another rat is no longer present, the trained rat directs his aggressive behavior toward the "innocent bystander," a rubber doll previously ignored. Thus aggression is transferred from an inaccessible to an accessible object (Miller, 1984a).

There are many interesting problems connected with the processes of displacement. Just what kinds of objects will become attacked in displaced aggression? The more similar they are to the objects of direct aggressive attack, the more likely they are to be attacked. As brought out earlier in the text, when one stimulus is similar to another, the response to the second is said to *generalize* from the first. Thus in the experiment just described, the rubber doll looks more like a rat than do the walls of the compartment, so that when the second rat is absent, the doll is attacked. However, the displacement may come about in another way: when attack on the frustrating object is inhibited through punishment. Thus the child cannot retaliate against the parent who frustrates him. In that case he is likely to displace his aggression, but will he choose another adult, similar to his parent? He is now in a conflict situation, of the kind described earlier: he would like to attack the parent, but that satisfying response is prevented by his fear of punishment. If another adult resembles the parent too closely, the fear of punishment will be aroused by him also, and so the second adult is unlikely to become the object of attack. Some distance is needed; when displacement occurs because of fear of retaliation, the object of displaced aggression must not be *too* similar to the object of direct aggression. It is often easier to blame foreigners for our troubles than to blame our neighbors.

71

Apathy

One baffling feature of human behavior is the tendency for similar situations to lead to diametrically opposite behavior by different individuals. While a common response to frustration is active aggression, another response is its opposite—apathy, indifference, withdrawal, inactivity, inattentiveness. A study of fifth- and sixth-grade children showed that disturbed children were more hesitant in turning to direct aggression after frustration than the more "normal" children, that is, those with fewest "neurotic" symptoms (Zander, 1944).

When resistance is futile, the frustrated person may become sullen and detached instead of angry and defiant. Apathy often indicates that aggressive tendencies are being held in check or inhibited, but they may express themselves indirectly.

Fantasy

When problems become too much for us, we sometimes seek the "solution" of escape into a dream world, a solution through *fantasy* rather than on a realistic level. This was the solution of the child who lay on the floor reciting nursery rhymes in the frustration experiment and of other children in the experiment who crossed the barrier by talking about the whole toys on the other side. One little girl fished through the wire, imagining the floor on the other side to be the pond that was actually out of reach.

It will be recalled that one approach to the study of the achievement motive is through fantasy. This suggests that the desired level of accomplishment is often not achieved and hence appears as an imagined success.

Unrealistic solutions are not limited to children. The pin-up girls in the soldiers' barracks symbolize a fantasy life that goes on when normal social life with women is frustrated. But experiments have also shown that men on a starvation diet lose their interest in women and instead hang on their walls pictures of prepared food cut from magazines (Guetzkow and Bowman, 1946).

Stereotypy

Another consequence of frustration is *stereotypy* in behavior, that is, a tendency to blind, repetitive, fixated behavior. Ordinary problem-solving requires flexibility, striking out in new directions when the original path to the goal is blocked. When repeated frustration baffles a person, especially if the frustration arises through punishment, some of this flexibility appears to be lost, and he stupidly makes the same effort again and again, though experience has shown its futility.

Stereotypy has been most carefully studied in rats, but parallels can be found in human behavior.

A white rat can be taught to jump to one of a pair of stimulus cards attached to windows by so arranging the cards that the rat finds food behind the positive card but is punished if he jumps to the negative card. The positive card may be one with a black circle on a white background, the negative one a white circle on a black background. The cards are so arranged that the rat knocks over the positive card when he hits it, opening the window that gives access to a platform where there is a food reward. If the rat jumps against the negative card, the card does not give way. Instead, the rat bumps against the card and falls into a net. By varying the positions of the cards, the experimenter can teach the rat to select the positive one and to jump consistently to it.

This discrimination experiment is converted into a frustration experiment by making the problem insoluble. That is, each of the two cards leads half the time to reward (positive reinforcement), half the time to punishment (negative reinforcement), regardless of its position at the left or the right. Hence, whichever choice the animal makes is "correct" only half the time. The result is that the rat, forced to jump, tends to form a stereotyped habit of jumping regularly to one side, either to the right or to the left, no longer paying attention to which card is exposed. The rat is still rewarded half the time and punished half the time after having adopted this stereotyped habit.

Once the stereotyped habit has been adopted, it is very resistant to change, so much so that it has been called an "abnormal fixation." For example, if the rat that has come to jump regularly to the right is now punished every time he jumps, he may continue to jump to the right for as many as 200 trials, even though the left window remains open as an easy and safe alternative. The behavior is so stereotyped that the alternative does not exist for the rat (Maier, Glaser, and Klee, 1940; Maier, 1949).

Further studies must be made before we know just what analogies are permissible between human behavior and these experimental results. It is quite possible, though not proved, that some forms of persistent behavior, such as thumb-sucking in young children or stuttering, have become more firmly fixed (i.e., stereotyped) because punishment and repeated frustration in efforts to get rid of them have intensified the undesirable responses. The persistence of difficulties in arithmetic and reading and spelling among bright children (and some adults) may be explained in part as a consequence of errors similarly stereotyped by early frustration.

Regression

Regression is defined as a return to more primitive modes of behavior, that is, to modes of behavior characterizing a younger age. There are two interpretations of regression. One is that in the midst of insecurity the individual attempts to return to a period of past security. The older child seeks the love and affection once bestowed upon him by again behaving as he did when younger: crying, seeking parental caresses, and so on. This type of regression is called *retrogressive* behavior, a return to behavior once engaged in. Such returns to earlier habits, when more recently acquired ones are blocked, have frequently been demonstrated in animal experiments (Mowrer, 1940).

The second interpretation of regression is that the childish behavior following frustration is simply of more primitive quality, but not actually a return to earlier behavior. This kind of regression, in contrast to retrogression, is called *primitivation.* Thus the adult accustomed to the restraints of civilized behavior may become so upset by frustration as to lose control and start a fist-fight, even though he did no fist-fighting as a child. Both forms of regression may, of course, occur together. In the frustration experiment with half-toys and restricted space earlier discussed, regression was shown through decrease in the constructiveness of play. We consider that this decreased constructiveness is a form of primitivation, rather than retrogression, because we do not ask whether the child returns to a mode of play characteristic of *him* at an earlier age. Without careful case studies we have no way of being sure, however, that the behavior was not retrogressive. It is a safe conjecture that it was retrogressive in some instances. Through a careful device of rating, each child's play in both the free and the frustrating situation was appraised as to its degree of constructiveness, that is (1) according to its likeness to the well-thought-out and systematic play of older children, or (2) according to its similarity to the fragmentary play of younger children. As a consequence of frustration the play tended to deteriorate. Drawing became scribbling; instead of pretending to iron clothes on the ironing board, children would knock the board down. The total loss in maturity shown amounted to 17 months of mental age; that is, the play of the children, who were two to five years of age, became like that of children about a year and a half younger. Not all children showed regression; some few showed little change, and a small minority even showed increased constructiveness. The prominence of regression is shown in which the changes in constructiveness of play for individual children are plotted.

The immediate consequences of frustration—the evidence that a person has been thwarted—are themselves ways of fighting the frustration. They are not merely signs of trouble but are also attempts at solution. If the solution is successful, the obstacles are overcome, the needs met, the conflicts resolved, and the frustrating episode is ended. However, some personal problems endure for a long time. They have continuing histories, and ways of dealing with them become habitual. These ways become so typical of the person that they help reveal what he is like. When we say that a person is aggressive or retiring, that he stands up for his rights, that he lets himself get pushed around, that he lives in a dream world, that he has a suspicious nature, we are talking about ways in which he habitually meets frustration.

Summary

Frustration results when individuals fail to attain their goals. Among the various symptoms of frustration are the following six: (1) restlessness (and tension), (2) destructiveness and aggression, (3) apathy, (4) fantasy, (5) stereotypy, and (6) regression. These consequences of frustration show us how important it is to understand the behavior of individuals when their goal-seeking behavior is blocked. (Adapted from Hilgard, E. R. *Introduction to Psychology.* 3d ed. New York: Harcourt, Brace & World, 1962.

Vocabulary Quiz on the Frustration Chapter

Directions: Circle the letter of the best definition for the term. You may refer to the text to find the answers. If you have used PQMR correctly, you should be able to finish this quiz in less than three minutes.

1. Opaque
   a. white
   b. colored
   c. something which blocks light
   d. a consequence of frustration

2. Displaced aggression
   a. hostile actions against an innocent person
   b. anger which occurs for the wrong reasons
   c. a communist plot
   d. a physical fight

3. Apathy
   a. indifference or withdrawal
   b. a type of aggression
   c. fear of punishment
   d. the true cause of frustration

4. Stereotypy
   a. blind, stupid, repetitive behavior
   b. sexist and racist thinking
   c. aggression against those of a different race
   d. music therapy for psychopaths

5. Insoluble
   a. fantasy dilemma
   b. will not mix with water
   c. cannot be figured out
   d. the best solution

6. Futile
   a. hopeless
   b. occupational
   c. extreme frustration
   d. in the future

7. Consequences
   a. truth
   b. actions or events caused by other actions or events
   c. an illusion of goal-seeking which results in aggression
   d. emotional disturbances

8. Engendered
   a. hidden
   b. discouraged
   c. sexually controlled
   d. caused

9. Frustration
   a. anger
   b. lack of interpersonal relationships
   c. the result of failure to attain goals
   d. displaced aggression

10. Intangible
   a. describes violent behavior resulting from frustration
   b. refers to something which is hard to see or understand
   c. refers to the release of tension
   d. refers to regressive behavior

Hidden Word Puzzle: Vocabulary about Vocabulary

Directions: This is a hidden word puzzle involving new words and concepts from this chapter. Listed below are brief definitions of these words or concepts. As you figure them out, circle them in the hidden word box. The terms may appear diagonally, horizontally, or vertically; and they may be printed from top to bottom or from bottom to top. Answers may be found in your text on the page indicated in parentheses. Do not just hunt for words. The word box contains wrong answers as well as the correct ones.

M	O	B	I	J	S	T	R	E	B	Y	O	O	T
D	I	C	T	I	O	N	A	R	Y	R	U	I	B
G	T	R	T	E	F	R	E	W	R	A	H	E	S
A	M	N	I	O	C	E	N	T	E	S	I	S	G
A	W	F	N	W	E	H	W	Q	C	S	P	K	E
R	I	N	D	S	A	W	N	O	R	O	Q	U	N
E	A	T	E	X	T	N	N	I	K	L	M	E	E
A	Z	R	X	O	O	T	X	Q	C	G	J	O	R
D	V	T	I	R	E	G	K	I	E	A	W	E	A
L	A	S	T	X	W	N	S	T	A	L	L	N	L
S	E	E	T	E	A	C	H	E	R	T	O	M	B

1. Indicates the page number where terms are explained (   )
2. A "little dictionary" in the back of a textbook (   )
3. A meaning clue provided by the words surrounding the unknown word (   )
4. Words like *amnion, photon,* and *isotope* (   )
5. Multiple definitions are one of the confusing things about this reference book. (   )
6. Words like *boon* and *plagued* (   )
7. Usually carries the "knock up" (   )
8. A procedure for detecting congenital diseases (   )

Definitions of vocabulary words in context clue exercise
Convivial—jovial or festive
Ambiance—atmosphere
Myriad—a great number
Tyro—a beginner
Capitulate—to give in or surrender
Devastating—extremely destructive
Prescient—foreseeing, one who looks into the future is prescient
Circumspect—careful
Scholastic—refers to school or scholarship

6
How to Improve Your Reading Comprehension

What Do You Believe about Reading Comprehension?

Directions: Read each of the statements below. Place a checkmark on the line in front of each statement you believe is true.

1. _____ If you become interested in what you are reading, your comprehension will improve.

2. _____ When interpreting a graph or chart it is always best to study the center of the graph first.

3. _____ Listening comprehension and reading comprehension are just about the same thing.

4. _____ The main idea is usually located in the first sentence of each paragraph.

5. _____ Every paragraph has a main idea.

We hope these statements have made you curious about reading comprehension. Perhaps you have developed a few questions of your own, such as, "What strategies can I use to improve my comprehension?" or "What exactly is a main idea?" Search for the answers to your questions as you read and work your way through this chapter.

What Is Reading Comprehension?

Read the following story about Rocky. Then, in the space provided, tell what you think the story is about.

Rocky

Rocky slowly got up from the mat, planning his escape. He hesitated a moment and thought. Things were not going well. What bothered him most was being held, especially since the charge against him had been weak. He considered his present situation. The lock that held him was strong but he thought he could break it. He knew, however, that his timing would have to be perfect. Rocky was aware that it was because of his early roughness that he had been penalized so severely—much too severely from his point of view. The situation was becoming frustrating; the pressure had been grinding on him for too long. He was being ridden unmercifully. Rocky was getting angry now. He felt he was ready to make his move. He knew that his success or failure would depend on what he did in the next few seconds. (Anderson, R. C., et al. "Frameworks for Comprehending Discourse." *American Educational Research Journal* 14 (1977): 367–81.)

In the original research, this story was read by sixty college students, thirty of them planning careers in music education and thirty of them taking weight lifting classes. Most of the weight lifters believed Rocky was a wrestler trying to break away from an opponent who was holding him. Most of the music majors, on the other hand, believed that Rocky was planning an escape from prison.

If you are a sports fan and know a lot about wrestling, the chances are that you put Rocky on a wrestling mat instead of in a jail cell. Why?

The reason is simple. Comprehension is determined by the information in your head as much as by the words on the page. Your beliefs, past experiences, and knowledge all fit together to direct your comprehension. Understanding what you read depends upon your ability to relate the information on the page to knowledge which you already have. Only your prior knowledge of wrestling, prisons, and human emotions allows you to understand the story about Rocky. Without such prior knowledge, "Rocky" would mean as little as the paragraph below. Read the passage and then estimate your comprehension as a percentage; for example, 20%, 50%, or 80%.

> One consequence of the parallel transmission is that the acoustic cues cannot be divided on the time axis into segments of phonemic chunks. The acoustic cue for the same perceived consonant /d/ is different in two different vowel contexts, /di/ and /du/, and there is no acoustic segment corresponding to the consonant segment /d/. Thus acoustic cues are presented in contrasts in terms of articulatory features. (Downing, J., and Leong, C. K. *Psychology of Reading.* New York: Macmillan, 1982, p. 129.)

ESTIMATED COMPREHENSION _____

If your comprehension was next to nothing, don't feel guilty, and don't put a curse on the authors. You are not stupid, and there is nothing wrong with the way the passage is written. The problem is probably that the topic is altogether unfamiliar to you, which means that you don't have the right prior knowledge to understand the passage. Without some prior knowledge of the particular subject you are reading about, there is no way you can read with understanding. This leads us to our definition of comprehension:

Comprehension is relating what you already know to new information.

Research shows that nothing is more critical to your comprehension than the knowledge you have before you begin to read. We believe this is just as true for listening comprehension as it is for reading comprehension. The box below shows other research findings about reading comprehension.

---

1. The more interested you are in what you are reading the better your comprehension will be.
2. The largest part of reading comprehension is knowing the meanings of the words.
3. Strategies such as PQMR can improve comprehension.
4. Writing short summary sentences while you read improves comprehension and recall.
5. Forcing yourself to make decisions when you read, such as deciding what to underline, improves comprehension.

Understanding Comprehension Failure

Just about everyone, at one time or another, has taken a course and failed to comprehend as well as they wanted. That's normal. Think of a course you have taken in which you felt your comprehension of the textbook was unsatisfactory. Based on the research summary, you should be able to figure out the reasons for your poor comprehension. Place a checkmark next to the reason(s) for not understanding the textbook.

SUBJECT: _____

_____ Didn't know enough about the subject before taking the course. (Low prior knowledge)

_____ Too many difficult words in the text.

_____ Subject/textbook was boring so I didn't pay attention.

_____ Didn't use a study plan or strategy such as PQMR.

Chances are excellent that you marked one or more of the four causes of comprehension failure. The question now is: What can be done to prevent these problems in other courses? Here are our recommendations:

1. Select courses with care. Make sure that you have taken all of the necessary prerequisites before enrolling. Try to find courses on topics that you already know something about. At the very

least, don't register for a full load of courses in which you have low prior knowledge. The lower your prior knowledge is, the harder it is to relate the new information in the book to the information already in your mind.

2. Try to select courses which interest you. When you can't do that, force yourself to look at the course from a positive point of view. Instead of griping about the boring book and the somnolent (sleep producing) teacher, think of ways in which the course might benefit you later. Try to see the course as interesting. Remember, every subject is interesting to somebody.

3. Use a study strategy such as PQMR. Plan to comprehend by setting a purpose for reading, previewing the assignments, looking up unknown words, and writing and marking important information in the text.

Finding Main Ideas

Probably one of your first impressions of college classes after your first week was the huge amount of reading you had to accomplish in a single semester. If you fit into the shoes of the typical college student, you are taking four or five classes each semester. Most courses have one or more required texts plus outside readings. At times you may feel smothered in a jungle of reading material. "How can I digest everything?" you ask yourself. "How is it possible to comprehend and remember all this stuff?" The answer is that it is not possible, nor is it necessary to know every bit of information you find in your textbooks. However, it is crucial that you learn to identify important ideas and important generalizations.

In Chapter 3 you learned how to use the PQMR system of study. This system includes writing and marking important information in your textbook as you read. The issue now is: How do you know what is important and what isn't? The answer to this question centers on something called *the main idea.*

Depending upon which textbook or reading program you are looking at, "the main idea" of a passage or paragraph might be defined as

1. the topic of the passage;
2. a good title for the passage;
3. the most important statement in the passage, sometimes called "the topic sentence"; or
4. an important generalization which holds the paragraph together.

Actually these are all just different ways of stating what the main idea is. To illustrate, read the following paragraph and then answer the questions that follow it. (Remember to use the dictionary and the index.)

One of the most common misconceptions about psychoanalysis arises from Freud's discovery that sexuality governs many of our hidden impulses and tendencies. Certain individuals and groups who do not clearly understand psychoanalysis accuse it of putting too great an emphasis upon sex. Sexuality does not necessarily mean genitality, or gratification derived from sex relations. Psychoanalysis uses the term *sexuality* in a very broad sense, to encompass the entire love life of the individual and all the gratifications that are necessary to his well-being. Thus, sexuality may include the love of parents for children, the love of children for parents or for other children, gratifications associated with mouth activity or activity of other external organs, as well as genital activity. It can be seen, therefore, that sex relations are only one part of this large concept of sexuality. (Polatin, Philip, and Philtine, Ellen. "Psychoanalytic Treatment." In *How Psychiatry Helps.* New York: Harper & Row, 1949, p. 135.)

Sample quiz on getting the main idea: Circle the letter of the *best* answer.

1. What is the topic of the paragraph?
   a. Freud
   b. Typewriters
   c. Sexuality
   d. Freud and Sexuality
   e. Freud and Typewriters
   f. Sexuality and Typewriters

2. What would be a good title for this paragraph?
   a. Fun with Freud
   b. Sexuality and the Typewriter
   c. Limitations of Freud's Theory of Psychoanalysis
   d. Sexuality as a Global Concept in Freud's Theory
   e. True Love

3. What is the most important sentence (topic) in the paragraph? Go back and underline the sentence which you think is most important.

4. In twenty-five words or less describe this paragraph's important generalization about Freud's theory.

_____

_____

_____

The best answer to question number one is (d) Freud and Sexuality. Some people would claim that if you can answer this question you understand the main idea of the paragraph. However, even with the words in the passage scrambled into nonsense you can still tell that the passage is about Freud, sex, and psychoanalysis. You could answer question number one without comprehending the passage at all. Give it a try:

> the of about misconceptions One psychoanalysis discovery governs most Freud's from many that tendencies governs common sexuality and hidden our arises of impulses. Sex individuals who do groups Certain clearly not it accuse psychoanalysis great too upon and understand of putting an emphasis.

As you can see, it doesn't take much comprehension to identify the topic. Knowing the broad topic of this paragraph is fine, but it fails to explain anything. The main ideas you need must go deeper than knowing the topic of what you have read. You will never score big on Professor Flipwhipple's final exam just by knowing, in this most limited way, what a reading assignment is about.

If you answered (a), (b), or (e) for question number two you are in deep trouble. (c) is not the best answer either, because the author does not see "sexuality" as a limitation of Freud's theory; he is defending Freud. The best answer to question number two is (d), Sexuality as a Global Concept in Freud's Theory. If you answered this correctly, you are one step ahead of someone who only knew the broad topic. This information is specific. It really describes what the paragraph is about.

The topic sentence should include the information that would go into a good title. In this paragraph both the first sentence and the last sentence might be considered topic sentences. If you underlined either one, count it right. Both sentences contain important information. The first sentence indicates that the paragraph is going to deal with Freud's concept of sexuality. The last sentence doesn't mention Freud or psychoanalysis; however, it does tell us that sex is only a part of the larger concept of sexuality. This is the important generalization in the paragraph.

Question number four asked you to write down the most significant generalization about Freud's theory. In our opinion, this calls for combining the information in the first and last sentences in the paragraph. Here is one way this could be written: In Freud's psychoanalytic theory sex is a complicated, general concept which means a lot more to a person's life than just sexual relations (foolin' around). This, in our judgment, is the main idea of the passage.

When you use PQMR, underline topic sentences and sentences which contain important generalizations about the topic. This is a strategy for finding main ideas.

Underline the main idea or topic sentence in each of the following passages. Then, in the space provided, write the most important generalization.

HINT: The topic sentence is often the first or last sentence in the paragraph.

Paragraph #1

Citizen participation and community involvement are concepts that stand at the heart of American life. A flourishing democracy flows from the active and creative participation of its citizens in the continuing work for the common good. More than a hundred years ago, Chief Tecumseh said: "A few chiefs have no right to barter away hunting grounds that belong to all the Indians for a few paltry presents or a keg or two of whiskey. . . . It requires all to make a bargain for all." Citizen participation has a firm basis in American law and the trend is toward even more explicit demands for maximum feasible participation in every practical part of the process. (Barber, Daniel. *Citizen Participation in American Communities*. Dubuque, Iowa: Kendall/Hunt Publishing Company, 1981, p. 7.)

Paragraph #2

It used to be thought that blood was particularly important in inheritance. Even those of us who ought to know better still speak of "blood lines," "bad blood," "blue-blooded," and the like. It was supposed that the blood of our ancestors mingled and was finally poured into us. According to this concept, your inheritance is a half-and-half blend of blood from your father and mother, and, hence, a quarter each from your grandparents, an eighth each from your great-grandparents, etc. This erroneous notion about heredity probably springs from two sources. First, people believed that blood is fundamental to life; therefore, it must be what we inherit. Second, there is the intuitive but false notion that all our ancestors must necessarily contribute their share to our make-up. (Fox, Elliot. *Heredity and You*. Dubuque, Iowa: Kendall/Hunt Publishing Company, 1977, p. 2.)

Paragraph #3

Sometime during the next week watch a late-night movie on television. If it is a typical western, sometime during the course of the film a mob will attempt to break into a small-town jail and drag an innocent victim into the streets to be strung up. The moral, of course, is that a group of otherwise upstanding citizens, when formed into a mob, will do all sorts of unusual and dastardly things. But do individuals always take extreme risks when placed in a group or mob? The answer, according to a large body of research, seems to be yes. People take greater risks when they are acting as part of a group than when acting alone. (Rosenfeld, Lawrence. *Analyzing Human Communication*. Dubuque, Iowa: Kendall/Hunt Publishing Company, 1980, p. 123.)

Paragraph #4

Sports do for the popular culture of America what "circuses" did for the Roman culture at the height of the Empire. They let the populace take part in a crucial ritual that binds them to one another and to the culture. Every people, no matter how civilized, must have a chance to yell for blood. Americans express this barbarism daily in their gladiatorial arts—in acting as spectators and psychic participants while other men fight, wrestle, and race with one another, break through human walls to make a goal in football, on ice, or in basketball arenas. (Lerner, Max. "Spectator and Amateur Sports." In *The Humanities: An American Experience*. By Robert Frazer et al, Arizona State University, 1977, p. 83.)

Limitations of a Main Idea Strategy

On the surface it may seem easy to find main ideas. Unfortunately, main ideas are sometimes hard to find for several reasons.

Limitation #1

Many paragraphs don't have a topic sentence or a clearly stated main idea. Some paragraphs are simply lists of events. For example, in the paragraph below there is no topic sentence and no clear main idea, just a series of actions in a story.

He stood there alone, and he could feel the dampness chilling along his spine. He turned, wondering if the other riders were watching him. He glanced both ways; most of the bronc riders were waiting to watch the roping. He saw Sunny Grebb tying his bronc rein around his rolled chaps. He heard someone hazing a horse into the chutes, and with a feeling of panic he realized it was his bronc. (Lofting, Colin. "Last Bronc." *The Saturday Evening Post,* Curtis Publishing Company 227:24. 28 August 1954.

Limitation #2

The main idea or the most important thought in a paragraph is not always the same for every reader. Comprehension is determined as much by what is in the mind as by what is on the page. For this reason different readers may find different main ideas in the same paragraph. What the author thinks is important, what your instructor thinks is important, and what you think is important may not always be the same thing. Read the following paragraph and underline the topic sentence or the main idea. If you can't find either one, make a generalization about the paragraph or summarize it in the space provided.

As the National Guard moved out from the ROTC building, Company A was on the right flank, Company C was on the left flank and Troop G was between the two. General Canterbury moved with the troops. As they approached the students, teargas was fired at the crowd. The combination of the advancing troops and the teargas forced the students to retreat. Some students retreated up Blanket Hill to the northeast of the advancing troops. The majority of the students were forced up Blanket Hill to the south of Taylor Hall. Some rocks were thrown by the students at the National Guard at this time but were for the most part ineffective. (Payne, J. G. *Mayday: Kent State.* Dubuque, Iowa: Kendall/Hunt Publishing Company, 1981, p. 175.)

GENERALIZATION OR SUMMARY: _____

_____

_____ .

What is your opinion? Would the important information in this paragraph be the same for the following people:
1. A Kent State student?
2. A National Guardsman?
3. A historian?
4. Someone writing the history of Taylor Hall?

We worked hard on this paragraph and could not come up with a main idea. The broad topic is the 1970 Kent State tragedy in which four students were killed and nine were wounded by Ohio National Guardsmen during a student protest. The paragraph itself describes a part of the confrontation between the students and the National Guard, but that isn't a significant generalization or a particularly important piece of information.

On the other hand, the paragraph contains a number of important details; for example, the fact that the Guardsmen were shooting teargas at the students, and the fact that the students were throwing rocks at the Guardsmen. In our opinion, the significance of each fact would depend upon who was reading the passage.

What this example points out is that main ideas and important facts are not a cut-and-dried matter. There is no easy formula for identifying important ideas. In fact, research shows that it is your EFFORT to find and mark important facts and ideas that brings about better comprehension and recall. You are better off underlining the wrong things than having the right things underlined for you by someone else.

Searching for main ideas isn't easy, especially when you consider that there are no sure-fire rules for finding them. However, you should still hunt for important topic sentences and main idea statements. Just don't be disappointed if you don't find them in every paragraph.

When you are underlining in a textbook, try to underline about 10–15% of the text. This is a general rule of thumb, however; the amount you will underline will vary from chapter to chapter and from class to class. You want to mark only *really* important information: topic sentences, main ideas, critical details. Too much underlining only messes up the text.

Sometimes you will mark what you believe is important. Other times you will mark what you think your instructor believes is important. In the long run, the only thing that matters is that you put your brain to work in sorting out the treasure from the trash.

Summarizing

The research on summarizing is similar to the research on underlining. It is the EFFORT you put into making the summary rather than the information itself that makes the difference. In other words, if the author of a geography book wrote a nice little summary for you at the end of each chapter subheading, it wouldn't help your comprehension and recall as much as if you had written the summaries yourself. This would be true even if your summaries were not as good as those provided in the book.

The summarizing technique improves comprehension and is simple, but it takes some time. All you have to do is write a sentence or two at the end of each major paragraph or chapter subheading. The sentence should summarize the paragraph, or it should state what you consider to be the main idea of the paragraph. Obviously, you should not write down anything that is directly stated in the text. That, you would underline.

In the following passage we have underlined what we consider important information. At the end we have written a short summary statement. (Remember to use the dictionary, glossary, or index if necessary.)

Human Sexual Response Cycle

All the various changes that occur in our bodies during sexual stimulation and sexual intercourse Masters and Johnson have called <u>the sexual response cycle</u>. To help explain these changes they have divided the sexual response cycle into four phases; <u>(1) excitement phase, (2) plateau phase, (3) orgasmic phase, and (4) resolution phase</u>. These four <u>phases occur progressively</u> during the response cycle of <u>both the male and the female</u>. There is <u>considerable variation</u> in the sexual response cycle between individuals and even for the same individual depending upon the circumstances. Nevertheless, for both the male and female there are two common physiological responses during the sexual response cycle, (1) a generalized congestion of the blood vessels and (2) an increased muscular tension. (Brum, G. D., Castro, P., and Quinn, R. D. *Biology and Man,* 3d ed. Dubuque, Iowa: Kendall/Hunt Publishing Company, 1978.)

Summary: *Describes the four-phase cycle of body changes which both men and women experience during sex.*

In this paragraph as in thousands of others you will face, it may seem that you could underline just about the whole thing. After all, all of the facts seem important, and a professor could quiz you on any of them. This is true. However, in addition to marking important information, the purpose of underlining is to force yourself to discriminate, to make decisions, to focus your attention. These things stop happening when the highlighter becomes a dot which shows where your eyes are on the page. That's the dead end students come to when they give up and say, "What's the use? Everything's important." Force yourself to decide which things are MOST important.

Read the following passage. Underline the MOST important information and write a one- or two-sentence summary of it.

Playing It Cool*

Playing it cool was conceived by Black people. Cool was born in the compressed, hot, and oppressive ghettoes. Playing it cool probably originated, in part, when the first African male ancestors discovered that they needed a new synthesized adaptable lifestyle to survive the horrors of the White man's ways. Cool is not simply an urban phenomenon. It has African roots. City living has simply refined cool and given it an adaptive and coping style for ghetto living. Cool, then, is not a product of either White America or the Black middle-class. Black middle-class people, however, who are not alienated from their roots, usually incorporate elements of cool. Playing it cool can be defined as a distinctive street cultural lifestyle which involves the art of learning how to be both detached and intimate. When a brother says, "man, you lost your cool," he is saying that a particular brother became unnecessarily boisterous, loud, angry, immature, and silly in a verbal exchange. To lose your cool means "acting like a child" rather than like an "adult in charge of the situation." The brother who loses his cool loses that cold, objective, nothing-phases-me detachment a man must have to survive in the high-tensioned inner city situation. The practice of cool is another Black ritual which prepares young Blacks for coping and survival in White society. (Porter, J. R., *Dating Habits of Young Black Americans: And Almost Everybody Elses Too*. Dubuque, Iowa: Kendall/Hunt Publishing Company, 1979, p. 55.)

Summary: _____

_____

_____

GRAPHIC COMPREHENSION

Graphic comprehension is the ability to understand maps, charts, graphs, and other visual presentations of information. Most college textbooks use pictures or graphics of one sort or another to illustrate important ideas. These graphic aids are valuable additions to books for two reasons:

1. Some ideas or pieces of information are easier to understand when they are presented as graphics.
2. A graphic is efficient. Information presented in maps, graphs, diagrams, and charts save space and time. "A picture is worth a thousand words."

Many students skip over graphic aids because they find them hard to understand. However, the PQMR strategy can be used to comprehend and study graphics. The steps of the strategy should be applied in the following manner:

Preview

1. Read the title.
2. Figure out what kind of graphic you are looking at.
3. Read any explanations which are on the graphic itself.

Question: Ask Yourself

1. What important idea does the graphic present?
2. What do the symbols, if there are any, represent?
3. Do I understand the information presented?
4. How does the graphic information fit into the chapter?
5. What am I supposed to learn from this material?

Mark

1. Circle or underline any important information.
2. Write down definitions and main ideas in the margins.
3. Write down any questions you have for your instructor.

Review

1. Make sure your questions have been answered.
2. Read over written comments and the things you underlined.
3. Close your eyes and make a mental image of the graphic.

Maps

A *map* is a scaled-down (smaller) representation of an area, usually some part of the earth. Maps are often drawings that use symbols and labels so that mountains, cities, or other features on the map can be found easily. Most maps are drawn so that North is at the top, South is at the bottom, East is to the right, and West is on the left side of the map.

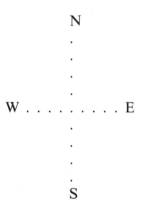

There are many kinds of maps. However, the three most common kinds of maps are political maps, physical maps, and special feature maps.

A *political map* shows the borders and locations of political units; that is, countries, states, capital cities, etc. Only major physical features such as oceans and high mountain ranges are included. Shown below is a political map of the United States. In the space provided list information provided by the map in addition to the type of information mentioned above.

Somerfield, B., *Skills in Reading 2,* New York: Cambridge Book Company, 1974, p. 45.

A *physical map* shows the natural features of a region; that is, mountains, lakes, rivers, elevations above sea level, etc. Only the boundaries of nations and states and the names of important land and water areas are included.

Below is a physical map of the United States. Look at the key in the lower left hand corner. It tells you that different shades show how high the land is above sea level in various parts of the country. For example, the map shows that the area of the Rocky Mountains in the west (the black splotch) is over 8,000 feet above sea level. How high above sea level is the state of Mississippi (Miss.)?

_____

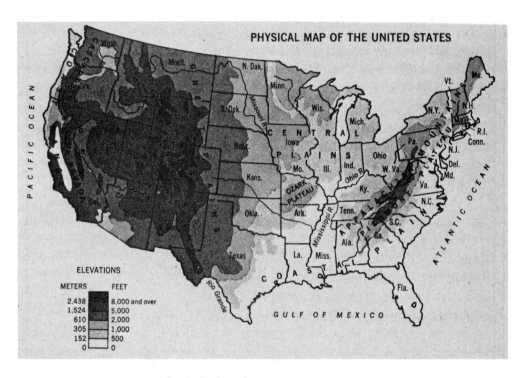

Somerfield, B., *Skills in Reading 2,* New York: Cambridge Book Company, 1974, p. 44.

Special feature maps show one special thing on a map of a particular geographical area. Below is a map showing important coal deposits in the United States. Read the message below the map and study the map. Then name a state that has no major coal deposits. (If you have trouble placing the states, look back on the political map on p. 85.)

(Lignite)

Rocky
Mountain
Region

Mid-continent
Region

Eastern
Region

Numerous
small lignite fields

From GEOLOGY: A SYNOPSIS, PART I: PHYSICAL GEOGRAPHY by J. Allan Cain and Eugene J. Tynan, copyright © 1980 by Kendall/Hunt Publishing Company. Reprinted by permission of Kendall/Hunt Publishing Company.

Charts

Charts present information by combining labels, special shapes, and drawings. Charts come in many shapes and sizes. For example, a *pie chart* uses a circle to present information. The whole circle equals 100% with each part representing a percentage of the whole.

The pie charts shown compare the occupations of working populations of five different countries. The key on the left shows the patterns, such as the wavy lines, which stand for a particular occupation. Here is what the pie chart shows for the Netherlands:

42% of the people work in industry
 8% of the people work in agriculture or fisheries
24% of the people work in trade and transport
26% of the people do some other kind of work

See if you can answer the following questions:

1. Which country has the smallest percentage of agricultural workers? _____

2. Which country has the second-largest percentage of its people working in industry? _____

3. How much greater is Mexico's percentage of agricultural workers than Japan's? _____

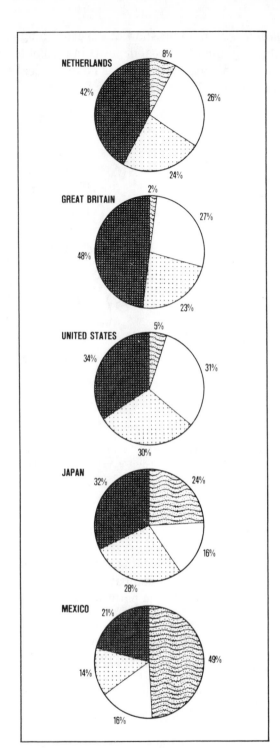

WORKING POPULATION

Agriculture and fisheries

Industry (including mining)

Trade and transport

Other professions

The graphs reveal the small percentage of northern Europeans engaged in agriculture and the high percentage in industry. Mexico, a country of southern European culture, is noticably different. Japan is an anomaly: technologically it resembles the northern European pattern.

A Compact Geography of the Netherlands, N. V. Cartografisch Instituut Bootsma, 's-Gravenhage, 1970.

Taken from Fuson, R. H. Introduction To World Geography Regions and Cultures, Kendall/Hunt Publishing Company.

A *hierarchical chart* orders things and shows how they relate to one another. For example, the chart below is drawn like a tree (these are sometimes called *tree diagrams*) and shows how different kinds of animals are related to each other. The lines show which creatures are related to each other and how closely. You can use the "word" *isa* to describe the relationships. For instance, a snake "isa" reptile and a reptile "isa" animal. Snakes belong to a larger group called *reptiles;* and reptiles belong to the even larger group called *animals*. You can also see that a snake is more like a crocodile than a fly because snakes and crocodiles belong to the same higher group called reptiles.

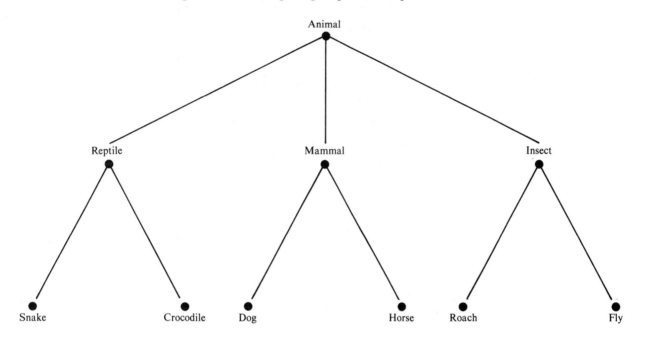

Diagrammed below is a skeleton of a hierarchical tree diagram. Using the words listed below the diagram, see if you can fill in the tree.

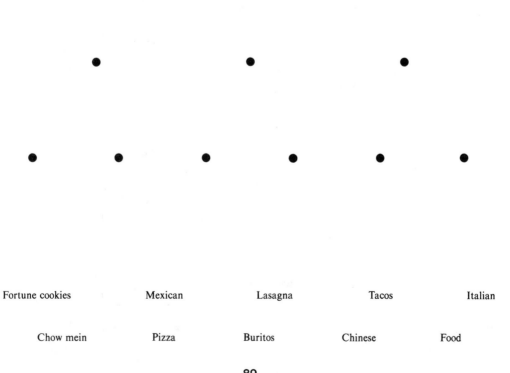

| Fortune cookies | Mexican | Lasagna | Tacos | Italian |
| Chow mein | Pizza | Buritos | Chinese | Food |

A different kind of hierarchical chart is drawn below. This one shows the sales organization of a large company. The person who holds a certain sales job is in charge of those people who hold jobs below him/her on the chart. Those who are higher in the chart are also higher up in the sales organization. For example, the District Sales Manager is in charge of one-hundred people in a major city. These people include branch sales managers, sales supervisors, and sales representatives. Study the chart and answer the following questions:

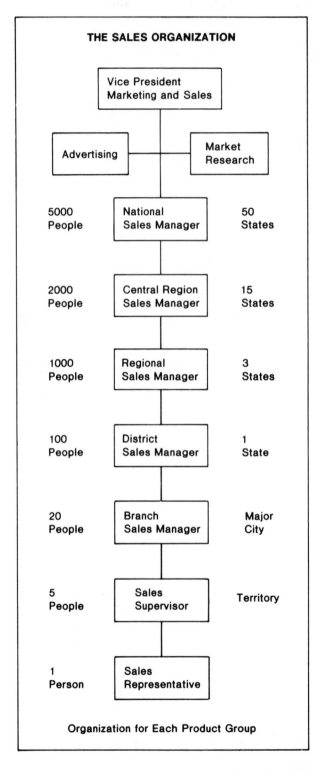

THE SALES ORGANIZATION

	Vice President Marketing and Sales	
	Advertising — Market Research	
5000 People	National Sales Manager	50 States
2000 People	Central Region Sales Manager	15 States
1000 People	Regional Sales Manager	3 States
100 People	District Sales Manager	1 State
20 People	Branch Sales Manager	Major City
5 People	Sales Supervisor	Territory
1 Person	Sales Representative	

Organization for Each Product Group

1. Who is the Central Region Sales Manager's immediate boss?

_____

2. To what group can the Sales Supervisor give orders?

_____

3. Who is in charge of a three state area?

_____

Another kind of chart is the *flowchart*. This graphic shows the steps for solving a problem. The symbols that are used to make flowcharts come from computer language. In order to understand flowcharts you should be familiar with the following symbols:

1. *Flowlines:* These lines show the direction to follow (flow) when going from step to step.

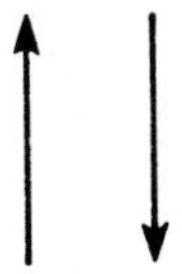

2. *Terminal Symbol:* This symbol shows the starting point and the end point in the chart.

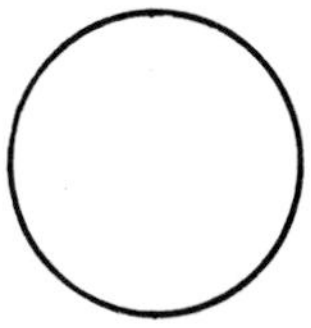

3. *Input/Output Symbol:* This symbol shows what information is needed to solve a problem.

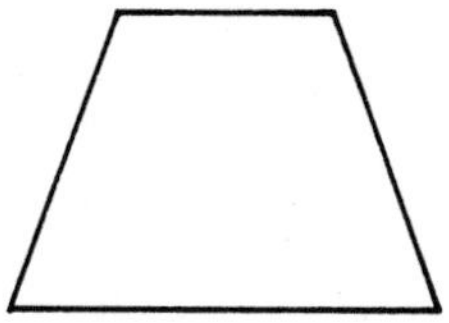

4. *Process Symbol:* This symbol tells what action must be taken to get a desired result.

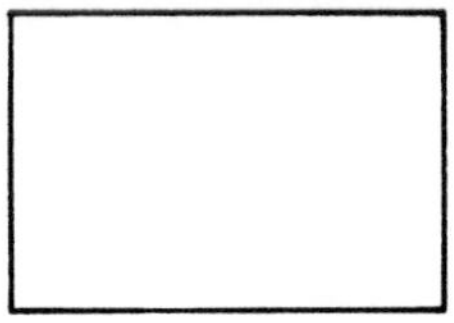

5. *Decision Symbol:* This symbol asks a question that is answered by a "yes" or a "no." The answer to the question determines which direction you will go in the chart when there are two possibilities.

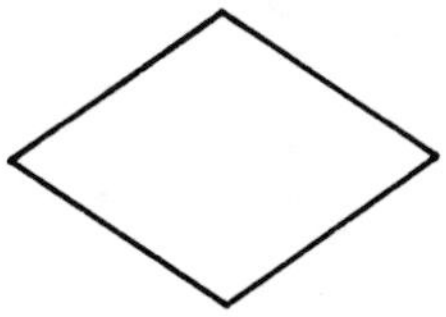

Now that you have studied the symbols, you are ready to interpret the flowchart shown below. It is a simple chart designed to compute wages. See if you can answer the following questions.

1. What decision must be made in this flowchart?

   _____

2. What words are written on the terminal symbols?

   _____ and _____

3. If Juan worked 20 hours of overtime, what would his overtime pay be? He normally makes $8 per hour.

   _____

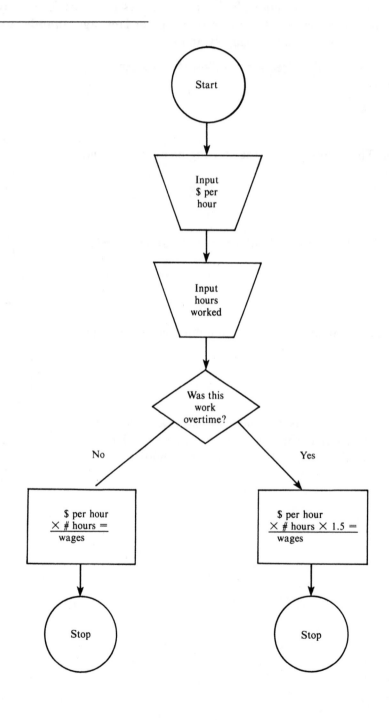

A *process chart* shows the individual steps in a process. Often, each step is illustrated. The process chart is like a flowchart in that it shows direction and movement. However, a process chart is also like a picture and uses names of things rather than symbols.

The process chart below shows where rain comes from. This process is called the hydrologic cycle (*Hydro* is Greek for "water.") The various processes in the hydrologic cycle are labeled on the chart, and the arrows show the movement of the water within the cycle. Study the chart and answer the following questions. (Remember to use the glossary, dictionary, and index if necessary.)

1. What are the three ways that water gets into the air?

   _____ _____ _____

2. Name three kinds of precipitation labeled on the chart.

   _____ _____ _____

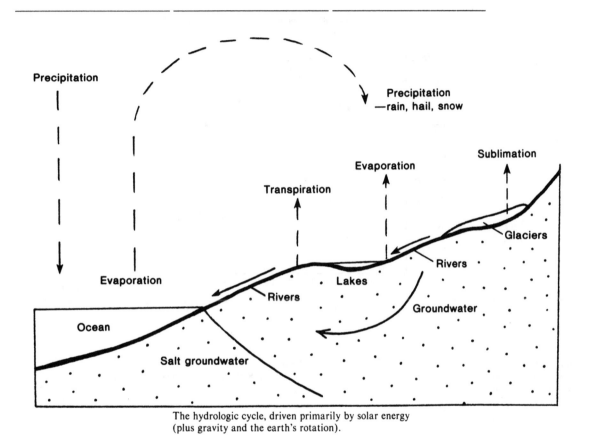

The hydrologic cycle, driven primarily by solar energy
(plus gravity and the earth's rotation).

From GEOLOGY: A SYNOPSIS, PART I: PHYSICAL GEOLOGY by J. Allan Cain and Eugene J. Tynan, copyright © 1980 by Kendall/Hunt Publishing Company.

Graphs

A *graph* is a drawing or picture which shows stages or changes in something over a period of time. For example, a graph could show how the weight of a baby changes from week to week or from month to month. The three kinds of graphs presented here are line graphs, bar graphs, and pictographs.

Line graphs use connected lines to show changes. For instance, the line graph below shows the numbers of males and females employed each year from 1971 to 1978. The numbers on the left-hand side of the graph stand for the number of people employed. The years are marked off along the bottom of the graph. The dotted line shows male employment and the solid line shows female employment.

Here is how the graph works. Imagine that a line is drawn straight up and down from each year to the top of the graph. Then imagine that a line is drawn from each number on the left side of the graph to the far right side of the graph. Wherever two lines cross on the graph, information can be plotted, or placed. For example, the number 9,340 is directly above 1971 on the graph. This means that 9,340 women in a certain city were employed in 1971. When the dots are connected you can see the changes in employment that occurred from year to year. Study the graph, then answer the following questions:

1. Which year had the greatest number of males employed?

   _____

2. What is the difference in female employment between 1975 and 1976? _____

3. What two generalizations can you make in comparing male and female employment?

   A. _____

   B. _____

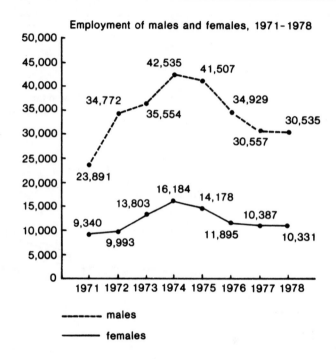

Employment of males and females, 1971–1978

Adapted from TOPICS IN SMALL BUSINESS MANAGEMENT Volume I, Second Edition, by Richard M. Hodgetts and Pamela Keel, copyright © 1982 by Kendall/Hunt Publishing Company. Reprinted by permission of Kendall/Hunt Publishing Company.

A *bar graph* uses bars of different lengths to show relationships. Exact amounts usually are printed on the top of each bar. The bar graph below shows how much stock prices have gone up between August 1982 and August 1983. The percentages on the bars show the increases in stock prices reported by each of the five investment houses. Which investment house reported the greatest increase in stock prices?* Now try these questions:

1. Which investment house reported the least gain in stock prices? _____ .

2. If a stock with the same gain reported by E. F. Hutton on the bar graph sold for 20 cents a share in August 1982, what did the same share of stock sell for in August 1983? _____

*Answer: Merrill Lynch.

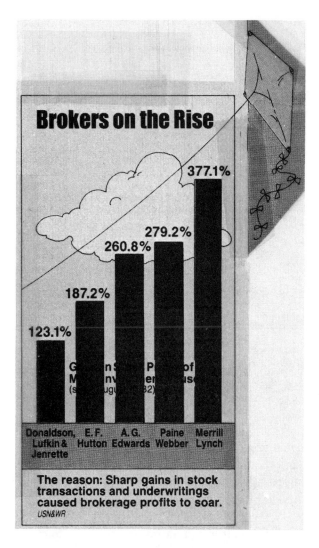

Reprinted from *U.S. News and World Report* issue of August 15, 1983. Copyright, 1983, U.S. News and World Report, Inc.

Diagrams

A diagram, like a map, is a scaled-down drawing. However, a diagram illustrates the important parts of a thing rather than a land area. Below is a diagram of a humidifier. A humidifier is used to add moisture to the air in a dry room. Water is added at the base of the humidifier. The water is then drawn up through a spinning pump and through a screen where it is changed from water to water vapor. A motor forces the water vapor out of the humidifier into the dry air through a spout. Now see if you can answer the following questions by inspecting the diagram.

1. Which part of the humidifier is removable?

   _____ _____

2. Where is the vapor spout located? _____

   _____ .

CONSTRUCTION DETAILS

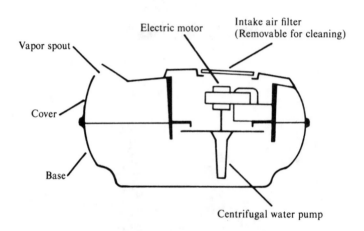

Major Review Exercise

It is now time for you to use everything you have learned about study strategies, vocabulary, and comprehension. Read the following chapter on stress and health. Be sure to use the PQMR technique, which we have summarized below.

PQMR Summary

    A. To preview: (Underline previewed material for this exercise.)
        1. Read the title and the first paragraph.
        2. Read the closing paragraph (or chapter summary).
        3. Skim the assignment by reading all headings and the first sentence that comes directly after each heading.
        4. As you skim, focus your attention on italicized words, pictures, graphs, and charts.
    B. To Question:
       Write down at least five questions which you have about the subject matter.
    C. To Mark:

_____	Underline or highlight main ideas and important details.
[ ]	Use brackets to mark important paragraphs.
Jargon	Circle new technical terms.
(1) (2) (3)	Number important steps, causes, or reasons.
* ! ?	Use the asterisk or exclamation point to indicate EXTREME IMPORTANCE. Use the question mark to show confusion or disagreement.
Super! Barf! True	Use personal comments and summarize each major subheading.

Stress and Health

Recently many psychologists and physicians have been struck by the fact that people in stressful life situations seem to be ill more frequently than those in less stressful situations.

Life change. During our lives, each of us experiences events which demand that we change our habits, adjust to new conditions, make new friends, or change our lifestyle. Marriage, divorce, the birth of a child, the death of a relative, or a promotion at work are all examples of these kinds of life changes. For the past several years, Thomas Holmes and his colleagues have investigated the impact of these life changes upon health (Holmes and Rahe, 1967; Holmes and Masuda, 1973).

Holmes theorizes that each life change introduces some stress into your life. That is, you have to cope with the change and adapt your behavior to new conditions. The greater the number and severity of these life changes, the greater is the amount of stress which is, in varying degrees, partly psychological, partly physical, and partly physiological. And while each person can tolerate a moderate amount of stress, greater amounts may interfere with normal psychological, physical, and physiological functioning.

In order to test out these ideas, Holmes and Rahe (1967) designed a questionnaire called the Social Readjustment Rating Scale, which is reproduced in Table 6.3. All of the events on the questionnaire are things that require adaptation and coping. Each item has been assigned a number of "Life Change Units" which reflects how much adaptation and coping it requires. One hundred

Table 6.3 The Social Readjustment Rating Scale

Life Event	Mean Value
1. Death of spouse	100
2. Divorce	73
3. Marital separation from mate	65
4. Detention in jail or other institution	63
5. Death of a close family member	63
6. Major personal injury or illness	53
7. Marriage	50
8. Being fired at work	47
9. Marital reconciliation with mate	45
10. Retirement from work	45
11. Major change in the health or behavior of a family member	44
12. Pregnancy	40
13. Sexual difficulties	39
14. Gaining a new family member (e.g., through birth, adoption, oldster moving in, etc.)	39
15. Major business readjustment (e.g., merger, reorganization, bankruptcy, etc.)	39
16. Major change in financial state (e.g., a lot worse off or a lot better off than usual)	38
17. Death of a close friend	37
18. Changing to a different line of work	36
19. Major change in the number of arguments with spouse (e.g., either a lot more or a lot less than usual regarding child-rearing, personal habits, etc.	35
20. Taking out a mortgage or loan for a major purchase (e.g., for a home, business, etc.)	31
21. Foreclosure on a mortgage or loan	30

From pp. 196–206 in THE DEVELOPING PERSON: A Life-Span Approach by Helen L. Bee and Sandra K. Mitchell. Copyright © 1980 by Helen Bee Douglas and Sandra K. Mitchell. By permission of Harper & Row, Publishers, Inc.

Table 6.3—*Continued*

Life Event	Mean Value
22. Major change in responsibilities at work (e.g., promotion, demotion, lateral transfer)	29
23. Son or daughter leaving home (e.g., marriage, attending college, etc.)	29
24. Trouble with in-laws	29
25. Outstanding personal achievement	28
26. Wife beginning or ceasing work outside the home	26
27. Beginning or ceasing formal schooling	26
28. Major change in living conditions (e.g., building a new home, remodeling, deterioration of home or neighborhood)	25
29. Revision of personal habits (dress, manners, associations, etc.)	24
30. Trouble with the boss.	23
31. Major change in working hours or conditions	20
32. Change in residence	20
33. Changing to a new school	20
34. Major change in usual type and/or amount of recreation	19
35. Major change in church activities (e.g., a lot more or a lot less than usual)	19
36. Major change in social activities (e.g., clubs, dancing, movies, visiting, etc.)	18
37. Taking out a mortgage or loan for a lesser purchase (e.g., for a car, TV, freezer, etc.)	17
38. Major change in sleeping habits (a lot more or a lot less sleep, or change in part of day when asleep)	16
39. Major change in number of family get-togethers (e.g., a lot more or a lot less than usual)	15
40. Major change in eating habits (a lot more or a lot less food intake, or very different meal hours or surroundings)	15
41. Vacation	13
42. Christmas	12
43. Minor violations of the law (e.g., traffic tickets, jaywalking, disturbing the peace, etc.)	11

Reprinted with permission from Journal of Psychosomatic Research 11:213–218, by T. H. Holmes and R. H. Rahe, The Social Readjustment Rating Scale. Copyright 1976, Pergamon Press, Ltd.

Life Change Units are given for "death of a spouse," marriage gets 50 Life Change Units, and the lowest score of all (11) is for minor violations of the law such as traffic tickets. A person fills out the Social Readjustment Rating Scale by checking off all of the events which have occurred in her life for the last year. The sum of the Life Change units for those items is her score.

In one of his early studies, Holmes gave this questionnaire to a group of 88 young doctors. Along with their reports of life changes, they were also asked to report any health problems that they experienced. From these records, the researchers looked to see whether or not health problems occurred within two years of the time a Life Crisis (score of 150 Life Change Units or above) had occurred. The results of this analysis are shown in Figure 6.9.

It is clear that the likelihood of illness was much greater for people who reported major life crises than for those who reported moderate or mild life crises. In fact, 79 percent of those with scores over 300 on the questionnaire experienced some change in health.

You should notice, however, that the amount and type of life change which occurs does not predict what *kind* of health change will occur. In Holmes' study, health changes included everything from infectious diseases to broken legs. All the score seems to predict is that *some* change in health status will occur.

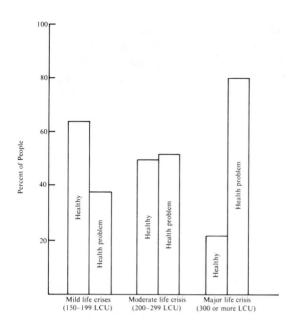

Figure 6.9. Impact of life crises upon health. People who had experienced a major life crisis (more than 150 Life Change Units) were very likely to have a health problem. In general, the lower the amount of life change, the lower the chance of a problem. (*Source*: Holmes, T. H. and M. Masuda, p. 175. Copyright 1973 by the American Association for the Advancement of Science.)

Of what use is this kind of research? Well, one application of this study might be to help people keep *down* the number of life changes they experience at one time. Suppose that a woman has a new baby. Her Social Readjustment Rating Scale might look like this:

13.	Pregnancy	40
19.	New family member	39
5.	Major change in sleeping habits	16
7.	Major change in eating habits	15
9.	Revision of personal habits (a diet to regain her figure)	24
		134

We might suggest to her that she refrain from moving (item 20, 20 points) or beginning work (item 30, 26 points), or beginning school (item 42, 26 points) for the time being, since any one of these events, added to her present situation, would constitute a life crisis.

Earlier we suggested that people who are poor or members of minority groups may be under more stress than more affluent, white people are. In fact, studies using the Social Readjustment Rating Scale have shown just this result. It may be that one reason for the difference between races and social classes in health during adulthood is the difference between these groups in the amount of life change they experience.

Type A behavior. Some researchers have gone even farther than Holmes, and have suggested that some kinds of stress may be the direct cause of specific illnesses. One of the best known theories of this kind was developed by two cardiologists (physicians specializing in heart disease), Meyer Friedman and Ray Rosenman (1974). Their research began when, just out of curiosity, they asked a group of businessmen what *they* thought was the cause of heart attacks in their friends. More than 70 percent thought that "excessive competitive drive and meeting deadlines," was the outstanding characteristic of their own friends who had had heart attacks. Friedman and Rosenman were about to dismiss this as an old wives tale, when they asked the same question of a group of doctors. The doctors, too, mentioned "excessive competitive drive and meeting deadlines."

Based on these observations, Friedman and Rosenman were able to describe a whole lifestyle characterized by what they call "Type A Behavior." The central trait in this lifestyle is the sense of time urgency, of too much to be done in too little time. There are other aspects of Type A Behavior (listed in Table 6.4), but the sense of being late, or of being behind schedule, is the most important part.

At the time this theory was being devised, most physicians thought (and many still do) that the primary cause of heart disease was a high level of cholesterol in the blood. If Type A Behavior was supposed to cause heart disease, it was important to show that that behavior pattern was related to levels of cholesterol.

To do this, Friedman and Rosenman devised a very clever study of tax accountants, checking their levels of cholesterol in the blood regularly from January until June.

> *When the April 15 tax deadline approached, and the sense of time urgency of these accountants rose sharply, so did the level of their serum cholesterol. Conversely, in May and early June, when their sense of time urgency almost disappeared, their serum cholesterol fell. (Friedman and Rosenman, 1974, p. 59.)*

Table 6.4   Characteristics of Type A Behavior Pattern.

You possess Type A Behavior pattern:

1. If you have (a) a habit of explosively accentuating various key words in your ordinary speech . . . and (b) a tendency to utter the last few words of your sentences far more rapidly than the opening words. . . .
2. If you *always* move, walk, and eat rapidly.
3. If you feel an impatience with the rate at which most events take place.
4. If you indulge in *polyphasic* thought or performance, frequently striving to think of or do two or more things simultaneously. . . .
5. If you find it *always* difficult to refrain from talking about or bringing the theme of any conversation around to those subjects which especially interest and intrigue you, and when unable to accomplish this maneuver, you pretend to listen but really remain preoccupied with your own thoughts.
6. If you almost always feel vaguely guilty when you relax and do absolutely nothing for several hours to several days.
7. If you no longer observe the more important or interesting or lovely objects that you encounter in your milieu. . . .
8. If you do not have any time to spare to become the things worth *being*, because you are so preoccupied with getting the things worth *having*.
9. If you attempt to schedule more and more in less and less time, and in doing so make fewer and fewer allowances for unforeseen contingencies. . . .
10. If, on meeting another severely afflicted Type A person, instead of feeling compassion for his affliction you find yourself compelled to "challenge" him. . . .
11. If you resort to certain characteristic gestures or nervous tics. . . .
12. If you believe that whatever success you have enjoyed has been due in good part to your ability to get things done faster than your fellow man and if you are afraid to stop doing everything faster and faster.
13. If you find yourself increasingly and inelectably committed to translating and evaluating not only your own but also the activities of others in terms of "numbers."

You can see that this kind of research has many important applications. Anything a person can do to reduce his Type A Behavior should reduce the risk of heart attack. Friedman and Rosenman offer many suggestions for ways to do this, but they all boil down to simply relaxing and letting time go by. That's good advice, but still very difficult for most people to follow.

Nutrition

Earlier in this book we emphasized the importance of good nutrition for optimal prenatal development and for the normal growth and physical development of the infant and child. You should not be surprised, then, to learn that nutrition also plays an important part in the health and development of adults.

One of the most important nutritional changes which occurs during the adult years is the gradual decrease in the number of calories eaten each day. Calories, as any of you who have dieted must know, measure how much energy is in the food we eat. Careful studies of adult males have shown the diet of the average 28-year-old man contains about 2700 calories per day, while that of an 80-year-old man is only about 2100 calories a day (see Figure 6.10).

Why do younger people eat more than older ones? There are two possible answers, because the body uses food energy in two quite different ways. First, it uses energy to maintain all of the cells and organs in the body. This is technically referred to as the "basal metabolism rate," because it describes how much energy is necessary to maintain the basic functions of the body. Secondly, food energy is used for physical activity—walking, climbing stairs, doing chores, and so forth. Older people might need fewer calories because their needs for basal metabolism are lower, or they might need fewer calories because their levels of activity are lower.

Figure 6.10. Average diet of adult men. People usually eat less as they get older, partly because their bodies require fewer calories for basic bodily needs (basal metabolism), and partly because they use fewer calories for physical activity. (*Source:* Shock, 1972, p. 18.)

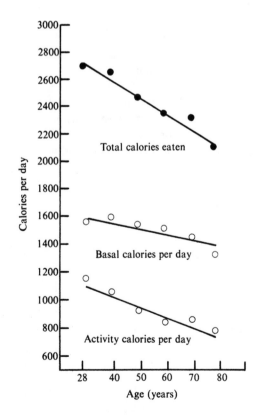

If you look at the bottom of Figure 6.10, you can see that, in fact, both of these changes are occurring. The number of calories needed for basal metabolism declines from about 1550 calories a day in 28-year-old men to about 1350 calories a day in 80-year-old men. That difference equals about the number of calories (200) in a piece of apple pie or a hot dog in a bun. Part of the change in diet, then, is really due to changes in the body's basic requirements. But it is also true that the number of calories used in activities declines even *more* dramatically during adulthood—from about 1150 calories in 28-year-old men to 750 calories in 80-year-old men. That 400 calorie drop is about equal to a chocolate ice cream soda every day.

When a diet decreases from 2700 calories to 2100 calories a day, the supply of specific nutrients goes down, too. A diet with fewer calories is also likely to provide fewer vitamins and minerals and less protein than a diet with more calories. This drop in the *quality* of nutrition may be just as important as the drop in the *quantity* of food eaten.

To give just one example, the diets of many elderly people are mildly deficient in the mineral potassium. T. G. Judge, a nutritionist, was interested in whether this deficiency had any impact on the behavior of elderly people. In his study (1972), Judge used a kind of IQ test called "Raven's Progressive Matrices," which is a measure of nonverbal reasoning. He gave this test to a group of elderly people both before and after they were administered a vitamin supplement. For half the group, this supplement included potassium; for the other half, it did not (this is called the "placebo"). Both groups of patients, as you can see in Figure 6.11, improved their scores the second time they took the test. But the group who received the potassium supplement improved significantly *more* than the group who did not.

This study does *not* show that all elderly people need to take potassium pills, or that taking potassium would make them smarter. It *does* show that even minor nutritional deficiencies may have a noticeable effect on some kinds of behavior. When we look at people's behavior, particularly if they are elderly, we need to remember that nutrition may be responsible for some of the behavior we observe.

A decrease in the amount and quality of food is not the only nutritional problem faced by the aging. On the contrary, there are a large number of factors which make eating well increasingly difficult for them. Some of these reasons are summarized in Table 6.5. They include fairly straightforward problems, such as loss of teeth or loss of coordination, and some indirect problems, such as low income, which may influence diet in a number of ways, nearly all of them negative.

Figure 6.11. Influence of potassium supplements on nonverbal reasoning scores. Although scores rose for both groups on the second test, the increase for the group who received a potassium supplement was greater than the increase for the group who got the placebo. (*Source:* Judge, 1972, p. 93.)

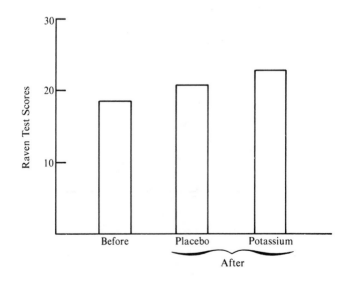

Table 6.5   Factors that Determine Eating Habits in the Elderly.

Loss of teeth or denture problems. Denture wearer must chew food four times as long to get the same effect as a person with natural teeth.

Decrease in salivation may make chewing more difficult.

Diminished sense of smell and taste (which may lead to oversalting of food, a problem for those with high blood pressure).

Loss of neuromuscular coordination (inability to feed self easily).

Chronic diseases.

Food preferences and habits.

Decreased physical activity, which limits caloric needs and may lead to weight problems.

Decreased physical activity, which makes it more difficult to shop and prepare foods.

Decreased basal metabolism rate, which supports basic bodily functions.

Long-term dietetic habits.

Income, which may limit availability of different foods.

Emotional upsets and problems, especially widowhood and widowerhood.

Lack of adequate food storage and cooking facilities.

Even though nutrition would seem to be an important concern for the elderly, quite little is actually known about the nutritional needs of older people. For example, the United States government has suggested nutritional requirements for infants, children, and adults, but not for the elderly. In fact, very few doctors are trained to look for nutritional deficiencies in their patients, especially the elderly ones. And even less is known about the long-term effects of diet—both good and poor—on the behavior of older people, or on the aging process itself. This is an area where a great deal of research, both basic and applied, still remains to be done.

Exercise

As we just saw, the amount of energy spent in activity declines rather dramatically over the adult years, resulting in an accompanying decline in the amount of necessary food intake. Unfortunately, another result seems to be that the level of physical fitness also declines.

Until fairly recently, most people accepted a decrease in fitness, of activity, and of the feeling of well-being as part of the process of aging. However, as you all know, sports and exercise have lately become enormously popular in this country. For the first time, many of us have realized that although it may be *typical* to be overweight and out of shape, it is not necessarily *normal*.

One study of exercise which illustrates this fact was a longitudinal study done by Fred Kasch (1976). Kasch was interested in two different groups of adult men. One was a group of former athletes, men who had continued to compete or at least participate in sports after their college years. These men were in good physical shape when the study began. The second group of men were those who were in poor physical shape at the start of the study. Some had been athletic during their youth, but had been inactive for many years; others had never been much interested in physical activities. Kasch enrolled men in these two groups into a vigorous program of physical training: running or swimming for at least an hour a day, at least three times a week.

One of the most common measures of physical fitness is the efficiency of the lungs at using oxygen. Using special equipment, Kasch measured the amount of oxygen each man could make use of per minute at the beginning of the program, and again after eight to ten *years* of training. The results of these measurements are shown in Figure 6.12. The men who were physically fit at the beginning of the study continued to show superior ability in oxygen efficiency, with very little change occurring in their capacity from the beginning to the end of the training program. For those men who had been unfit at the outset, though, the results of the program were dramatic: Their ability to

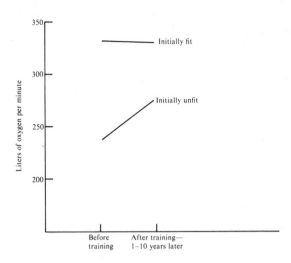

Figure 6.12. The effects of exercise upon breathing efficiency. After 8–10 years of vigorous exercising, the breathing capacity of former college athletes shows no decline. The capacity of the men who were initially out of shape has increased greatly, although it is not as high as for the men who had exercised continuously since adolescence. (*Source:* Kasch, 1976, p. 66.)

make use of oxygen improved significantly. Rather than getting worse as they got older—the average pattern among those who do not exercise—they got better. Granted, they were still not as well off as the men who had stayed fit since adolescence, but they were significantly better off than they had been at the start of the experiment. Vigorous exercise, then, is one way to improve the capacity to send oxygen and nutrients to all parts of the body, which is an important aspect of adult health. Regular exercise is a good habit for all adults to adopt.

Good Health Practices

Avoiding stress, eating nutritious foods, and exercising regularly have all been shown to improve health and to partially counteract the effects of aging. But just how much good do these good habits really do? How much difference does it make to keep yourself relaxed, well nourished, and physically fit? If you do all those things, will you really feel any better or live any longer than your friends who are nervous, overweight, and malnourished? Indeed you will. Studies by Nedra Belloc and her co-workers (Belloc, 1973; Belloc and Breslow, 1972) have shown that these and other health practices are clearly related to expected life duration. Belloc began by compiling a list of seven desirable health practices, which we've noted in Table 6.6. Each of the items on the list has been shown to reduce the death rate among adults. That is, people who usually sleep seven or eight hours have a lower death rate than people who sleep more or less than that amount. In the same way, people who eat breakfast almost every day are less likely to die young than people who do not.

But Belloc was also interested in whether combining these good practices would reduce the death rate. To test out this possibility, she made use of some data which had been collected in a large-scale (6928 persons) survey of citizens in Alameda County, California. All of these people answered questions about their health habits. Belloc was able to obtain public health records including death certificates for this county, and therefore could tell the habits of those individuals who had been surveyed and then had died. The results of this analysis are shown in Figure 6.13.

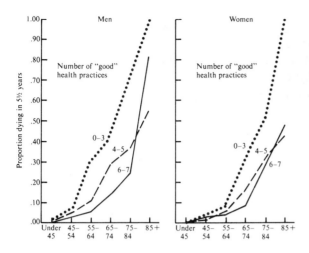

Figure 6.13. The effects of good health practices upon death rates. The more good health habits a person has, the smaller is his or her chance of dying. This difference is especially pronounced among men. (*Source:* Belloc, 1973, p. 75.)

Table 6.6   Good Health Practices.

1. Usually sleep 7 or 8 hours.
2. Eat breakfast almost every day.
3. Eat between meals once in a while, rarely, or never.
4. Weight for a man between 5% under and 19.99% over desirable weight for height. Weight for women, nor more than 9.99% over desirable weight for height.
5. Often or sometimes engage in active sports, swim, or take long walks, or often garden or do physical exercises.
6. Drink not more than 4 drinks at a time.
7. Never smoke cigarettes.

(*Source:* Belloc and Breslow, 1972, p. 415.)

For both men and women, the highest death rates were found for those who had the smallest number of good health practices. This effect was particularly dramatic for the older subjects in the study, although it was true to some extent at all ages. People with moderate numbers of good habits had intermediate mortality rates, while those with the greatest numbers of good habits had the very lowest rates. Clearly, the more good health practices you observe, the greater your chances for survival.

Answer the following questions about stress and health.

1. Which of the following produces the most stress in an individual's life?
   a. Pregnancy
   b. Retirement
   c. Being fired
   d. Divorce

2. A person with 300 LCU's would probably be less healthy than a person with 200 LCU's.
   a. True
   b. False
   c. No difference

3. Which of the following statements is true?
   a. People require more activity calories than basal calories.
   b. As age increases the need for activity calories decreases faster than the need for basal calories.
   c. On the average, adult men aged 40 take in 1600 calories per day.
   d. Someone who is 50 needs only half as many calories as a person who is 25.

4. The term *placebo* refers to
   a. a special potassium diet.
   b. a treatment or medicine which has no important ingredients.
   c. a test of nonverbal reasoning abilities.
   d. the conditions under which stress leads to poor health.

5. What is the proportion of men who die within 5.5 years if they have four or five good health habits and are between the ages of 65 and 74?
   a. 19%
   b. 28%
   c. 42%
   d. 56%

6. A common measure of physical fitness is
   a. efficiency of the lungs in using oxygen.
   b. LCU's.
   c. amount of potassium in the diet.
   d. basal calories.

7. Which is not a factor that determines the eating habits of the elderly?
   a. Loss of teeth
   b. Income
   c. Number of children
   d. Decrease in salivation

8. *Chronic* refers to a condition which
   a. goes on for a long time.
   b. is quite severe.
   c. can't be cured.
   d. the person is unaware of.

9. Which of the following is not characteristic of a Type A personality?
   a. Works fast.
   b. Dies sooner than other people
   c. Is overweight
   d. Indulges in polyphasic thought

10. Which of the following do you think is the most important idea in this chapter?
    a. Stress can affect your life.
    b. Good health practices can keep you alive longer.
    c. Physical fitness is mostly in your mind.
    d. The influence of hormones and mental discipline can make you a happier person.

7
How to Become a Critical Reader

What Do You Believe about Critical Reading?

Directions: Read each of the statements below. Place a checkmark on the line in front of each statement you believe is true.

1. _____ Thoughtful reading comes with maturity.
2. _____ College students believe too much of what they read.
3. _____ You should not be critical of your college textbooks.
4. _____ Facts are true, whereas opinions are false.
5. _____ Propaganda techniques are discouraged in a democracy.

We hope these statements have made you curious about thoughtful, critical reading. Perhaps you have developed a few questions of your own: "Should I be more critical of my textbooks?" or "What *is* critical reading?" Search for the answers to your questions as you read and work your way through this chapter.

Which Kind of Reader Are You? Which Kind Do You Want to Be?

> There are four kinds of readers. The first is like the hourglass; and their reading being as the sand, it runs in and runs out, and leaves not a vestige behind. A second is like the sponge, which imbibes everything, and returns it in nearly the same state, only a little dirtier. A third is like a jelly-bag, allowing all that is pure to pass away, and retaining only the refuse and dregs. And the fourth is like the slaves in the diamond mines of Golconda, who, casting aside all that is worthless, retain only pure gems.
> —Coleridge

College students have often been described as "sponges." They sit in class soaking up lectures and then go home to soak up more information from textbook assignments. They memorize facts and opinions as if they were the same thing. And if they happen to disagree with their textbook or professor, they usually remain silent—at least until the professor is out of earshot! You can do better than this. You can be a critical reader.

What Is a Critical Reader

Critical readers are people who judge the truth and value of what they are reading. Critical readers are not sponges.

Why Is Critical Reading Important

As a college student you are constantly making decisions about things, events, and people. You must also learn to evaluate what you read, and your textbooks are no exception. Like all mortals, the authors of magazine articles, textbooks, and other literature have opinions which are reflected in their writing. The college student who reads critically can judge the accuracy and merit of those opinions.

In order to become a critical reader you must

1. learn to distinguish fact from opinion,
2. search out the author's true purpose, and
3. learn to identify and resist propaganda techniques.

What Does Research Have to Say about Critical Reading?

> 1. College students accept most of what they read in textbooks.
> 2. Most authors try to influence our thinking in some way.
> 3. Humans interpret what they read based on prior knowledge and past experiences.
> 4. Changes in our attitudes are based on our willingness to be influenced.

Distinguishing Fact from Opinion

Read these two statements:

1. Toyota was the largest selling automobile in the United States in 1983.
2. America's favorite automobile is the Toyota.

Sentence (1) is a statement of *fact;* that is, it can be tested to see if it is true. In addition, a statement of fact is *neutral;* it doesn't takes sides. Sentence (2) is an *opinion* since it cannot be tested for truthfulness. It is a judgment, bias, or belief.

The truth of the first sentence can be tested by looking at the statistics for cars sold in the U.S. in 1983. This would determine if Toyota really did sell more than any other car-maker. Statement (2) is an opinion. How do you prove something is the favorite? How do you define favorite? Does favorite mean best-selling? Least expensive? Largest? Most fuel efficient? Favorite suggests an opinion or belief that cannot be measured, counted, or made objective. To see another example, read these statements:

1. Ralph made a serious error in judgment.
2. Ralph broke the law.

Statement (1) is an opinion. How would you define *error in judgment*? It might depend upon who is doing the judging. Statement (2), however, is different. If Ralph broke the law, he committed a specific crime, and it can be proven.

Here are some other statements. In each space provided place an F if the statement is a Fact or an O if it is an Opinion.

1. _____ It was the largest six-month setback in the organization's ten-year history. It amounted to an average loss of more than $400,000 per day between January 1 and June 30.

2. _____ National pride is essential. Waving the flag and bragging about greatness can be fun and reassuring. But if such attitudes are symptomatic of a return to simplistic, "we're-the-best" chauvinism, they are also dangerous—unworthy of a nation that desires to be great. (Huffman, J. L. "Bellicose Patriotism Ill Serves The United States." In *The Miami Herald,* 4 September 1984, p. 23A.)

3. _____ The special effects in the movie *E.T.* were much better and more exciting than the special effects in *Poltergist.*

4. _____ Bill Smith, who is entering his third NFL season, has been shifted from running back to wide receiver.

5. _____ Big newspapers are always getting together with big TV to find out how well the American public has learned its lessons on current events. Usually, the newspapers and the TV poll takers come away shocked. No matter how many times people are instructed on the big issues by editorial writers; no matter how many columnists weigh the pros and, of course, the cons, no matter if Dan Rather opens the evening news looking seriously sincere instead of anxiously twitty, it seems the American public just won't do its homework. (Miami Herald, 1983)

6. _____ The Times-CBS poll found that only 25 percent of the people surveyed knew that the Reagan Administration supports the existing government in El Salvador, only 13 percent knew that it sides with the insergents in Nicaragua, and only 8 percent got both answers right, even if they didn't like them. (Miami Herald, 1983)

Identifying the Author's Intent

A critical reader is aware of the author's intent or purpose in writing. Authors usually write with one or more of these five purposes in mind: to describe, to inform, to explain, to persuade, or to entertain. It is important for you, the reader, to be aware of the author's intent. This allows you to be in control of what you read. For example, when authors are trying to persuade you to think in a certain way, you should know that they have biases. Knowing this makes it possible for you to reject or accept their points of view logically.

In most textbooks the author's first intent is to inform or explain by presenting factual information. Keep in mind, however, that since textbook authors are human too, they may not be able to—or want to—keep their opinions out of what they write.

Some authors set out to describe the death of a president, a rodeo, or a beautiful Hawaiian sunset. Other authors entertain with adventure, wild humor, or erotic love stories. Whatever the intent, one of your tasks as a critical reader is to discover the purpose behind the pen.

The following passages provide examples of the five kinds of author intent:

1. *Description:* Presents a picture for your mind

   The room reeked of chaos. Chairs and tables were overturned. Lampshades were askew. Everywhere I looked I saw disorder.

2. *Information:* Presents only the facts

   Worldwide, many nations—such as Great Britain, the Netherlands, Denmark, Australia, and Israel—use as much or more sugar per capita than the United States. And consumption is rising in other lands, especially in developing nations. The U.N. reports an increased use of sugar unmatched by any other food for humans, predicting that by 1980 the world will consume some 186 billion lbs. a year. (Deutsch, R. M. "Sugar in the Diet of Man: A Summary." In *Human Ecological Issues: A Reader.* Edited by F. M. Clydesdale and F. J. Francis. Dubuque, Iowa: Kendall/Hunt Publishing Company, 1980, p. 113.)

3. *Explanation:* Tells why

   Public opinion polls in the United States indicate that the foremost concern in the minds of most Americans is inflation. This is a complex phenomenon and has many causes. Basically, inflation occurs when demands for goods and services exceed supplies. Since the beginning of history supplies of resources such as arable land, clean water, timber and minerals has far exceeded the number of people dependent on them. But in the past few decades that picture has changed. Today, throughout much of the world, there are more people than resources and in this transformation of our global economy may well lie the seeds of worldwide inflation on a scale and of a character never before known. (Green, M., & Fearey, R. A. "Today's children—Tomorrow's parents." In *Human Ecological Issues: A Reader.* Edited by F. M. Clydesdale and F. J. Francis. Dubuque, Iowa: Kendall/Hunt Publishing Company, 1980, p. 180.)

4. *Persuasion:* Tries to convince you

   Walking is a lot better than jogging. Walking strengthens the heart and facilitates the loss of excess fat without creating the arthritic joints that come from pounding the pavement. Walking is also less dangerous Every year hundreds of unsuspecting joggers are ruthlessly run down by jealous fat people in Volkswagens. So for heaven sakes walk, don't run!

5. *Entertainment:* Gives you pleasure, thrills, or satisfaction

It is cold at 6:40 in the morning of a March day in Paris, and seems even colder when a man is about to be executed by firing squad. At that hour on March 11, 1963, in the main courtyard of the Fort d'Ivry a French Air Force Colonel stood before a stake driven into the chilly gravel as his hands were bound behind the post, and stared with slowly diminishing disbelief at the squad of soldiers facing him twenty meters away.

A foot scuffed the grit, a tiny release from tension, as the blindfold was wrapped around the eyes of Lieutenant-Colonel Jean-Marie Bastien-Thiry, age thirty-five, blotting out the light for the last time. The mumbling of the priest was a helpless counterpoint to the crackling of twenty rifle bolts as the soldiers charged and cocked their carbines.

Beyond the walls a Berliet truck blared for a passage as some smaller vehicle crossed its path towards the centre of the city; the sound died away, masking the "Take your aim" order from the officer in charge of the squad. The crash of rifle fire when it came, caused no ripple on the surface of the waking city, other than to send a flutter of pigeons skywards for a few moments. The single "whack" seconds later of the coup-de-grace was lost in the rising din of traffic from beyond the walls. (Forsyth, F. *The Day of the Jackel.* New York: Viking Press, 1972, p. 3)

Keep in mind as you attempt to determine the author's intent that the author can have more than one purpose at the same time. For example, the passage above describes as well as entertains. Read the passages below and write the author's *main intent* in the space provided:

Description   Information   Explanation   Persuasion   Entertainment

1. _____ In a sudden burst of spectral splender the sun peaked over the ragged canyon wall, lighting little crags and sending the shadows scuttling away to wait out the heat of the desert day.

2. _____ Do not be easily drawn into the crowd. Continue to enter into relationships with individuals, not crowds. Often the crowd is the manipulated result of a small group's will to power. Think long and hard before joining any crowd. Be absolutely certain you understand its rhetoric. The crowd too easily becomes a mob; and an eruption of two crowds, as Elias Canetti put it, is an outbreak of war. It is true that, on occasion, the accomplishments of a crowd have been constructive. Still, there has to be a better way to get good things done. I leave that challenge to your generation. (Potak Chaim in *The Pennsylvania Gazette,* 1983, p. 41.)

3. _____ A difference between suppression and repression is that suppression is conscious, deliberate control of behavior, while repression is unconscious. You repress or push back or bury what is unacceptable either to you or to others. There are some ideas or desires that are taboo and that people do not allow themselves to think about. The memory of an experience may be so frightening or disgusting that you "forget" by submerging the memory in the subconscious. These repressed ideas and memories in an emotionally disturbed person are sometimes revealed during psychoanalysis. Repressed ideas may also be activated in dreams, in which the dreamer has no conscious control. (Baltus, P. *Personal Psychology for Life and Work.* New York: McGraw Hill, 1983, p. 145)

4. _____ Fred Rosewater was a good sailor and had attended Princeton University, so he was welcomed into the homes of the rich, though, for Pisquontuit, he was gruesomely poor. His home was a sordid little brown-shingle carpenter's special, a mile from the glittering waterfront.

Poor Fred worked like hell for the few dollars he brought home once in a while. He was working now, beaming at the carpenter and the two plumbers in the news store. The three workmen were reading a scandalous tabloid, a national weekly dealing with murder, sex, pets, and children—mutilated children, more often than not. It was called *The American Investigator,* "The World's Most Sparkling Newspaper." *The Investigator* was to the news store what the *Wall Street Journal* was to the drugstore.

"Improving your minds as usual, I see," Fred observed. He said it with the lightness of fruitcake. (Vonnegut, K. *God Bless You Mr. Rosewater.* New York: Delacourte Press, 1965, p. 100.)

5. _____ A steam bath is often a substitute for exercise as a means of weight reduction. Any weight loss however, is from dehydration and is quickly recovered as soon as water is ingested. A serious health hazard is created if thirst is ignored and water is not replenished. Steam baths are certainly relaxing but useless as a method of weight control. (Melograno, V. J., and Klinzing, J. E. *An Orientation to Total Fitness.* Dubuque, Iowa: Kendall/Hunt Publishing Company, 1974, p. 160.)

Propaganda Techniques

All of us are constantly pressured by various interest groups to vote for their candidates, support their causes, or buy their products. Many techniques are used to persuade us to act in certain ways. Often these techniques appeal to people's emotional needs and are not based on facts or evidence of real worth. Arguments or techniques that distort facts or appeal to our emotions are called *propaganda techniques.*

What follows is a description of specific propaganda techniques that are commonly used. As you read about each technique, try to think of your own examples.

Name Calling Name calling is a propaganda technique which uses emotionally charged "bad names" to arouse feelings of fear, distrust, and hate. Examples of bad names are *imperialist, warmonger, commie,* and *redneck.* Sometimes the person doing the name calling implies the bad name rather than stating it directly. For example, saying that a politician takes his orders from Moscow would be implying that the politician is a communist or a communist sympathizer.

Glittering Generality The glittering generality technique uses vague, "nice-sounding" words to praise a person, idea, or product. The main thing to remember is that the complimentary words cannot be proven; they are opinions, not facts. Words such as *better, improved, loyal, honest,* and *outstanding* are common examples of words which are used to make someone or something "glitter."

Card Stacking This technique uses facts to support a person, product, or cause, but carefully omits certain other facts. Because there is a factual presentation, it is often difficult to detect this form of propaganda. When politicians running for reelection list all of their successes and none of their failures, it's an example of card stacking. To detect card stacking you must always ask yourself, "Are all sides of the issue being fairly presented?"

The Testimonial This common technique uses famous people to promote a person, cause, or product. The most important thing to remember about the testimonial is that the people who are doing the selling are not experts about the product in question; for example, a football player selling pantyhose or a famous actor pushing health insurance. In addition, these people are usually paid for their endorsement, so we must question whether the endorsement is for real or for bucks.

Transfer In this technique characteristics are transferred from one object or person to another. For example, a beautiful woman demonstrating bath oil on TV is trying to make viewers believe that if they buy and use the bath oil they too will become beautiful. They are supposed to think that the characteristic "beauty" will transfer to them. The real goal, of course, is to convince the viewers to spend their money on the product.

Flattery This technique appeals to our desire to be famous, important, or special in some way. The propagandist may imply that we have good taste, superior brains, or terrific judgment. For instance, an advertisement for wine may boast that it does not appeal to everyone, but only to people with "class."

Plain Folks This propaganda technique attempts to gain our confidence by making us think that the person seeking our support is just like us. This technique is often used by politicians during election campaigns. They will purposely be seen kissing babies, fishing, mowing the grass, or going to church, etc. People tend to be comfortable with their own kind and suspicious of those who are different. Politicians know this and go to great lengths to show us that they are just home grown, down-to-earth, simple, plain folks. (If you believe that, we know of a nice bridge for sale. . . .)

The Bandwagon This kind of propaganda coaxes us to do what everyone else is doing. The bandwagon approach capitalizes on our herd instinct. If "everyone" is supporting Snidely Whiplash for governor, then he must be the best! If "everyone else" is charging off to buy a bottle of Warthog aftershave, how can we go wrong if we buy some too? We tend to feel that if we are following the crowd we must be doing the right thing. It seems that we never outgrow the desire to be one of the gang, and that makes us ripe for pickin' when the propagandist uses the good old bandwagon approach.

Read the following examples of propaganda techniques. In the space provided write the letter of the propaganda technique being used. The first one has been done for you.

A. Name Calling   E. Transfer
B. Glittering Generality   F. Flattery
C. Card Stacking   G. Plain Folks
D. Testimonial   H. Bandwagon

1. __H__ Nine out of ten people read *The National News.*

2. _____ Diamonds by Julius Cordono may cost more, but you're *worth it.*

3. _____ According to Runway Rhoda, star of stage and screen, "a day without Mountain Clover Mouthwash, is like a day without friends."

4. _____ Laboratory tests show that Agent Orange Bug Spray is safe to use in the home because it is nonflammable.

5. _____ "Billy John, a hard workin' family man, is what we need in the Congress of these here United States."

6. _____ My opponent, Malcolm Meeks, is a wimp.

7. _____ Beautiful women shop at The Gallery.

8. _____ For the most exciting meal of your life, dine at the romantic Log Cabin Retreat.

Now that you have some experience in identifying propaganda techniques, test your knowledge on the advertisement on the next page. Write your answers in the space provided.

1. What does smelling a plastic flower have to do with banking?

2. Why is a robot used in this ad?

3. Which emotional needs does this ad appeal to?

4. Which propaganda technique is being used?

5. What is the purpose of the ad?

_____

_____

Bias

At this point you may be thinking that critical reading is mostly a matter of recognizing how writers deliberately lie or try to influence us in other ways. However, even when their intentions are to present information objectively, all authors have biases, that is, beliefs that are not based entirely on facts.

Read the editorials on the next two pages. Both writers have recorded their observations of the same event, the 1977 National Women's Conference. As you read, think about *fact versus opinion, author's intent,* and *propaganda techniques.* Be prepared to answer a few questions when you have finished.

The Ladies, God Bless 'em, Survived Their Clambake

By JAMES J. KILPATRICK
Washington Star Syndicate

THE National Women's Conference wound up at 1:30 Monday afternoon in something close to pure bedlam, with the pro-family contingent walking out to the strains of God Bless America and the rest of the ladies, God bless them, still chanting it up for the E.R.A.

Kilpatrick

The three-day clambake produced little in the way of surprises and almost nothing in the way of hard news, but it was an interesting affair nonetheless. It may even have had its useful aspects. Whether the results justified the expenditure of $5 million in public funds depends upon one's point of view. I would rather have the $5 million back, but I have seen far more federal money wasted in much worse ways.

The one small surprise came toward the very end, when the delegates voted down a recommended resolution for the creation of a Cabinet-level Women's Department. This was the last of 26 pro-

posals, and the general idea was that without a Women's Department the other 25 might be ignored. As it turned out, the delegates felt that if a Women's Department were created, a Men's Department might be required in the name of Holy Equality, and the thought was unbearable. The ladies shouted the proposition down; the pro-lifers took to their heels; and in a final gurgle of oratory the conference adjourned *sine die.*

Otherwise, no surprises. The apprehensive sponsors, fearful that hair might literally be pulled, had fortified the conference rules with some bristling provisions against punching, gouging and performing on the bullhorn, but none of these rules had to be invoked. With only a handful of exceptions, the combatants behaved with remarkable civility. If the opposing forces lusted in their hearts for mutual mayhem, they kept such felonious impulses to themselves.

THE 25 approved resolutions had been well publicized over the past two years. Most of them earlier had been approved in most of the state women's conventions. The Houston ratifications thus amounted to little more than *pro forma* rubber stamps, and indeed this was the stifled cry that arose now and then from the dissident seats: "Rubberstamp! Rubberstamp!"

Proponents dominated the affair by a margin of four or five to one, though the

standing vote on the pro-abortion resolution appeared to be a good deal closer. The abortion issue was the most emotional issue, generating even more heat than a resolution on sexual preference. This latter resolution is intended to protect lesbian women against discrimination. For the record, there were plenty of lesbian women in evidence—they conducted a "dyke vigil" Sunday evening—but I saw none of the offensive conduct reported at a few of the state meetings last summer.

THE official International Women's Year sessions at the Coliseum understandably dominated the news, but the unofficial pro-family rally at the Houston Astro-Arena deserved more coverage than it got. Phyllis Schlafly's troops turned out 15,000 strong in a rally that one speaker said was "just like revival in a black Baptist church." The affair united Catholics who oppose abortion and fundamentalists who oppose any tampering with what they perceive as women's God-given role in the scheme of things.

The pro-family folks impressed me as just as sincere in their convictions as the IWY supporters are sincere in theirs. We saw extremism on both sides. Bella Abzug equated the dissidents with the Ku Klux Klan and the John Birch Society, and the dissidents equated their foes with lesbianism and free love.

AFTER listening to these ladies for the better part of three days, I left Houston with the heretical thought—a thought that ought to be suppressed—that it was a mistake ever to teach little girls to read. They grow up to be women who read *Robert's Rules of Order*. They learn to holler "Point of personal privilege!" and "Point of parliamentary inquiry!" and they can tie a meeting into knots.

The most outstanding women at Houston were Dr. Mildren Jefferson, a Boston surgeon who heads the National Right to Life Committee, and Ms. Anne Saunier of Ohio, who chaired most of Sunday's sessions at the Coliseum. Dr. Jefferson is a five-foot package of dynamite. Ms. Saunier, a long-legged militant, man-hating tiger, is the best presiding officer I ever watched in action. If she wanted to make her services available to the presidential conventions of 1980, we could wrap up the business in 24 hours and go home.

HOUSTON CONFERENCE IN PERSPECTIVE

Women Emerging as New Political Force

By ELLEN GOODMAN
of The Boston Globe

ABOUT six years ago I wrote that women would be the most important new force in politics. About three years ago I started really believing it.

Now, after four days in Houston spent listening to people at the National Women's Conference and at the counter-rallies, it's obvious that the women's movement has literally "moved women," thousands of them, into the political arena. They are the ones who now have the pivotal role in the shifting conservative and moderate alliances in the country at large.

Goodman

Women's rights groups have grown in numbers and in savvy. Once, feminist conferences would be paralyzed on the finer philosophical points, or disrupted on personality politics. Houstin, however, marked the shift from philosophy to public policy concerns by women who—despite strong feelings—learned to make compromises and coalitions.

HALF a dozen years ago, women's rights advocates didn't have the experience or the troops to put on this kind of massive national event. Last week they ran the show with a virtually all-woman team, from planners to security aides, with only the normal run of mishaps, disruptions and "points of order." In fact, the main problem of the conference was that, until the end, the leadership ran too light a show. Many delegates, not just the "antis," left unhappy at the lack of open debate.

The conference also showed the broadening coalition of women's groups who stuck together on the ERA—probably the only issue in the country that could bring three President's wives onto the same podium at the same time.

The organization of the conference was remarkable since most of the delegates (despite having had some previous involvement in women's issues) had not been to a national political convention before.

BUT I also saw in Houston the number of women who are being activated into political life as part of what is called the new conservative coalition.

The minority delegates at the conference, and the women at the so-called "Pro-Family" counter-rally, were also recruited on "women's issues." They entered politics against the ERA or abortion or homosexuality. Now they have become a chorus chanting the favorite themes of conservatism. The code phrase heard again and again on the floor was, "The federal grab for power."

The anti-ERA delegates I talked with usually insisted that they were in favor of equality, but against the ERA and, especially, the "Washington Bureaucracy" as its enforcement agency.

Phyllis Schlafly, a woman who made her name off the women's movement, has changed her line a bit, as she plans to run for the Senate in Illinois against Chuck Percy. She, too, talks less about housewives and more about the federal government: "Why would anyone want to give the Washington bureaucracy more power than they already have?"

The IWY conference itself proved to be a political training ground for both the pro- and anti-change groups. These women are in politics to stay. Even those who speak against change have changed enough to speak out. And to seek political power.

THE women's movement encourages all women to have a voice in the system. They have that voice, but they're using it to say different things.

I wonder what will happen as conservative women want to move into leadership roles in more than token numbers on more than "women's issues." Will they encounter political discrimination and become feminists in their time?

Conversely, will the moderate and liberal men who still control their party hierarchies realize that their political future is invested in the women's rights coalition? Those women shouldn't be treated as supplicants, but as saviors. They're the only significant source of energy for change around.

Now, as I pack my "Houston Survivor" T-shirt, and head home, I'm sure of one thing: There'll be more sexual politics in party politics from now on.

1. List three emotionally charged words that are used in one of the editorials. Circle these words in the text.

   _____ _____ _____

2. List two propaganda techniques used in the Kilpatrick editorial. Underline and label them in the text.

   _____

   _____

3. In your opinion, what are the authors' intents:

   Kilpatrick: _____

   Goodman: _____

4. Which editorial would you trust as being more factual?

   Kikpatrick __

   Goodman __

Even textbook authors are not immune from having bias. Although they primarily present information, they are still biased by their background knowledge and personal experiences. The following excerpt is from a critical review of a state history textbook called *Your Mississippi*. It certainly illustrates the bias that can be present even in textbooks.

> The Stars and Bars of the Confederacy are emblazoned upon the jacket of this book both front and back; this brazen assertion of white supremacy is not contradicted by the contents. The black presence in Mississippi is almost totally absent from the text and illustrations. The slave appears only briefly, and then as a faceless statistic, not as a human being. The Black Code approved by the legislature November 21–29, 1865 is characterized by the author, with almost one hundred percent inaccuracy, as "a group of vagrancy laws. . . ." Members of the Ku Klux Klan, we are told, rode around in hoods and bedsheets to serenade their girls. Not one of the bloody crimes committed by this group against black people in Mississippi is mentioned. The life of black people in the century after Reconstruction receives hardly more than a mention. There is no hint of the tragic reality of a whole people living in rickety shacks, toiling on the white man's fields, surviving on cornbread and beans, with young folks working as hard as the adults and growing up in ignorance and illiteracy. (Scott, J. A. "History Textbook Adoption Challenged in Mississippi." *Inequality in Education,* 1977, p. 130.)

As the review excerpt suggests, textbooks do not always represent the truth, nor do they always state all points of view objectively.

The quote which follows is from the National Education Association's Educational Policies Commission of 1966 and was included in a college textbook called *Social Foundations of Education*. Using the PQMR strategy, again summarized below, read the quote and then answer the questions at the end. (Westby-Gibson, D. ed. New York: The Free Press, 1967.

PQMR Summary

    A. To preview: (Underline previewed material for this exercise.)
        1. Read the title and the first paragraph.
        2. Read the closing paragraph (or chapter summary).
        3. Skim the assignment by reading all headings and the first sentence after each heading.
        4. As you skim, focus your attention on italicized words, pictures, graphs, and charts.
    B. To Question:
    Write down at least five questions you have about the subject matter.

C. To Mark:

_____	Underline or highlight main ideas and important details.
[ ]	Use brackets to mark important paragraphs.
⟨Jargon⟩	Circle new technical terms.
(1) (2) (3)	Number important steps, causes, or reasons.
* ! ?	Use the asterisk or exclamation point to indicate EXTREME IMPORTANCE. Use the question mark to show confusion or disagreement.
Super! True!	Use personal comments and summarize each major subheading.

D. Read

The Need for Early Childhood Education
NEA Educational Policies Commision

Research shows clearly that the first four or five years of a child's life are the period of most rapid growth in physical and mental characteristics and of greatest susceptibility to environmental influences. Consequently, it is in the early years that deprivations are most disastrous in their effects. They can be compensated for only with great difficulty in later years, and then probably not in full. Furthermore, it appears that it is harder to modify harmful learnings than to acquire new ones. Finally, experience indicates that exposure to a wide variety of activities and of social and mental interactions with children and adults greatly enhance a child's ability to learn. Few homes provide enough of these opportunities. It is reasonable to conclude that the postponement of an educational contribution by society until children reach the age of six generally limits the flowering of their potentials.

Family life and family love are among the most cherished of American values. In addition, they are important to the healthy development of the individual physically and spiritually, and they are basic to his happiness. They are regarded as a birthright of every child and parent. Moreover, except in extreme cases of neglect and mistreatment at home, it is hard to conceive of an institutional alternative to the home and family that could do as well.

Therefore, although early schooling is needed, family life must be strengthened, not replaced. The need is for a complement, not an alternative, to family life. But the need is compelling.

Those children commonly called "disadvantaged" are in the greatest need of early schooling, for they are most in need of help in developing their ability to live independently and creatively in a modern society. They are disadvantaged precisely because the cultures into which they are born prepare them poorly for modern life. Many are further disadvantaged because, victimized by racial prejudice, they develop a disparaging image of themselves by the age of five or six. It is imperative that American society provide these children, in their most formative years, with helpful cultural characteristics and the healthy image of their human worth that their personal progress requires. At the present time, schooling for four-year-olds is rarely free of cost to the parents and therefore is least available to many children in most desperate need of it.

But not only those commonly considered disadvantaged are disadvantaged in their lives at home. The pampered also are disadvantaged; so are those whose parents are obsessed with the need to impress and achieve; so are those, whatever their economic background, whose parents show them little love; so are those who have little chance to play with other children or with children of other backgrounds; so are those with physical handicaps. Early education could help all these children.

Early education is advisable for all children, not merely because of the need to offset any disadvantages in their background, but also because they are ready by the age of four for a planned fostering of their

Educational Policies Commission, National Education Association, University Opportunity for Early Childhood Education. Washington, D.C.: NEA, 1966, pp. 3–5. Reprinted by permission of the publisher.

development and because educators know some of the ways to foster it through school programs. Early education has long been available to the well-to-do, and it is commendable that governments are now acting on the need to make it available to some of the poor. But the large middle group should have the same opportunities.

The opportunity for early education at public expense should therefore be universal. The nation would benefit in the greater development of its people's talents and in the reduction of the need for expensive remedial work and of the incidence of dropout with its attendant economic and social ills. The nation would benefit, too, from the knowledge that public educational funds are being spent with greater efficiency, from a new national unity based on increased respect for nonwhite groups as they develop their talents more completely, and from the awareness that greater recognition is being given to the ideal of human dignity. Individuals would benefit in all these ways, as well as in the enjoyment of a richer childhood and a lifetime lived at a higher level of achievement than is typical today.

Beginning at what age should the opportunity for education be offered at public expense?

For several reasons, the Educational Policies Commission recommends that it begin at the age of four. These two additional years are years about which there is considerable knowledge regarding the contribution that organized education can make. These are years in which many parents deem it desirable for children to have a few hours away from home during the day. A two-year extension is also more feasible financially than a longer extension; indeed, public kindergartens are already common, and for many places the extension would amount to only one year.

1. What is the authors' purpose? _____

_____

2. In what ways are the authors biased? _____

_____

3. What emotions are being aroused? _____

_____

4. What propaganda techniques are used? _____

_____

5. Do you question the accuracy of any of the information? _____

_____

6. How has this selection influenced your thinking? _____

_____

In Summary

There is no substitute for critical thinking and critical reading in college. Sorting fact from opinion, detecting author bias, and recognizing propaganda are skills which will serve you well in college, and in your future professional life. However, as a critical reader you also have certain rights and responsibilities.

Hear Ye! Hear Ye!
The Bill of Rights and Responsibilities for Critical Readers

Responsibilities

1. You have the responsibility of getting all of the facts, and getting them straight.
2. You are responsible for separating verifiable facts from opinion when you read.
3. You are responsible for resisting fallacious lines of reasoning and propaganda.
4. You are responsible for deciding what is relevant and irrelevant when you read.
5. You have a responsibility to entertain the author's point of view objectively. Negativism and criticism are not the same thing.
6. For better or for worse, you are responsible for the conclusions you draw when reading, even if the author provides you with false or misleading information.

Rights

1. You have a right to all of the facts, though you may have to root them out for yourself.
2. You have a right to be exposed to contrasting points of view.
3. You have a right to ask questions, even if it annoys the professor.
4. You have a right to your own opinion, even if it contradicts recognized authority.

Mangieri, J. N., and Baldwin, R. S. *Effective Reading Techniques: Business and Personal Applications.* San Francisco: Canfield Press, 1978, p. 60.

8
How to Take Tests

What Do You Believe about Taking Tests?

Directions: Read each of the statements below. Place a checkmark on the line in front of each statement you believe is true.

1. _____ If you don't know the answer to a test item, all you can do is guess blindly.

2. _____ Memory ability is inherited and can't be improved.

3. _____ Some tests are not good measures of your knowledge.

4. _____ Essay tests are easier than true–false tests.

5. _____ Test grades are entirely determined by how much you know about the subject matter of the test.

We hope these statements have made you curious about tests. Perhaps some questions of your own come to mind, for example, "How can I improve my test scores?" Look for the answers to your questions as you work your way through this chapter.

Tests Are One of the Facts of Life in College

Nobody likes tests. Students hate taking them and professors hate making them up and grading them. Unfortunately, as a college student you are doomed to take tests since there must be some way of determining if, and to what extent, students have mastered the material presented in the course.

Although you must resign yourself to taking tests, you needn't resign yourself to performing poorly on them. In fact, the research on test preparation and test taking makes it clear that you can improve your test performances by using intelligent test taking strategies and study techniques such as those discussed in Chapter 4. Here is what research has to say about testing:

> 1. Test taking strategies improve test scores.
> 2. Test scores are higher for students who do not cram.
> 3. Answering practice questions in study sessions improves test scores.
> 4. Bits of information are best remembered when they are grouped into meaningful categories.

To illustrate the effectiveness of test taking strategies, we have constructed a test below. At the end of the chapter you will have an opportunity to take the test again as a way of testing your knowledge of test taking strategies.

Testwiseness Pretest

Directions: Circle the letter of the best answer.

A. Multiple Choice
1. An action designed to stop a behavior is a
    a. negative reinforcement.
    b. punishment.
    c. associations.
    d. hanging.

2. According to Jerome Kagan
    a. the first year of life is totally critical.
    b. children can recover from early environmental impoverishment given normal stimulation and care.
    c. punishment should not be used on children.
    d. sex differences are culturally determined.

3. Which of these statements is untrue?
    a. IQ tests and achievement tests really test the same thing.
    b. The best IQ tests are really achievement tests.
    c. IQ really stands for *Intelligence Quotient*.
    d. Individualized IQ tests assess genetic potential.

4. The results of the Milwaukee Project support
    a. an environmentalist position with regard to intelligence.
    b. behaviorism.
    c. Jenson.
    d. Piaget's.

5. *Intelligence Quotient* is a function of
    a. the relationship between mental age and chronological age.
    b. MA.
    c. CA.
    d. luck.

B. True or False
6. T F Intelligence always declines rapidly in later life.

7. T F Social learning theory, as proposed by Albert Bandura, emphasizes the impact of the environment on the individual.

8. T F Since most college students drink to excess, college students on probation frequently suffer from anxiety.

9. T F The Harlows found that monkeys with normal peer relations develop into socially and sexually normal adults even if they have been deprived of a mother.

10. T F Women are shorter than most men.

How to Improve Your Memory for Tests

Few college professors give open book tests. Tests usually take the objective or essay form and require you to be able to recognize or remember the information from texts and lectures. Therefore, a good memory is essential to test success. Fortunately, it is possible to improve your memory if you are willing.

What Do We Remember?

We remember what we understand.
We remember what we think is important.
We remember what has personal meaning for us.
We remember what we have just learned.
We remember what we overlearn.

Why Do We Forget?

1. We forget because information is not clearly understood.
   Solution: Use the PQMR study strategy.
2. We forget things that do not have personal meaning for us.
   Solution: Try to relate new information to things you already know and care about. Try to think of some way that you might eventually use the information. There is probably no such thing as impractical knowledge.
3. We forget because we did not learn the information well enough in the first place.
   Solution: Overlearn information. Overlearning is what occurs when you keep studying something even after you have learned it. Most people overlearn their multiplication tables as children and remember them for a lifetime.
4. We forget previously learned information when new information interferes with it. This is called *retroactive inhibition.*
   Solution: Follow each study session with an entirely different activity, such as a bike ride. Avoid cramming, and NEVER pull an all-night study session before an exam. A modest review the evening before and a good night's sleep will bring better results.
5. We forget when we fail to organize information.
   Solution: Use mnemonics.

Mnemonics

Mnemonics are techniques used to aid remembering. They are especially useful for memorizing information. The following mnemonic techniques should be useful additions to your study strategies.

Grouping. When items are grouped together, memory is improved. Read the following numbers. Then look away and try to repeat them.

49738526

Now read these groups of numbers. Then look away again and try to repeat them.

831   254   96

If you are like most people, you found the grouped numbers easier to remember.

Grouping is especially helpful when the groups are meaningful. Read the three lists of words below. Then look away and see how many words you can remember from each list.

A	B	C
zebra	pear	five
apple	canary	frog
seven	three	banana

How many words did you remember altogether? _____

Now do the same experiment with these three lists:

A	B	C
elephant	orange	two
parrot	lemon	four
toad	plum	six

How many words did you remember this time? _____

As you can see, grouping words into logical categories makes them easier to remember.

Making Associations. An *association* is a relationship. Sometimes you associate or relate two things because one causes the other. Other times we associate things simply because they exist together. For example, we associate the color red with apples, fire engines, and enraged bulls. Any association you can make that links new information with things you already know will help you remember the new information.

Suppose you need to learn the definition for the word *potable* (pronounced so that "pot" rhymes with "coat"), which means "suitable for drinking." You could form a mental picture of a big pot filled with cool, fresh spring water sitting on a table in the shade of a big oak tree. Imagine that you are very thirsty. Now picture lifting the pot off the table and pouring the potable water down your parched throat. You have just improved your ability to remember the word *potable* and its meaning by forming a mental association.

Use the association technique to learn the meanings of the words below. First, look up the definition. Then, describe the association you will use to help you remember the word and its definition.

Idiosyncrasy:

Definition _____

Association _____

_____

Porcine:

Definition _____

Association _____

_____

Vivisection:

Definition _____

Association _____

_____

Acronyms. To form an acronym you take the first letter of each word in a concept and use these letters to form a word or a sentence. Music students are often taught to remember the notes of the treble clef, E G B D F, with the acronym *Every Good Boy Does Fine*. Many math students learn the order of mathematical operations (parentheses, powers, multiplication, division, addition, subtraction) by using the acronym *Please Pardon My Dear Aunt Sally*.

Now try your hand at acronyms. The Swiss psychologist, Jean Piaget, has divided human intellectual development into four stages:

1. Sensorimotor
2. Preoperational
3. Concrete Operational
4. Formal Operational

Make up an acronym that could help you remember these stages in the proper order. _____

How to Get Tough on Tests

"Getting tough" on tests is mostly a matter of good study strategies and good personal organization. The rest of this chapter will help you to develop the strategies you need to be an aggressive test taker.

Pre-Test Organization

The month before the test you should be reviewing text material, class notes, and other assigned materials frequently. Remember, lots of short study sessions are better than a few giant cramming sessions.

Find out as much as you can about the test itself.

1. Find out exactly when the test will be given.
2. Ask your professors to discuss the kinds of questions that will be on the test: multiple choice, true–false, essay, completion, matching, or short answer.
3. If your professors give essay tests, ask them what they look for in a good essay answer.
4. Ask your professors to give you examples of test items and good test answers. Many professors will be willing to do this, but almost none will do it if you don't ask!
5. Talk with students who have taken the course before. They may even have copies of old tests.
6. Try to guess which questions your instructor will ask.

On the night before the test

1. A light study session should be enough. Do not cram!
2. Make sure you have pencils, pens, bluebooks, a watch, a calculator (if permissible), and any other materials you may need for the exam.
3. Get a good night's sleep.

On the day of the test you should

1. eat a good breakfast,
2. tell yourself that you will do well on the exam,
3. make sure you have all the materials you need for the exam, and
4. allow plenty of time to get to the exam on time.
5. Do not cram right before the test. That is the worst thing you can do. Cramming can result in retroactive inhibition, which causes students to forget important information. Cramming also causes needless test anxiety.
6. In the hours right before the test review the material lightly. Then go for a walk or a swim.

Testwiseness

Once you are seated in the examination room, there is no more time for preparation. You are as prepared as you are going to be. However, there is something you can do during the exam that will positively affect your grade. You can exercise your testwiseness skills. *Testwiseness* is the ability to take tests effectively using good principles of organization, critical reading skills, and knowledge of the flaws that commonly appear on professors' tests.

Multiple Choice Tests. As a college student you will probably take more multiple choice tests than any other kind. The most typical multiple choice item consists of a *stem* and several *options*. For example:

The Civil War ended in   (Stem)
1. 1880
2. 1492   (Options)
3. 1865
4. 1855

Use the following strategies to be testwise on multiple choice tests.

1. Read all directions carefully. It is not unusual for students to get poor grades on exams simply because they fail to read and follow directions.
2. Budget your time so that you are certain to finish the test. Students sometimes spend too much time on one part of the test and then fail to finish another. Nothing seems to hurt a test grade as much as leaving items blank.
3. Do not waste time on very difficult items. Come back to them after you've worked through to the end of the exam.
4. Assume that each item has a correct answer and that you know enough to figure it out one way or another.
5. Always guess if you don't know the answer. Never leave a multiple choice question blank.
6. If the correct answer is not obvious to you right away, try to eliminate obviously wrong or silly options and then guess from among those that remain. For example:

    The speed of light is
    A. 3700 miles per hour
    B. 186,000 miles per second
    C. 0
    D. 186 miles per second

    You should be able to eliminate option C right away. That gives you a one-in-three chance of guessing correctly instead of a one-in-four chance.
7. Whenever two of the options are identical, then both answers must be wrong. For example:

    A kilogram is equal to
    A. 2.5 pounds
    B. 1000 grams
    C. 22 pounds
    D. 2 pounds 8 ounces
8. Whenever two of the options are opposites, one of them is always wrong and the other is often, but not always, right. For example:

    A proton is a
    A. positively charged particle
    B. free atom
    C. negatively charged particle
    D. displaced neutron
9. Be aware that the answer to a question may appear in the stem of another question. For example, the answer to item *1* can be found in the stem of item *26*.

    1. A z-score is a
    A. percentile equivalent
    B. concept in criterion referenced testing
    C. measure of standard error
    D. standardized score

       26. Standardized scores, such as z-scores and t-scores, are based on
          A. standard deviations
          B. stanines
          C. chi squares
          D. grade equivalents

10. Be alert for alternatives which do not match the stem grammatically. Professors sometimes make this mistake. For example:

     The smallest unit of sound capable of making a meaning distinction in language is a
     A. morpheme
     B. allophone
     C. phoneme
     D. tagmeme

11. When alternatives seem equally good, select the one which is longest and seems to hold the most information. For example:

     In the United States inferior intellectual development is most often caused by
     A. Poor nutrition
     B. Divorce
     C. The combined effects of heritability and environmental deprivation
     D. Television

12. When all else fails, select an option which is neither the first choice nor the last. For example,

     The probability of rolling a 12 with two dice is
     A. 3 in 12
     B. 1 in 12
     C. 1 in 36
     D. 2 in 19

True–False Tests. True–false questions are actually statements which students must decide are true or untrue. Major examinations are seldom composed entirely of true–false questions. However, many professors like to include some of these on their tests. True–false tests are feared by many students because they believe that professors are trying to trick them into a lower grade. In reality, most professors are just interested in finding out how much their students know. Here are some testwise principles for true–false tests.

1. Read all directions carefully.
2. Budget your time so that you are certain to finish the test.
3. Guess if you don't know the answer. Never leave a true–false question blank.
4. If any part of the statement is false, the correct answer for the item is "false." For example, the item below is false because the second part of the statement is false.
   The United States entered World War II after the Japanese attacked San Francisco.
5. Be alert for such words as *never* and *always*. These absolutes often signal a wrong answer. For example, item *A* is false because it does occasionally rain in the desert. On the other hand, item *B* is true because *never* is qualified.
   A. It never rains in the Sahara Desert.
   B. It almost never rains in the Sahara Desert.
6. Long statements are somewhat more likely to be true than short statements. For example, *A* is true and *B* is false.
   A. In the poem "Ozymandias," Shelley uses irony to make a statement about the mortality of man.
   B. Ozymandias was a monk.
7. Assume that the professor is asking straightforward questions. In other words, do not turn an obviously true statement into a false one by creating wild possible exceptions in your mind. For example, item *A* is true in spite of the fact that *B, C,* and *D* contradict the statement, if you have a strong imagination.
   A. Shoes are an important part of the business person's physical appearance.
   B. Business people don't wear horseshoes.
   C. Brake shoes are not part of the business person's appearance.
   D. If your pants are so long that they cover your shoes, the shoes won't make any difference.

129

Matching Tests. A matching test is usually composed of two lists, a question list and an answer list. The answer list contains words or statements which have to be matched to a word or statement on the question list. In other words, each item on the answer list must have some special association or relationship with an item on the question list. Frequently the answer list contains extra choices which will not be used. Here are some testwise principles for matching tests.

1. Read all directions carefully. For instance, find out if answers can be used more than once.
2. Budget your time so that you are certain to finish the test.
3. Always guess if you don't know the answer. Never leave a matching item blank.
4. Do the items you are sure of first.
5. Cross out answers which obviously don't belong on the list.
6. If answers can be used only once, cross off answers you are sure of after you have used them.

Now apply your testwiseness skills on the following matching exercise.

Directions: Match the correct answer with the appropriate statement. An answer can be used only one time. Put the letter of the correct answer in the space provided. The correct answers can be found on page 134.

Questions	*Answers*
1. _____ Lee surrendered to him at Appomattox.	A. Picket
2. _____ President of U.S. during the Civil War.	B. Grant
3. _____ President of the Confederacy.	C. Sherman
4. _____ He made a famous charge at Gettysburg.	D. Napolean
5. _____ The Union's Secretary of State.	E. Davis
6. _____ He burned Atlanta on his march to the sea.	F. Kennedy
7. _____ Commanded the Army of Virginia.	G. Stuart
8. _____ A famous confederate cavalry officer.	H. Booth
9. _____ Secretary of War for the Union.	I. Patton
10. _____ He assassinated the president.	J. Lincoln
	K. Stanton
	L. Seward
	M. Lee

Short Answer Tests. A short-answer test requires you to recall specific information. This kind of test is often more difficult than multiple choice, true–false, and matching tests which only require that you recognize the correct answer when you see it. There are two main types of short-answer items, completion and definition. A *completion* item (example A) contains a blank which has to be filled with the appropriate word. A *definition item* ((example B) requires you to write out an entire definition.

A. Hawaii is located in the _____ Ocean.
B. Define *iconoclast:*

Here are some testwise principles for short-answer tests.

1. Read all directions carefully.
2. Budget your time so that you are certain to finish the test.
3. Always guess if you don't know the answer.

*(If your score is less than 60%, you might want to consider picking up an American history elective.)

4. Do the items you are sure of first.

5. On completion tests make sure that the answer fits in grammatically. For instance, in example A the word *psychological* will fit, but *psychology* and *psychologist* will not.

The formal study of personality began with the _____ observations of Sigmund Freud.

6. On definition tests be certain to define the concept properly. Say what it is. Perhaps give an example. But don't talk *around* the definition. The best way to start a definition answer is to say: "An isotope is . . .," or "The regression effect is . . .," and then go right on and define the term as specifically as possible. In the example below check each definition which you believe is adequate (Answers are on page 134).

1. Define *positive reinforcer*

_____ It makes you feel good.

_____ When you do things you like to do more often than you do things you don't like to do.

_____ A stimulus that causes an increase in behavior.

_____ A positive reinforcer is something that makes a person or animal behave in a certain way more often.

_____ A positive reinforcer is a stimulus that makes you happy.

Essay Tests. Essay tests are among the most difficult of exams because they require recall of information, good writing skills, and good organization. Here are some testwise principles for essay tests.

1. Read all directions carefully. Essay tests often use in their directions key words that you must clearly understand. Here are some of the key words and their meanings:

Key Word	*Meaning*
enumerate	to name one at a time
illustrate	to explain with examples
trace	to tell the history or development of something from the earliest to the most recent time
compare	to point out similarities and differences
contrast	to point out differences
outline	give a general description, plan, or summary
summarize	to give a brief version of the most important points
evaluate	to judge the merit of
justify	to give reasons for
critique	to summarize and evaluate

Two essay answers (A and B) are given below for the same essay question. One answer followed directions and is better organized than the other. It would probably receive a better grade. Read both answers and place a check mark next to the best one. (Answer is on page 134)

Directions: Compare saccadic and pursuit eye movements.

_____ *Answer A:* There are two basic kinds of eye movements: saccadic and pursuit. Saccadic movements are used when you go from object to object when the objects are at rest. Pursuit movements follow a moving target. During the act of reading, saccadic movements allow the reader to stop on a line of print and pick up information. The word saccade means little jerk.

_____ *Answer B:* There are two basic kinds of eye movements: saccadic and pursuit. They are the same in the sense that both of them are used to locate visual information. However, they are physically different. Saccadic movements are jumps while the pursuit movement is smoothe. Another difference is that saccadic movements let the eyes go from one still object to another while pursuit movement follows a moving target.

Write a brief essay comparing Nevada with Vermont.

_____

_____

_____

_____

_____

_____

2. Budget your time so that you are certain to finish the test. Check to see how many points each essay question is worth. Spend the most time on the questions which are worth the most points.

3. Always give some kind of answer, even if you don't understand the question.

4. Unless the directions say otherwise, never give a minimal answer. Professors expect you to elaborate and to give full explanations in your essays. For the essay question below, responses *A, B,* and *C* all technically answer the question, but only *C* meets the spirit of the essay exam by giving an explanation.

Questions: Do you believe that cohabitation is as practical as marriage?
Answer A: No.
Answer B: Yes. I think cohabitation is a good idea.
Answer B: Yes. I think cohabitation is practical since recent research shows that cohabitation is just as likely to result in a stable relationship as marriage. Cohabitation also gives people an opportunity to judge whether or not they want to spend a lifetime with someone before they go through all the legalities of marriage.

5. Use the technical language of the course when writing an essay. Remember, the professor wants to find out how much you know, and that includes your knowledge of the subject-area vocabulary. Compare answers *A* and *B* for the essay question below. *B* is a better answer because it uses more technical language.

Question: Summarize the process of conception and the initial stage of prenatal development.
Answer A: The male cell goes up to the egg and digs its way inside. Once this happens the genetic material from the man and the woman mix to form the genetic pattern for the baby. After this happens the cell begins to split up again and again as the fertilized egg works its way down to the uterus where it will attach itself to the woman's body.
Answer B: The male sperm cell digs its way into the ovum and the egg is fertilized. Once this happens the chromosomes from the sperm cell and the chromosomes from the ovum mix to form the genetic pattern for the baby. After this happens the fertilized ovum begins to reproduce itself though a process called mitosis. As this process continues, the fertilized egg, now called a zygote, works its way down the fallopian tube to the uterus where it will attach itself to the wall of the uterus.

6. Pay attention to capitalization, punctuation, spelling, grammar, and neatness. Proofread for these things as you reread your answers. Remember, the grading of essays is largely subjective. A sloppy answer can only reduce your grade.

After the Test

Test preparation and test taking can provide you with valuable learning experiences. If you are pleased with your results, you should feel confident that you can do it again and again. If you are not pleased, try to figure out where you went wrong. Often, we learn more from our failures than from our successes. Make an appointment with your instructor to go over your test. Most professors are willing to spend some extra time with you if you show them that you really care about the quality of your work. Professors have office hours; take advantage of them. The important thing to remember is that one poor test grade is not the end of the world, but just a step in the learning process.

Testwiseness Posttest

Directions: Circle the letter of the best answer.

A. Multiple Choice

1. An action designed to stop a behavior is a
   a. negative reinforcement.
   b. punishment.
   c. associations.
   d. hanging.

2. According to Jerome Kagan
   a. the first year of life is totally critical.
   b. children can recover from early environmental impoverishment given normal stimulation and care.
   c. punishment should not be used on children.
   d. sex differences are culturally determined.

3. Which of these statements is untrue?
   a. IQ tests and achievement tests actually test the same thing.
   b. The best IQ tests are actually achievement tests.
   c. IQ stands for *I*ntelligence *Q*uotient.
   d. Individualized IQ tests assess genetic potential.

4. The results of the Milwaukee Project support
   a. an environmentalist position with regard to intelligence.
   b. behaviorism.
   c. Jenson.
   d. Piaget's.

5. An *I*ntelligence *Q*uotient is a function of
   a. the relationship between mental age and chronological age.
   b. MA.
   c. CA.
   d. luck.

B. True or False

6. T   F   Intelligence always declines rapidly in later life.

7. T   F   Social learning theory, as proposed by Albert Bandura, emphasizes the impact of the environment on the individual.

8. T   F   Since most college students drink to excess, college students on probation frequently suffer from anxiety.

9. T   F   The Harlows found that monkeys with normal peer relations develop into socially and sexually normal adults even if they have been deprived of a mother.

10. T   F   Women are shorter than most men.

One Final Caution

Do not be fooled into thinking that testwiseness is a good substitute for knowledge. In fact, most of the testwiseness tips presented in this chapter, especially for multiple choice and true–false tests, will not work with well-written tests. This is also true for standardized tests such as the SAT. In the final analysis testwiseness is far less important than your understanding of course content.

Answers to matching test on page 130.
1. B
2. J
3. E
4. A
5. L
6. C
7. M
8. G
9. K
10. H

Answers for definition item on page 131.
1. Define *positive reinforcer*
___ It makes you feel good.
___ When you do things more that you like.
X A stimulus that causes an increase in behavior.
X A positive reinforcer is something that makes a person or animal do a behavior more often.
___ A positive reinforcer is a stimulus that makes you happy.

Answer for essay test item on page 131. *B* is the better essay because the writer followed the directions and compared (noted similarities and differences) saccadic and pursuit eye movements.

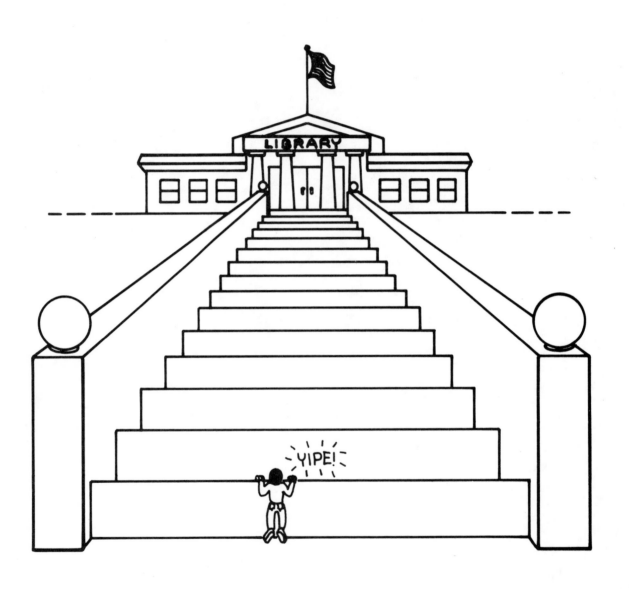

9
How to Use the Library

What Do You Believe about the Library?

Directions: Read each of the statements below. Place a checkmark on the line in front of each statement you believe is true.

1. _____ You should ask for help from librarians only as a last resort.

2. _____ *World Book Encyclopedia* is one of the best references to use when you are writing a college term paper.

3. _____ *Nonprint materials* refer to materials in the library that have no letters or words on them.

4. _____ Microfiche are very small rodents that infest libraries and eat the covers off books.

We hope these statements have made you curious about the library. Perhaps you have a few questions of your own. Search for the answers to your questions as you read and work your way through this chapter.

The What, Where, How, Why, and When of Library Use

The library is probably the most important building on your campus. Unfortunately, the library strikes fear into the hearts of freshmen everywhere. The main reason for the students' trepidation is their lack of familiarity with the library. Most students are overwhelmed by the hundreds of thousands of books and other materials housed there.

You, too, may be unaware of *what* materials and services the library can provide and *where* you can find them. You may also be uncertain about *how* to use the resources of the library, as well as *why* and *when*. Once you have learned the basic library facts presented in this chapter, you will be able to walk into your college library with a feeling of confidence.

Basic Question #1: What Can the Library Do for Me?

The library is your most important resource for writing term papers and research papers. Since libraries contain the facts and literature that you need as a student, you can think of the library as the most knowledgeable teacher you will ever have. Any questions you need to have answered, any projects you need to complete, any research you need to do, all can be accomplished with the help of the library. In addition, you have available librarians who are willing to help you find the information you need.

The library is also a good place to study, away from the TV, stereo, phone, refrigerator, and other distractions that are so common to your home or dorm. Distractions cause your attention to wander. When this happens you may find yourself merely going through the motions of studying, wasting time and not getting any results. Since the quiet and convenience of the library encourages studying, you should consider making it your study headquarters.

Most libraries have set aside special sections for group study. Here you and your classmates can work on group projects, discuss possible exam questions, or tutor (or be tutored) without interruption. The library can also be a "thinking place." Quiet distraction-free places far away from video games are becoming harder and harder to find.

```
796
D659c      Dolan, Edward F., 1924-
           Calling the play : a beginner's guide
           to amateur sports officiating / Edward
           F. Doland, Jr. -- New York : Atheneum,
           c1981.

                232 p.  :  ill.  ;  23 cm.
                Bibliography

                1. Sports officiating    I. Title

FM    03 MAY 82   7775684   DZMMof   81-66014
```

Author card

```
                 SPORTS OFFICIATING
796
D659c      Dolan, Edward F., 1924-
           Calling the play : a beginner's guide
           to amateur sports officiating / Edward
           F. Doland, Jr. -- New York : Atheneum,
           c1981.
                232 p.  :  ill.  ;  23 cm.
                Bibliography

                1. Sports officiating   I. Title

FM    03 MAY 82   7775684   DZMMof   81-66014
```

Subject card

```
           Calling the play

796
D659c      Dolan, Edward F., 1924-
           Calling the play : a beginner's guide
           to amateur sports officiating / Edward
           F. Doland, Jr. -- New York : Atheneum,
           c 1981.
                232 p.  :  ill.  ;  23 cm.
                Bibliography

                1. Sports officiating    I. Title

FM    03 MAY 82   7775684   DZMMof   81-66014
```

Title card

Figure 1. Types of cards in the card catalog

The *reserve reading room* is also an important spot in the library. This is where professors set aside books, magazines, tapes, and other materials they have suggested or assigned. Sometimes these materials may be used only in the library. In other cases you will be allowed to take them out for a limited period of time. In any event, you should know where your library reserve reading room is located.

Basic Question #2: How Do I Find Things in the Library?

The first and most important step in learning to use the library efficiently is to understand how to use the card catalog. The *card catalog* is a big set of drawers which contain many thousands of individual cards (like notecards). The cards—and the drawers—are arranged in alphabetical order. They index (list and describe) all of the books and other materials in the library.

Some colleges and universities are now using computerized systems which replace the traditional card catalog. Instead of walking to a drawer and looking up cards, students use computer terminals to find the location of materials in the library. On some campuses, faculty and students can use remote terminals to see if a book is in the library before going there.

Every item in the library is listed in the card catalog in three different ways: (1) by subject, (2) by author, and (3) by title. This makes it easier for you to find materials if you don't have complete information. For example, if you know only the title of a book, you can look in the card catalog under the title to see if the book is part of the library's collection. On the other hand, if you know only the author of the book, you can look in the card catalog under the author's name. A given author may have written many books, in which case you can flip through that author's cards until you come to the right title of the book you want. Even if you don't know a specific author or title of the book you can look in the card catalog under the book's subject.

The three cards shown in Figure 1 are examples of title, author, and subject cards. Notice that the only difference among the cards is at the top of the card. The title card has the title typed above the author's name. The subject card has the subject typed above the author's name.

The Call Number. The call number for a book is like the address for your home. It tells you where in the library a certain book can be found. Books on the same subject usually have similar call numbers. For example, if you were hunting for a specific book, say *The Mating Habits of the Hummingbird*, you might come across several other books on the same topic just because they have similar call numbers and have been shelved together. The call number is in the upper left-hand corner of the catalog card. (See the three lines shown there in Figure 2.)

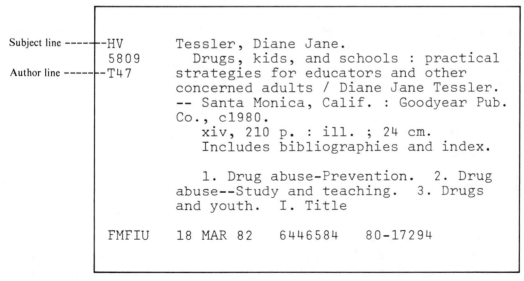

Subject line ----- HV
5809
Author line ----- T47

Tessler, Diane Jane.
   Drugs, kids, and schools : practical strategies for educators and other concerned adults / Diane Jane Tessler. -- Santa Monica, Calif. : Goodyear Pub. Co., c1980.
   xiv, 210 p. : ill. ; 24 cm.
   Includes bibliographies and index.

   1. Drug abuse-Prevention. 2. Drug abuse--Study and teaching. 3. Drugs and youth. I. Title

FMFIU   18 MAR 82   6446584   80-17294

Figure 2. Subject and author lines in Library of Congress classification system

A	General Works
B	Philosophy, Psychology, Religion
C	Archaeology
D	History—Not including United States
E	United States History
F	History: U.S. States and Western Hemisphere
G	Geography, Anthropology, Sports, Recreation
H	Sociology, Business, and Economics
J	Political Science
K	Law
L	Education
M	Music
N	Fine Arts
P	Language and Literature
Q	Science
R	Medicine
S	Agriculture
T	Technology
U	Military Science
V	Naval Science
Z	Bibliography and Library Science

Figure 3. Library of Congress Classification letters

Libraries classify call numbers by using either of two classification systems: The Dewey Decimal system or the Library of Congress system. Since almost all colleges and universities use the Library of Congress classification system, that is the one we will discuss here. A general understanding of how the Library of Congress system works is vital for learning how to use the card catalog efficiently.

Library of Congress Classification System. The Library of Congress system uses twenty-one letters to broadly classify all knowledge (see Figure 3). These letters can be used one at a time or in combinations. Look at the first line of the card in Figure 2 for an example.

The second line of a call number based on the Library of Congress system is a number that breaks down the category into a more specific area. For example, Figure 4 is a page taken from the *Library of Congress Classification Outline*. It shows the subcategories under the letter G. This reference can help you to identity topics for research papers or it can help you to narrow down a topic that is too broad. For example, suppose a sociology professor assigns you a five-page research paper on the manners and customs of an American Indian tribe. You should probably go to the *Library of Congress Subject Headings* in order to pick a topic that you can discuss well in five pages. Under the letter G (see Figure 4), which includes the subject "anthropology," you will find the subclassification GT. Here you see the general topic of manners and customs narrowed down to such things as houses, costume, love, marriage, and town life.

The third line of the call number (see Figure 2) is the author line, which starts with the first letter of the author's last name.

Remember that books with similar call numbers are shelved together. Instead of thinking of the library as a mass of unrelated books lined up on shelves, think of the library as a series of mini-collections where books on similar topics are grouped together.

Other Library Resources

1. Periodicals

Periodicals are publications that appear at regular intervals—daily, weekly, monthly, or quarterly (four times a year). The two major kinds of periodicals are *journals* and *magazines*. Sometimes these words are used to mean the same thing, but there is a subtle difference. A magazine, such as *Ladies Home Journal* or *Popular Computing,* can be read by the average person with an interest in the topics covered by the magazine. On the other hand, journals, such as *Psychological Reports* or *Journal of Abnormal Child Psychology,* are more technical and designed for a smaller audience of specialists.

G		Geography (General)
		For geography and description of individual countries, *see* D–F
	149–570	Voyages and travels (General)
		Including discoveries, explorations, shipwrecks, seafaring life.
		For travel in special continents and countries, *see* D–F
	575–890	Polar regions
		Including exploration, history, description
	905–910	Tropics (General)
	912–922	Northern and Southern Hemispheres
	1000.3–3122	Atlases
	3160–9980	Maps. Globes
GA		Mathematical geography. Cartography
		Including topographical surveys of individual countries
GB		Physical geography
		Including arrangement by country
	400–649	Geomorphology
	651–2998	Water. Hydrology
		Including ground water, rivers, lakes, glaciers
	5000–5030	Natural disasters
GC		Oceanography
	100–181	Seawater
	200–376	Dynamics of the sea
	377–399	Marine sediments
	1000–1023	Marine resources. Applied oceanography
	1080–1581	Marine pollution
GF		Human ecology. Anthropogeography
GN		Anthropology
	49–296	Physical anthropology. Somatology
	301–673	Ethnology. Social and cultural anthropology
		For descriptions of individual ethnic groups, *see* D–F
	700–875	Prehistoric archaeology
		Including arrangement by country
GR		Folklore
	72–79	Folk literature (General)
	430–940	Folklore relating to special subjects
GT		Manners and customs (General)
		For works limited to special countries, *see* D–F
	170–474	Houses. Dwellings
	500–2370	Costume. Dress. Fashion
	2400–5090	Custom relative to private and public life
		Including love, marriage, eating, smoking, treatment of the dead, town life, customs of chivalry, festivals and holidays
	5320–6720	Customs relative to special classes, by birth, occupation, etc.
GV		Recreation
	191.2–200.5	Outdoor life. Outdoor recreation
		Including camping for individuals or small groups, organized camps, trailer camping, hiking, mountaineering
	201–555	Physical training
	561–1198.995	Sports
	1199–1570	Games and amusements
	1580–1799	Dancing
	1800–1860	Circuses, spectacles, etc.
		Including rodeos, waxworks, amusement parks, etc.

Figure 4.

Periodicals are very useful in writing research papers because they contain the most current information. Periodicals are kept together in a special place in the library. They are shelved alphabetically by name, with the most current ones located in a special reading area.

Each year the library sends the periodicals from the previous year to a bindery where they are bound into book form. The bound periodicals then become *volumes* which are numbered. Suppose you wanted to find the following article:

    Author   Title

Allen, G. J. The behavioral treatment of test anxiety: Recent research and future trends. Behavior Therapy. 3. 1972, 253–262.

    Journal   Volume Number   Date of Publication   Pages

You would first find the periodicals section of the library. Second, you would search in the *B*'s for the journal *Behavior Therapy*. Third, you would find volume 3 of the journal. And fourth, you would go to page 253 where the article begins. If the journal isn't there or if the volume you need is missing, ask the librarians for assistance. They are there to help you.

2. Reference Books

Bibliographies Bibliographies catalog or list books by their topics. Figure 5 shows a page from the popular bibliography, *Books in Print*. This bibliography provides a current listing of books that are on the market and published by major American publishers. Each book's entry shows its title, author, date of publication, price, and publisher. Books are grouped and cross-referenced by author, title, and subject area.

If, for example, you were doing a paper on the ill effects of smoking and wanted to know what current books deal with that topic, you could go to the Subject Guide of *Books in Print* and look up titles beginning with the word *smoking*. There are, of course, many other bibliographical works. When you are working on a paper in a particular area, for instance, zoology, go to the reference area of the library and ask one of the librarians to help you find the most appropriate bibliography.

Smoking & Arterial Disease. R. M. Greenhalgh. 320p. 1981. text ed. 49.50 (ISBN 0-272-79604-2). Pitman Pub MA.

Smoking & Arterial Disease. R. M. Green-Halgh. 350p. 1981. 110.00 (ISBN 0-272-79604-2, Pub. by Pitman Bks England). State Mutual Bk.

Smoking & Arterial Disease. Ed. by R. M. Greenhalgh. 315p. 1981. text ed. 57.95x (ISBN 0-8464-1215-2). Beekman Pubs.

Smoking & Behavior, Report No. 1. Division of Mental Health & Behavioral Medicine, Institute of Medicine, National Research Council. 1982. pap. text ed. 8.50 (ISBN 0-309-03290-3). Natl Acad Pr.

Smoking & Chemical Child Abuse. Michael Meftah. 1981. 5.75 (ISBN 0-8062-1616-6). Carlton.

Smoking & Health: A Comprehensive Bibliography. Compiled by Alberta D. Berton. (Biomedical Information Guides Ser.: Vol. 3). 535p. 1980. 95.00x (ISBN 0-306-65184-X, IFI Plenum). Plenum Pub.

Smoking & Its Effects on Health: Report. WHO Expert Committee. Geneva, 1974. (Technical Report Ser.: No. 568). (Also avail. in French & Spanish). 1975. pap. 3.60 (ISBN 92-4-120568-7). World Health.

Smoking & Politics: Policy Making & the Federal Bureaucracy. 3rd ed. A. Lee Fritschler. 208p. 1983. pap. 11.95 (ISBN 0-13-815027-3). P-H.

Smoking & Reproduction: A Comprehensive Bibliography. Ernest L. Abel .LC 82-15660. xviii, 163p. 1982. lib. bdg. 35.00 (ISBN 0-313-23663-1, ASR/). Greenwood.

Smoking & You. Arnold Madison. LC 75-1347. (Illus.). 64p. (gr. 4 up). 1975. PLB 6.97 (ISBN 0-671-32725-9). Messner.

Smoking Antiques. Amoret Scott & Christopher Scott. (Shire Album Ser.: No. 66). (Illus.). 32p. (Orig.). 1983. pap. 2.95 (ISBN 0-85263-540-0, 3380249, Pub. by Shire Pubns England). Seven Hills Bks.

Smoking by Children in Great Britain. Beulah R. Bewley & Isobel Day. 21p. 20.00x (ISBN 0-686-98311-4, Pub. by Social Sci Res) State Mutual Bk.

Smoking: Facilitator's Manual. Sabina M. Dunton & Melody S. Fanning. Ed. by Richard A. McNeely. (Well Aware About Health Risk Reduction Ser.). (Illus.). 186p. (Orig.). 1982. 29.95 (ISBN 0-943562-51-1). Well Aware.

Smoking Flax. Hallie E. Rives. LC 72-2026. (Black Heritage Library Collection Ser.). Repr. of 1897 ed. 15.25 (ISBN 0-8369-9057-9). Ayer Co.

Smoking for Two: Cigarettes & Pregnancy. Peter A. Fried & Harry Oxorn. LC 80-20054. (Illus.). 1980. 10.95 (ISBN 0-02-910720-2). Free Pr.

Smoking Gods: Tobacco in Maya Art, History, & Religion. Francis Robicsek. LC 78-64904. (Illus.). 1978. 39.50 (ISBN 0-8061-1511-4). U of Okla Pr.

Smoking Hazards-Reprints. 3.00x (ISBN 0-686-29965-5). Cancer Control Soc.

Smoking-Is It a Sin? Tom McDevitt. 80p. (Orig.). 1981. pap. 4.50 (ISBN 0-933046-03-0). Little Red Hen.

Smoking Land: A Novel of Super-Science & Amazing Adventure. Max Brand. LC 80-17333. (Max Brand Popular Classics Ser.). 112p. 1980. pap. 5.95 (ISBN 0-88496-155-9). Capra Pr.

Smoking Leg, & Other Stories. facsimile ed. John Metcalfe. LC 74-152950. (Short Story Index Reprint Ser.). Repr. of 1926 ed. 16.00 (ISBN 0-8369-3828-3). Ayer Co.

Smoking, Life & Health. rev ed. George Madis. (Illus.). 1964. 5.95 (ISBN 0-910156-02-6). Art & Ref.

Smoking on Health. 128p. 1977. 29.00 (ISBN 0-272-79412-0, Pub. by Pitman Bks England). State Mutual Bk.

Smoking or Health. Royal College of Physicians. 1977. pap. 12.00x (ISBN 0-8464-0853-8). Beekman Pubs.

Smoking Paradox: Public Regulation in the Cigarette Industry. Gideon Doron. LC 79-50400. 1979. text ed. 18.00 (ISBN 0-89011-531-1). Abt Bks.

Smoking: Psychology & Pharmacology. Heather Ashton & Rod Stepney. LC 81-18829. 250p. 1982. 22.00x (ISBN 0-422-77700-5, NO. 3604, Pub. by Tavistock). Methuen Inc.

Smoking Technology of the Aborigines of the Iroquois Area of New York State. Edward S. Rutsch. LC 73-92558. 252p. 1972. 25.00 (ISBN 0-8386-7568-9). Fairleigh Dickinson.

Smoking: Third World Alert. Uma R. Nath. (Illus.). 150p. 1983. 12.95 (ISBN 0-19-261402-9); pap. 2.95 (ISBN 0-19-261325-1). Oxford U Pr.

Smoking: Workbook. Sabina M. Dunton & Melody S. Fanning. Ed. by Richard A. McNeely. (Well Aware About Health Risk Redution Ser.). (Illus.). 109p. (Orig.). 1982. pap. 7.95 (ISBN 0-943562-52-X). Well Aware.

Smoky. Will James. (gr. 7-11). 1926. willow leaf ed. 12.95 (ISBN 0-684-12875-6, ScribT). Scribner.

Smoky God. Willis G. Emerson. (Illus.). 1908. pap. 4.95 (ISBN 0-910122-20-2). Amherst Pr.

Figure 5. Entries on smoking from *Books in Print*. (Reprinted with permission of the R. R. Bowker Company. Copyright © 1983 by Xerox Corporation.)

Dictionaries. Usually the word *dictionary* brings to mind a single book, perhaps a "Webster's." Actually, there are many kinds of dictionaries, most of which are not found in the average home. There are general dictionaries; dictionaries of slang, abbreviations, and synonyms; biographical dictionaries; and dictionaries for particular subject areas. Any time you need to find out how to spell, define, or use a word, expression, or symbol, the chances are excellent that your college library will have the dictionary you need. Again, check with the reference librarian if you need help.

Encyclopedias. No doubt, you are familiar with general encyclopedias such as *Britannica* and *World Book*. However, relying on these as your major source of information for college level projects isn't a good idea. Professors tend to take a dim view of papers based on general encyclopedias since they are very general and lack the sophistication which should characterize college work. A better bet is to search for information in specialized encyclopedias which provide detailed information in specific subject areas, for example, *The Encyclopedia of Philosophy, Encyclopedia of World Art, Encyclopedia of Educational Research,* and the *Encyclopedia of Advertising.*

Yearbooks, Atlases, and Gazetteers. These are reference books which contain thousands of facts on hundreds of subjects. A gazetteer is an alphabetized list of place names which includes pronunciations, locations, descriptions, and statistics. For example, *Webster's Geographical Dictionary* contains a gazetteer that lists more than 40,000 places in every part of the world. Gazetters are geographical dictionaries. Atlases are also geographical. An atlas is a collection of maps that are bound together in a single volume or book.

Yearbooks are annual (yearly) publications which update events or developments during a given year. For instance, almanacs such as the *World Almanac* are general yearbooks which give up to date information about everything from sports records to the results of political elections. With an almanac you can find such facts as the average winter temperature in Chicago or what day of the week April 9, 1865 fell on. (General Lee surrendered to General Grant to end the Civil War on this date.) There are also yearbooks for specific subjects; for example, *Year in American Music, Yearbook of Agriculture,* and *Yearbook of International Organizations.*

Indexes and Abstracts. These references are simply lists and sources (where to find something) of materials such as magazines. The big difference between an index and an abstract is that an index lists magazine articles and the like without giving any description of them, whereas an abstract provides brief descriptions of the articles or books. Figure 6 on the following page shows sample listings for an index and an abstract. Some of the most important indexes and abstracts are discussed below.

A. *Reader's Guide to Periodical Literature.* This index provides information about approximately 125 magazines of general interest, such as *Time* and *Scientific American.* Magazine articles are under alphabetized topic headings. For example, the excerpt on the following page (Figure 7) shows the major heading "Mental Illness." Underneath that is the subheading "Diagnosis." Below the subheading are listed two articles, one in *Newsweek* and one in *Psychology Today.* Both of these articles deal with diagnosing mental illness. If you were doing a paper on this topic and thought these articles might be useful, you would copy (1) the name of the periodical, (2) the number of the volume that contains the article, (3) the pages on which the article appears, and (4) the date of publication. The next step would be to go to the periodicals section of the library and find the articles.

B. *Specific subject indexes and abstracts.* Many indexes and abstracts deal with particular fields; for example, *Social Science Index, Business Periodicals Index, Chemical Abstracts,* and *Short Story Index.* Again, your reference librarian will help you to find the index or abstract which suits your particular needs.

C. *Periodical Directories.* Suppose you are doing a paper on marketing techniques, but you have no idea what the major journals are in the field of business. The following three useful guides list periodicals for every subject area.
    1. *Ulrich's International Periodical Directory*
    2. *The Standard Periodical Directory*
    3. *Magazines for Libraries*

Holtby, Michael. The origin and insertion of script injunctions. *Transactional Analysis Journal, 1976(Oct), Vol 6(4), 371–376.* 63:12351

Holte, Arne. [Toward a scientific concept of confirmation: II. Preparations for an empirical study.] (Norg) *Tidsskrift for Norsk Psykologforening, 1979(May), Vol 15(5), 199–205.* 64:7895

Holte, Carol S.—*See* Cummins, David E. 60:6456

Holthouse, Norman D.—*See* Tokar, Edward B. 60:12772

Holton, George C.—*See* Smaby, Marlowe H. 59:13329

Holton, Susan A. An exploratory study into the proxemic and verbal behavior of "normals" in dyadic interaction with the deaf. *Dissertation Abstracts International, 1977(Aug), Vol 38(2-A), 546.* 60:9617

Holton, Susan A. Not so different: Spatial and distancing behavior of deaf adults. *American Annals of the Deaf, 1978(Dec), Vol 123(8), 920–924.* 63:7849

Holtz, Jane L. Exploring the psychological contract over the life cycle. *Dissertation Abstracts International, 1978(Oct), Vol 39(4-A), 2399.* 62:9967

Holtz, Karl-Ludwig—*See* Eberle, Gerhard 64:186

Holtz, Sigrid—*See* Dickenberger, Dorothee 61:12335

Holtzman, Garry L.—*See* Lentz, J. Michael 61:12447

Holtzman, Jeffrey D.; *Sedgwick, Harold A. & Festinger, Leon.* Interaction of perceptually monitored and unmonitored efferent commands for smooth pursuit eye movements. *Vision Research, 1978, Vol 18(11), 1545–1555.* 63:8802

Holtzman, Jeffrey D.—*See* Festinger, Leon 64:2593

Index

4998. Flory, Randall K. & Smith, Catesby T. (Hollins Coll) **Effects of limited-target availability on schedule-induced attack.** *Physiology & Behavior,* 1983(Jan), Vol 30(1), 11–18.—Male White King pigeons ($N = 7$) exposed to a 180-sec fixed-time food schedule could attack a rear-projected conspecific target that was available either (a) continuously throughout the interfood interval, (b) randomly during 1 30-sec portion of each interfood interval, or (c) during the final 90 sec of each interval. During continuous-target availability, attack was maximal shortly after food ingestion and progressively decreased thereafter. During random-target availability, 5 Ss attacked less per target-access period the later that period occurred within the interfood interval; 2 Ss exhibited relatively high local attack rates even when access periods occurred within the final one-third of the interval. When the target was available only during the 2nd half of the interfood interval, attack occurred as soon as the target was presented and progressively decreased throughout the remainder of the target-access period. Results show that schedule-induced attack can be increased by limiting the availability of that target and that such attack can reliably occur at times other than shortly after food delivery. (36 ref)—*Journal abstract.*

Abstract

Figure 6. Samples of an Index* and an Abstract**

Magazine—*Psychology Today*
Volume Number—11
Page Numbers—34–35+
Publication Date—January 1978

MENTAL illness—*Continued*
Diagnosis
Beyond neurosis; new edition of the Diagnostic and statistical manual of mental disorders. D. Gelman. Newsweek 93:68 Ja 8 '79
Who's mentally ill? new version of the Diagnostic and statistical manual of mental disorders. D. Goleman. Psychol Today 11:34–5+ Ja '78

Genetic aspects
Creativity and madness; dopamine receptors. M. Thacher. il Hum Behav 8:50–1 Ja '79
Genetic marker for depression reported. Sci News 115:20 Ja 13 '79

Nutritional aspects
Is our diet driving us crazy? J. Schinto. Progressive 42:26–8 My '78

Social aspects
We have to stop running away. R. Carter. por McCalls 105:121+ Je '78

Figure 7. Excerpt from *Readers Guide to Periodical Literature.* New York: The H. W. Wilson Company, 1983, p. 986.

*Excerpt from *Psychological Index* from *The Accumalative Author Index to Psychological Abstracts, 1978–1980,* p. 313, American Psychological Association, 1981

**Excerpt from *Psychological Abstracts,* Granick, L. et al. eds. *70,* 3, American Psychological Association, Inc. Arlington, VA. Sept. 1983 p. 557.

MARRIOTT Corp
   Marriott Corporation reports 1st-quarter net income increased to $19.2 million, up 13.6% from $16.9 million year ago (S), Ap 12,IV,8:3
MARRON, Donald B. See also Paine Webber Inc, Ap 15
MARSEILLES (France). See also Waste etc, Ap 12
MARSH, Warne. See also Music—Recordings, Ap 13
MARSHALL, Prentice H (Judge). See also Trucks and Trucking, Ap 3,9,15
MARSTELLER Inc
   Marsteller Inc promotes Dale E. Landsman to executive vp/executive creative director (S), Ap 12, IV,16:4
MARTELLA, Luis Carlos (Lt). See also Falkland Islands, Ap 5
MARTIAL Law. See also Poland, Ap 9,14. Turkey, Ap 1
MARTIN, Barbara. See also Music—Concerts, Ap 10
MARTIN, Billy (Baseball Mgr). See also Baseball—New York Yankees, Ap 7,13
MARTIN, Lawrence N Jr (Judge). See also Fires and Firemen—NYS, Ap 8,11
MARTIN, Lucy. See also Educ—NYC, Ap 12
MARTIN, Luis. See also Fires and Firemen—NYS, Ap 8
MARTIN, Preston. See also Federal Reserve System, Ap 12

MARTIN Marietta Corp. See also Noranda Mines Ltd, Ap 5
MARTINEZ Ordonez, Roberto. See also Latin America, Ap 6
MARTINS, Peter. See also Dancing—Taylor, Paul, Dance Co. Ap 5
MARTISE, James B. See also National Enquirer, Ap 14
MARX, Groucho (1890–1977)
   Judge Jacqueline L. Weiss schedules hearing for April 1 on what will be done with physical property left by Groucho Marx to Erin Fleming; jury award of $221,843 in compensatory damages and $250,000 in punitive damages to Bank of America, executor of estate, is binding only with respect to cash; bank wants court to establish trust into which real property would be placed on ground that Fleming got it through fraud and duress; Fleming photo (M), Ap 1,I,17:1; Santa Monica, Calif, Superior Court Judge Jacqueline L Weiss denies defense motion for mistrial in Groucho Marx estate case; but she rules that Erin Flemming, Marx's companion for last years of his life, will not have to turn over to Bank of America two houses and other gifts (M), Ap 2,I,p2
   David Sabih, attorney for Erin Fleming, requests new trial on Groucho Marx estate, contending that Bank of America had hidden diary kept by Marx during his last years; says he has just learned that diary existed (S), Ap 6,I,18:6

Length of Publication—short article (About Groucho Marx)*
Publication Date—April 6 (The index itself shows the year.)
Section of the paper—1
Page—18
Column—6

Figure 8. Excerpt from the *New York Times Index*. New York: New York Times, April 1983.

3. Newspapers

Information about business, economics, government, and social events can be found in newspapers. Library holdings of newspapers are generally on microfilm. (More will be said about microfilm later in the chapter.) Newspapers, like periodicals, are important sources of information. They are also indexed. An example of a major newspaper index is the *New York Times Index*. All newspaper indexes have subject entries and cross references. The *New York Times Index* gives the date, section, page and column number of each entry. For example, *Ap 4, VI, 7:2* means that a particular story was published on April 4, in section 6 of the newspaper, page 7, column 2. Abstracts of news stories end with a length indicator; (*L*) indicates a long story, (*M*) indicates a story of medium length, and (*S*) indicates a short item. See Figure 8 for an excerpt from the *New York Times Index*.

4. Government Publications

These documents are published by local, state, and federal agencies. They contain a wealth of information on economics, marketing, energy, health, education, criminal justice, social work, and other areas of government research. Government publications are also indexed. The most current and comprehensive index is the *Monthly Catalog of Government Publications*. This catalog is arranged aphabetically by the name of the government agency that published the document.

   Government publications are kept in a designated section of the reference room. These documents are NOT listed in the regular card catalog. Government publications are very complicated. In fact, most university libraries have special librarians who work only with this type of publication. We suggest that you seek the help of this specialist if you need government documents.

5. Nonprint or Nonbook Materials

These include all library resources that are not printed on paper; for example, microfilm, audio tapes, slides, and filmstrips. Today many periodicals and newspapers are reproduced on microfilm or microfiche to save space in the library. The microfilm and microfiche look something like the frames of a film strip with the print so reduced in size that it cannot be read without magnification. Mechanical readers are used to magnify all microforms, which come in the following formats:

A. Microfilm—16mm or 35mm reels of film.

B. Microfiche—4″ × 6″ transparent cards on which the print has been reduced 24 times.

C. Microcards—3″ × 5″ opaque (can't see through it) cards which may have printing on both sides.

Be sure to ask a librarian for help in using the mechanical readers if you are unfamiliar with the equipment.

6. Computer-Assisted Research Services

You can save a lot of time if you order a computer search of the literature when you are faced with a major presentation or term paper. Libraries may charge a fee for this service, but it is generally faster and more complete than a literature search you could do on your own. The computer-assisted search consists of the following steps:

A. Select the topic you wish to investigate; for instance, "The Organization and Operation of a Small Business."

B. Make a list of terms that describe the content area of your topic. Usually, there are lists available from which you can select these terms. These key terms, called *descriptors,* are fed into the computer by library personnel. For the topic, "The Organization and Operation of a Small Business," you might use descriptors such as "small business," "financial planning," "locating," or "merchandising." The idea is to select descriptors that focus directly on the topic; otherwise you end up with a lot of references which don't pertain to your topic.

C. After the computer has processed the descriptors, you will receive a list of journal articles and other materials that deal with your topic.

D. Decide which articles are important and locate them in the library. (The more accurate and precise your descriptors are, the more "on target" the computer-generated articles will be.)

7. Interlibrary Loans

Since no library has every book and article ever written, you will probably find yourself at one time or another needing something your library doesn't have. Frequently, you will be able to get the desired book or article by asking your library to get it for you from another library. You will need to check first with the reference librarian and then fill out an order card or form. Typically, there is no charge for this service.

8. Other Library Services

A walking tour of the library will uncover services such as typing rooms, photocopy machines, and audio-visual equipment such as language tapes, records, and art slides. Remember, the library is not just a giant collection of books. Frequent use of the library's resources will help you to become a prepared, competent, and successful college student.

Review Exercise

Place the letter of the correct definition on the space in front of the term. The number in parentheses indicates the page on which the answer can be found.

1. _____ Abstract (143)

2. _____ Periodical (140)

3. _____ Index (143)

4. _____ Bibliography (142)

5. _____ Call Number (139)

6. _____ *Library of Congress Classification Outline*(140)

7. _____ Almanac (143)

8. _____ *Monthly Catalog of Government Publications* (145)

9. _____ Microfiche (146)

10. _____ Descriptors (146)

A. Shows subcategories in the Library of Congress classification system.

B. Tells where in the library a book can be found.

C. Key terms which are used in a computer search.

D. Gives brief summaries of journal articles.

E. The most commonly used yearbook.

F. Journals that appear at regular intervals.

G. Transparent 4″ × 6″ cards on which print is reduced 24 times.

H. Lists of materials and where to find them.

I. A catalog or list of books on a particular topic.

J. An index of materials published by local, state, and federal agencies.

Name _____

1. Who is the author of the book *Something of Value*?

   _____

2. What is the call number for the book *Beyond Freedom and Dignity* by B. F. Skinner?

   _____

   _____

   _____

3. What is the subject matter of the book *The Pyramid Climbers*?

   _____

4. The last word in the title of a book by Harvey Cox rhymes with *kitty*. What is the title of the book?

   _____

5. The following article appeared in the magazine *Psychology Today:* "Alcohol, Marijuana, and Memory," Vol. 13, Part 2, No. 10, March 1980, pp. 42–56, 92. Who is the author?

   _____

6. Find the author and title of the book with this call number:
   PS1305
   .A1
   1912

Author: _____

Title: _____

7. Use the *McGraw-Hill Dictionary of Scientific and Technical Terms* to find the meaning of the word *cranioplasty*.

   _____

8. What day of the week was April 12, 1886? _____

9. Use *Webster's Geographical Dictionary* to find where the city of Cunaxa is/was located. Location:

   _____

10. Describe the picture on Plate 290 of the *Encyclopedia of World Art*. Description: _____

   _____

11. How many home runs did Mickey Mantle hit in 1958? _____

12. Use volume 40 of the *Reader's Guide to Periodical Literature* to find the title of one article written by Bernard Price. Select the article which sounds most interesting to you.

   _____

   _____

13. What is the last word on page 283 of volume 24 of the *Education Index*? _____

14. The following article appeared in the magazine *Scientific American:* "How Continents Break Up," Vol. 249, No. 1, July 1983. What are the authors' names? _____

   and _____

15. What is *Lagenidiales?* _____

Appendix A
Supplemental Reading Passages

1. THE 800TH LIFETIME (445 words)

In the three short decades between now and the twenty-first century, millions of ordinary, psychologically normal people will face an abrupt collision with the future. Citizens of the world's richest and most technologically advanced nations, many of them will find it increasingly painful to keep up with the incessant demand for change that characterizes our time. For them, the future will have arrived too soon.

This book is about change and how we adapt to it. It is about those who seem to thrive on change, who crest its waves joyfully, as well as those multitudes of others who resist it or seek flight from it. It is about our capacity to adapt. It is about the future and the shock that its arrival brings.

Western society for the past 300 years has been caught up in a fire storm of change. This storm, far from abating, now appears to be gathering force. Change sweeps through the highly industrialized countries with waves of ever accelerating speed and unprecedented impact. It spawns in its wake all sorts of curious social flora—from psychedelic churches and "free universities" to science cities in the Arctic and wife-swap clubs in California.

It breeds odd personalities, too: children who at twelve are no longer childlike; adults who at fifty are children of twelve. There are rich men who playact poverty, computer programmers who turn on with LSD. There are anarchists who, beneath their dirty denim shirts, are outrageous conformists, and conformists who, beneath their button-down collars, are outrageous anarchists. There are married priests and atheist ministers and Jewish Zen Buddhists. We have pop . . . and op . . . and *art cinetique*. . . . There are Playboy Clubs and homosexual movie theaters . . . amphetamines and tranquilizers . . . anger, affluence, and oblivion. Much oblivion.

Is there some way to explain so strange a scene without recourse to the jargon of psychoanalysis or the murky clichés of existentialism? A strange new society is apparently erupting in our midst. Is there a way to understand it, to shape its development? How can we come to terms with it?

Much that now strikes us as incomprehensible would be far less so if we took a fresh look at the racing rate of change that makes reality seem, sometimes, like a kaleidoscope run wild. For the acceleration of change does not merely buffet industries or nations. It is a concrete force that reaches deep into our personal lives, compels us to act out new roles, and confronts us with the danger of a new and powerfully upsetting psychological disease. This new disease can be called "future shock," and a knowledge of its sources and symptoms helps explain many things that otherwise defy rational analysis.

2. Acceptance of Death (366 words)

Dr. Elizabeth Kübler-Ross has contributed greatly to our understanding of the psychological aspects of dying. After interviewing hundreds of dying patients, she concluded that there are five stages to approaching one's own death.[1] Dying patients generally go through these stages between the time when they learn about a terminal illness and the time they die.

The first stage is **denial.** The dying person refuses to believe that death is near. Relatives and friends may also try to deny the inevitable, either to protect the dying person from the truth or because they cannot accept the truth themselves. The second stage is **anger.** Once the reality of dying has been accepted, the person reacts in protest and anger, asking "Why me?" The patient may be angry with doctors and nurses, with relatives, and even with God. A person in this stage of approaching death may express anger at anyone who is well and at anyone who tries to help.

After the anger stage, for most people comes a period of **bargaining**—either with God or with whatever power the person believes in. Such bargains take the form, "If I get well, I will lead a better life" or "If I could only live until . . . I would dedicate my life to . . . ." The actual bargains depend on the values, past experiences, and personality of the individual. There are some who claim that their bargaining, to some extent, was successful. But in most cases the dying persons realize their bargaining does not work.

Depression is the stage following bargaining. By this time the patient realizes death is near. But emotional acceptance is not yet possible. It is heartbreaking to lose a loved one, but it can be many times harder for the dying person to cope with the idea of losing everyone and everything on earth. The opportunity to express this loss can be helpful to the patient. Those who care about the dying person should be willing to both talk and listen.

The fifth and final stage of dying is **acceptance.** The dying person has learned to accept death without undue fear and bitterness. Just how a person reacts in this stage varies with the individual. Some will want to do whatever they can as long as they are able. They may want to see friends and relatives. Others may wish to spend more time alone or with someone very close, in order to prepare for the death they have now accepted.

3. Too Much Sugar (471 words)

Which contains a greater percentage of sugar: *Heinz Tomato Ketchup* or *Sealtest Chocolate Ice Cream? Wishbone Russian Dressing* or *Coca Cola? Coffee-mate Non-Dairy Creamer* or a bar of *Hershey's Milk Chocolate?*

Unless you have a food-analysis laboratory in your basement, the answers might come as quite a surprise. The *Heinz Tomato Ketchup* is 29 percent sugar, compared to 21 percent for the ice cream. If you put *Wishbone Russian Dressing* on a salad, you're pouring 30 percent sugar, a proportion more than three times that of *Coke*. The *Coffee-mate,* which is supposed to be a substitute for cream, contains 65 percent sugar, against 51 percent for a *Hershey* bar.

Those were some of the results when CU analyzed 24 common food products to determine what proportion of their weight consisted of sugar. (When we use the word "sugar," we're referring to all varieties of sugars, including those in corn syrup, honey, fruit, and vegetables, as well as ordinary table sugar, or sucrose.)

When it comes to sugar, much of the food industry apparently operates on the assumption that the consumer has three taste preferences: sweet, sweeter, and sweetest. If you prepare your chicken with *Shake 'N Bake Barbecue Style,* you're getting a coating that's 51 percent sugar. A bowl of *Quaker 100% Natural Cereal* gives you 24 percent sugar. If you munch on a *Ritz Cracker,* you know you're not eating a cookie, but you might not know it's 12 percent sugar.

A look at product ingredients on supermarket shelves reveals the difficulty of finding almost any type of prepared food product without sugar in it. It's used not only in sweet baked goods, desserts, and soft drinks, but also in sauces, many baby foods, almost all fruit drinks, salad dressings, canned and dehydrated soups, pot pies, frozen TV dinners, bacon and other cured meats, some canned and frozen vegetables, most canned and frozen fruits, fruit yogurt, and breakfast cereals. If you eat a hot dog, there is likely to be sugar in the meat, in the ketchup or relish, and in the bun. There is even a bit of sugar in many brands of salt. And for Fido, there's sugar in *Gaines-burgers* dog food.

What is all this added sugar—an average of 128 pounds consumed by every man, woman, and child in the United States last year—doing to us? It depends on whom you listen to. The Sugar Association calls it "one of our cheapest sources of food energy" and "the catalyst that makes eating pleasurable." Kellogg Co., which makes various brands of pre-sweetened cereal, says that sugar is "a solution to some world hunger problems."

But to critics, sugar represents "empty calories," accompanied by a host of medical ills. Sugar has been blamed not only for heart disease and diabetes, but also for a list of afflictions ranging from acne to varicose veins—not to mention obesity and tooth decay.

4. Computer Worship (580 words)

Even in upbeat times, educating a child or coping with the loss of a job is a sobering experience. These days, with commissions denouncing the educational system and economists warning of obsolete skills, education and jobs are gloomy issues indeed. But advance men for the computer age, through a steady chorus of advertising, offer hope: computer literacy. Without computer literacy, they predict ominously, no one has a prayer of getting good grades, of graduating, of finding a job, of taking part in the world of higher technology.

Computer literacy embodies a set of skills, variously defined. In general, a computer literate person knows the parts of a computer and what they do, has learned to operate a few of the more popular programs, and can write some elementary programs, usually in the language called Basic.

Courses offering to teach these skills have popped up everywhere. In the San Francisco Bay area alone there are more than 500, not including the public schools. Local business institutes offer night classes to ambitious workers; museums promote hands-on computer projects for kids; four-year-olds at private preschools receive computerized tutoring. Major computer manufacturers encourage the busy march toward self-improvement. Tandy, which makes Radio Shack computers, runs a national program to introduce teachers to computers. Atari has a chain of summer computer camps. Apple has gotten a state tax break by donating a computer to every public and private school in California. Similar proposals at the national level would cost hundreds of millions of dollars in federal tax breaks.

What the computer literacy movement seems to be mostly enriching is its backers: sellers of computers and computer programs; promoters of retraining courses for workers and teachers; and writers and publishers of the industry's books and magazines. Last year, for example, U.S. schools spent nearly $500 million on personal computers and programs.

"I see computer literacy as the New Math of the 1980s," says Daniel McCracken, professor of computer science at the City College of New York, author of well over a dozen textbooks on computer languages and former president of the Association for Computing Machinery, a professional organization for computer scientists. "I suggest that we might save a lot of wasted opportunity to do more useful things if we were to pinch this one off before it has a chance to get well rooted."

Pinching it off won't be easy.

In a catchy ad by Program Design, Inc. for "Baby's First Software," for example, a confident toddler stares out at the reader and his future. "Your child becomes part of the action, while acquiring new skills," the ad proclaims. The Children's Television Workshop, which created *Sesame Street,* now is pushing *Enter,* a new computer magazine for children 10 to 16. "The computer is as basic to your child's life and lifestyle as paper was to yours and mine," states a letter to parents. "And learning computer skills *is* (not will be) as fundamental as learning to read and write was to you and me . . . you can consider these to be overstatements, but only at your youngster's peril." In a commercial for Commodore computers a college freshman returns home in disgrace. If his parents had bought a Commodore in the first place, suggests the voice-over, this never would have happened. Out of school? It's not too late. "Learn: computer programming or computer operations. Take the First Step . . . Now!" reads a newspaper ad for the Computer Learning Center, a business institute in the Washington, D.C., suburbs.

5. Behind A Smoke Screen (498 words)
by Susan West

The language is disarmingly reasonable. "Can we have an open debate about smoking?" pleads the first in a series of advertisements that the R.J. Reynolds Tobacco Company began running in January. "You've heard so many negative reports about smoking and health," it goes on, "that you may assume the case against smoking is closed." In the coming months, the ad promises, Reynolds will "discuss a number of key questions relating to smoking and health."

Not surprisingly, health organizations have declared the multimillion-dollar campaign completely absurd. "A smoke screen," American Cancer Society President Gerald Murphy called it. "A clever tactic," says Leonard Schuman of the University of Minnesota's School of Public Health. "If you lie often enough, people will start to believe you."

It is the thousands of studies on many different groups of people, all showing smokers have worse health than nonsmokers, that damns the tobacco industry's stance, says University of Minnesota's Schuman. Epidemiologists, he explains, will establish a causal link from a statistical association if the association meets these criteria: It is consistent and strong; nearly every person who gets the disease has been exposed to the same agent; the disease develops after, not before, exposure to the suspected cause; and the association fits all the facts. The massive amount of data linking smoking and disease, particularly lung cancer, meets these requirements, he says.

To ignore that link would be foolish. "Some people who run blindfolded across the New Jersey Turnpike at rush hour might not get hit by a car," says Douglas Lloyd, Connecticut commissioner of health services. "But few would be dumb enough to do it."

As for the animal experiments, it isn't necessary to duplicate human behavior to show a substance is harmful, explains University of California at Los Angeles epidemiologist James Enstrom. Tests such as painting cigarette "tar" on the skins of animals confirm that at least 20 carcinogens are present in tobacco. Autopsies of smokers also testify to the severe damage smoking wreaks on human tissue.

The fact that few animals—far less than one percent in most tests—contract lung cancer when forced to breathe cigarette smoke says more about animal instinct than about the dangers of smoking. Animals quickly learn to breathe shallowly when exposed to smoke; instead of lung cancer, they develop tumors of the larynx. Says one expert on carcinogens, "There is no animal stupid enough to smoke except man. When we find an animal that will inhale cigarette smoke as deeply as man, all the evidence indicates they will get the same tumors as man."

The constitutional predisposition argument doesn't hold up, says Enstrom. "We simply can't find any other factor with as strong a relation to lung cancer as smoking." The fact is, he says, people who don't smoke rarely get lung cancer.

The tobacco industry's protestations are specious, say scientists. But worse, says Enstrom, "At home base is the point that people who don't smoke have better health. Ignoring that fact is irresponsible and callous."

6. A killer star
(272 words)

BERKELEY, Calif.—First, the bad news. Somewhere beyond the solar system is a death star that periodically wipes out most life on Earth. That is the conclusion of scientists who have pieced together data on mass extinctions and craters in Earth's crust.

The researchers say the star, dubbed Nemesis, is in a 28-million-year orbit around the sun and at one point passes close enough to disturb the Oort Cloud, a celestial repository of fledgling comets surrounding the solar system. The star's gravitational backwash sends thousands of comets falling into the inner solar system; roughly 25 of these hit Earth. The impact of the comets darkens the skies with dust, killing plant and animal life.

The scientists' speculations stem from a recent report that much of life on Earth suddenly disappears about every 26 million years. There is evidence that at least one such mass extinction—the disappearance of the dinosaurs 65 million years ago—occurred at the same time that the Earth collided with a comet or asteroid.

A comet shower can be triggered by a wayward star. But the scientists, one group from the University of California and the other from the University of Southwest Louisiana and Computer Sciences Corp. in Houston, say that because the extinctions occur at regular intervals, the comet showers must be caused by a star that is in orbit around the sun. Furthermore, the Berkeley group has found that the ages of craters scarring the Earth coincide with the times of the mass extinctions.

Now for the good news: The last extinction was 12 million years ago, so it will be another 14 million before Nemesis returns.

Reprinted by permission of SCIENCE 84 Magazine, © 1984 the American Association for the Advancement of Science.

7. From What Color Is Your Parachute (449 words)
by Richard Bolles

    Okay, this is it.
    You've been idly thinking about it, off and on, for
  some time now, wondering what it would be like.
To be earning your bread in the marketplace.
Or maybe you're already out there,
And the problem is choosing another career.
Anyhow, the moment of truth has arrived.
For one reason or another, you've got to get at it—
Go out, and look for a job.
You've heard of course, all the horror stories.
Of ex-executives working as doormen.
Of former college profs with two masters degrees
  working as countermen in a delicatessen.
And you wonder what lies in store for you.

    Of course, it may be that the problem is all solved.
    Maybe you're going to "drop out" and just go
      "do your own thing." The subsistence-survival game.
      Or, if not, maybe some friend has button-holed you
      and said, "Why not come and work for me?"
      So, your job-hunt ends before it begins.
        Or, it may be that you came into your present
        career after a full life doing something else, and
          You know you're welcome back there, anytime;
        Anytime, they said.
        And, assuming they meant it,
        no problem, right?
        So long as that's still what you want to do.
        But for the vast majority of us,
        that isn't how it goes.
        Not for us the Horatio Alger role;
        ah no! In retrospect it seems
      We play a kind of Don Quixote; and
      the job-hunt is our windmill.

Those who have gone the route before,
  all say the very same thing.
    This is how we go about it, when our time has come:
      We procrastinate,
        that's what we do.
        Busy winding things up, we say.
        Actually, if the truth were known,
          we're hoping for that miracle;
          you know the one:
            that if we just sit tight a little longer,
            we won't have to go job-hunting, no

the job will come hunting for us.
Right in the front door, it will come.
To show us we are destiny's favorites.
But, it doesn't. And of course,
eventually, we realize that time
and money
are beginning to run out.
Time to begin in earnest.
And all of our familiar friends immediately
are at our elbow, giving advice—
solicited or unsolicited, as to what we should do.
"Joe (Jean), I've always thought you would make a great teacher."
So we ask who they know
in the academic world,
and, armed with that name,
we go a-calling. Calling, and
sitting, cooling our heels
in the ante-room of the Dean's office,
until he asks, at last,
"And what can I do for you, Mr. (Miss)?"
We tell him, of course, that we're job-hunting,
"And one of my friends thought that you . . ."
Oops. We watch the face change,

8. Today's College Freshmen: Do They Pass the Test? (670 words)

Steps to improve the nation's high schools and tougher standards in colleges are beginning to pay off in higher student achievement on American campuses.

That is the conclusion of a recent College Board study and of a group of educators from colleges across the nation who were interviewed by *U.S. News & World Report*. They say that after years of failure by high schools to educate students properly, results of better schooling are becoming evident.

Nevertheless, weaknesses persist. One notable example: Many students still need remedial work in college to make up for deficiencies in their high-school education. Another: Poor study habits.

Over all, however, things are looking up. Here is how five top college educators size up the strengths and shortcomings of new students—and offer advice to young people preparing for college.

Newcomers 'Significantly Better Prepared"

Diether Haenicke, Provost and
Vice President for Academic Affairs,
Ohio State University, Columbus

Freshmen entering Ohio State today are significantly better prepared than they were five years ago. But that has not happened without a lot of prodding on our part and a joint effort between high schools and the college. Until this fall, any student who graduated from a high school in Ohio had access to any public institution in the state, as long as space was available. It was essentially an open-admission system. But we found that a large number of students required help in the basic subjects.

In 1978, 26 percent of our entering freshmen needed remedial mathematics—math on the ninth-grade level. A high percentage also needed remedial work in English. The college—and state taxpayers—were spending 1 million dollars a year providing remedial courses, for which students received no college credit. We also experienced a high dropout rate in the first year. We enrolled 7,700 freshmen in 1978, but only 75 percent of them were here a year later. In other words, we lost 25 percent of the freshman class, mostly because they could not keep up in their studies.

To reduce these problems, we began an intensive program in which our faculty went into junior high schools and tested students to alert them to what courses they should take in high school if they wanted to succeed in college. This program has lessened the need for remedial courses and cut the dropout rate. In 1983,

just under 19 percent of our freshmen needed remedial math. With a class of more than 7,000 freshmen, a 7 percent drop means a lot more students are better prepared.

More students are finishing their first year of college, as well. In 1982, we admitted 7,200 freshmen, and 80 percent were still here a year later. That is a 5 percent improvement and, on our large-number base, rather nice progress. We expect even greater improvement as a result of a new college-preparatory curriculum that we recommend for high school students. Starting with freshmen entering this fall, we recommend that no person come to college with fewer than four years of high-school-level English, three of math, two of science, two of a foreign language and one unit of visual or performing arts. A student who does not have these qualifications may be admitted but must make up the work during the summer or in the first year of college.

Already, students are rising to the challenge. In 1982, nearly 17 percent would not have met our new science recommendations. In 1984, only 4 percent are deficient.

Kids want to succeed in college. By raising our standards, we are not discouraging students from furthering their education. Instead, we are telling them: "We want you to come to college, but we want you to be successful. We don't want you to drop out and waste your resources, your time, your parents'—or the public's—money. The best advice we can give is to take these courses, because students who have done so have a much higher chance of success."

9. On the Trail of America's "Serial Killers" (981 words)

How to stop criminals who murder for no apparent reason? That's the task now facing police in many areas.

At a time when violent crime is dropping, one category of deceptively dangerous men—called serial killers—is causing alarm from coast to coast, with seemingly motiveless murders.

The growth in this brand of law-breaking is a glaring exception to a trend, confirmed in an April 19 report by the Federal Bureau of Investigation, of declining violent crime, which fell by 5 percent in 1983.

Still, nearly 20,000 Americans are murdered each year, and more of the crimes are going unsolved. There are more than 4,000 such unexplained cases recorded yearly—twice the 1970 total.

One key reason, authorities say, is a surge in the number of men roaming from state to state looking primarily for female and juvenile victims. "They are killing for the sake of killing, and the crimes are very difficult to solve," comments Director Alfred Regnery of the U.S. Office of Juvenile Justice and Delinquency Prevention.

One crime spree ended in mid-April when Christopher Wilder, wanted for eight murders or disappearances in eight states, was shot to death with his own gun during a scuffle with police in a small New Hampshire town.

Investigators said Wilder was just one on a long list of criminals who are responsible for strings of homicides. In other recent cases:

• Henry Lee Lcuas, a drifter sentenced to death April 13 for a Texas murder, said he killed 360 persons while he and another man traveled across the South.

• Arthur Bishop, a former Eagle Scout convicted in Salt Lake City of murdering five boys, is a suspect in similar cases in Utah and California.

• Gerald Stano, a computer operator with a history of mental problems, confessed to killing at least 41 women in Florida, New Jersey and Pennsylvania.

• At least 20 women, most of them prostitutes or runaways, have been found dead near a Seattle river. Their slayings are blamed on a man known only as the "Green River killer."

The phenomenon of serial killings has been recognized since a man dubbed Jack the Ripper murdered seven London prostitutes in 1888. A few spectacular one-man crime waves have occurred since then in the U.S., but only in recent years have law-enforcement authorities noticed the increase in what the FBI calls murders with "unknown motives."

Each case has its own peculiarities, but interviews by experts with more than 40 persons convicted in multiple-murder cases reveal common threads.

Typically, serial killers have a desire to dominate others. Their targets usually are women and children, whom they can overpower. The murders often are accompanied by sexual assaults; if the defendants are caught, they frequently are found awash in pornography.

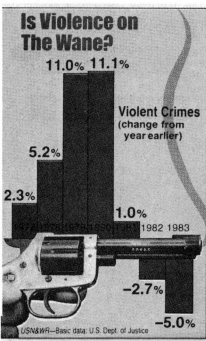

Is Violence on The Wane?

11.0% 11.1%

Violent Crimes (change from year earlier)

5.2%

2.3%

1.0%

1477 1978 1979 1980 1981 1982 1983

-2.7%

-5.0%

USN&WR—Basic data: U.S. Dept. of Justice

Some serial criminals are discovered to have set fires and tortured animals as youths, and many had been abused by their parents. "These victims later become victimizers," remarks Justice official Regnery.

What frightens many people about mass murderers is that despite mental aberrations that cause them to kill, they usually look and act normal. "They can deal well with society," says Robert Keppel, an investigator for the Washington State attorney general's office who has worked on 10 such cases. "They are not 'creatures' or 'animals' who can easily be identified."

In fact, assailants often befriend their victims. Wilder, a photographer, allegedly enticed many of the women he later killed or assaulted by suggesting that they be-

come fashion models and offering to take their pictures.

Some blame the mobility of U.S. society for making victims more available to murderers. "It's not unusual for people—especially if they're drug users—to just up and leave home," says Cmdr. Alfred Calhoun of the Ouachita Parish Sheriff's Office in Monroe, La. "Many become victims because they're vulnerable hitchhiking or wandering in deserted places."

As the toll of mysterious deaths accumulates, law enforcement is mounting an effort to identify and arrest serial murderers before their rampages go further.

Key clues at the scene. Although a series of killings gets attention when it is confined to one area, officials may be slow to notice crime patterns across state lines. To help overcome this problem, the Justice Department is setting up a computerized system at the FBI national training academy at Quantico, Va., that will list characteristics of all homicides with unknown motives.

"The crime scene itself often reveals a great deal about the personality of the killer," notes Roger Depue of the FBI's behavioral-science unit. "A homicide scene may portray evidence of hatred, rage and impulsivity or coolness, detachment and cunning."

This summer, police will be able to compare unusual deaths in their areas with those from other cities. "When officers see a bizarre crime scene, they should be able to call us for help, like a doctor might call Johns Hopkins University," says Depue.

The FBI already has compiled profiles of several types of repeat criminals. Analysts study data on more than 200 suspects each year. In 1982, they helped to locate or prosecute persons responsible for 50 killings and 126 rapes.

Some state and local authorities are taking matters into their own hands. Louisiana officials have hosted two conferences in recent months in which more than 150 investigators from two dozen states gathered to compare notes on serial killings from their areas. Similar meetings are planned later this year in Georgia and Wisconsin.

The U.S. also is commissioning research that might demonstrate the need for earlier treatment of problems such as child abuse that could contribute to a serial murderer's personality.

In the meantime, unprovoked crime remains rampant. A new compilation from the U.S. Bureau of Justice Statistics shows that despite a large number of offenses involving friends and relatives, nearly two thirds of violent crime is the work of assailants with no previous relationship to their victims.

by TED GEST

10. And a Child Shall Lead Them—Astray (568 words)

From the outside, the two-story house in Columbus, Ohio, looks much like the other residences in the quiet, middle-class neighborhood. But according to the Resch family, who lives there, and to newspapers and television stations across the country, what went on inside the house early in March was quite extraordinary—if not downright paranormal. Whenever the Resch's foster daughter Tina, 14, was around, telephones began to fly, lamps toppled, and glasses smashed against walls.

To harried Mrs. Joan Resch, who talks about "the force," this was obviously a case for Mike Harden, a columnist for the Columbus *Dispatch;* in more peaceful times he had written a column about the family, who over the years has taken in more than 250 foster children. After seeing a coffee cup crash near Tina, Harden called in Fred Shannon, a *Dispatch* photographer, to capture the proceedings on film. More strange things happened, but never when Shannon had his camera pointed at Tina. So, he recalls, "I lowered my camera and turned my head ninety degrees to the left. When I saw something begin to move, I snapped a picture."

Shannon eventually exposed most of a roll of film. When he returned to the *Dispatch,* his editors picked a frame that showed Tina rearing back in fright as a telephone flew by her. (Among the rejected shots was one showing Tina's arm in what resembled a big league pitcher's follow-through.) The picture appeared on the front page the next day over a story by Harden containing such passages as this: "Small objects in the house had begun to move unaided by human touch: candles, lamps, wall hangings. Upstairs, the shower began running. The hands of the clock began turning much faster."

By the next day the picture and Tina's story had appeared in newspapers across the country, distributed by the Associated Press in a straightforward, unquestioning way. Reporters converged on the house, and the family allowed Tina (who has seen the film *Poltergeist*) to be interviewed at a crowded press conference in the living room. Nothing untoward happened during the session, but as the crew from Channel 6 in Columbus was preparing to depart, they happened to leave a running camera unattended. The camera caught Tina pulling a lamp over onto herself, and the tape was broadcast the next day in slow motion. Tina's explanation, to the relief of the press, was that she had merely been joking. Although the Cleveland *Plain Dealer* mentioned that incident, the same article led off with a report that, on another occasion, "the lamp on the end table lifted itself slightly into the air and smacked her in the head."

The strange goings-on in Columbus attracted the attention of Bill Roll, director of the Psychical Research Center in Chapel Hill, North Carolina, who flew to Columbus and was invited into the house. He claimed that he witnessed a bar of soap falling into a bathtub, a picture falling off a wall, and his tape recorder flying a distance of seven feet. Although he conceded that he was not observing under "controlled conditions," he concluded that it looked very much as if Tina had demonstrated genuine RSPK (repeated spontaneous psychokinesis). To Skeptical Eye, it sounds more like TMFPP (Tina making fools of the press and paranormalists).

11. (An Introduction from) The Peter Principle (608 words)

by Raymond Hull

AS AN author and journalist, I have had exceptional opportunities to study the workings of civilized society. I have investigated and written about government, industry, business, education and the arts. I have talked to, and listened carefully to, members of many trades and professions, people of lofty, middling and lowly stations.

I have noticed that, with few exceptions, men bungle their affairs. Everywhere I see incompetence rampant, incompetence triumphant.

I have seen a three-quarter-mile-long highway bridge collapse and fall into the sea because, despite checks and double-checks, someone had botched the design of a supporting pier.

I have seen town planners supervising the development of a city on the flood plain of a great river, where it is certain to be periodically inundated.

Lately I read about the collapse of three giant cooling towers at a British power-station: they cost a million dollars each, but were not strong enough to withstand a good blow of wind.

This incompetence would be annoying enough if it were confined to public works, politics, space travel and such vast, remote fields of human endeavor. But it is not. It is close at hand, too—an ever-present, pestiferous nuisance.

As I write this page, the woman in the next apartment is talking on the telephone. I can hear every word she says. It is 10 P.M. and the man in the apartment on the other side of me has gone to bed early with a cold. I hear his intermittent cough. When he turns on his bed I hear the springs squeak. I don't live in a cheap rooming house: this is an expensive, modern, concrete high-rise apartment block. What's the matter with the people who designed and built it?

The other day a friend of mine bought a hacksaw, took it home and began to cut an iron bolt. At his second stroke, the saw blade snapped, and the adjustable joint of the frame broke so that it could not be used again.

Last week I wanted to use a tape recorder on the stage of a new high-school auditorium. I could get no power for the machine. The building engineer told me that, in a year's occupancy, he had been unable to find a switch that would turn on current in the base plugs on stage. He was beginning to think they were not wired up at all.

This morning I set out to buy a desk lamp. In a large furniture and appliance store I found a lamp that I liked. The salesman was going to wrap it, but I asked him to test it first. (I'm getting cautious nowadays.) He was obviously unused to testing electrical equipment, because it took him a long time to find a socket. Eventually he plugged the lamp in, then could not switch it on! He tried another lamp of the same style: that would not switch on, either. The whole consignment had defective switches. I left.

I recently ordered six hundred square feet of fiber glass insulation for a cottage I am renovating. I stood over the clerk at the order desk to make sure she got the quantity right. In vain! The building supply firm billed me for seven hundred square feet, and delivered nine hundred square feet!

Education, often touted as a cure for all ills, is apparently no cure for incompetence. Incompetence runs riot in the halls of education. One high-school graduate in three cannot read at normal fifth-grade level. It is now commonplace for colleges to be giving reading lessons to freshmen. In some colleges, *twenty percent* of freshmen cannot read well enough to understand their textbooks!

Abridged from Introduction by Raymond Hull in THE PETER PRINCIPLE by Dr. Laurence J. Peter and Raymond Hull. Copyright © 1969 by William Morrow and Company, Inc. By permission of the publisher.

12. How Safe Is Our Food Supply?
(330 words)

by Thomas H. Jukes, PhD

To judge from the fuss being made by "consumerists" in books, magazines, newspapers, and on the radio and television, we are in tremendous danger from our food supply. We are told that some of the substances added to foods or present as contaminants may give us cancer. Prominent in the list are nitrosamines, saccharin, food colorings, and diethylstilbestrol (DES). If we escape these dreadful intruders, we are warned that saturated fatty acids in our foods can cause cancer of the large bowel, and we are advised to devour large amounts of wheat bran to stave off this fate.

However, after eating three meals a day for a good many years, my own opinion is that food is one of the safest things that I encounter in my everyday life. Our food supply in the United States is in its golden age of safety, adequacy, variety, and abundance. It has reached this stage first as a result of a free and open marketplace in which producers and processors compete for the attention of consumers and second, because of the flowering of science and technology during the past century. These facts are evident to anyone who compares the contents of a modern supermarket with the flyblown grocery shop of past years with its cracker-barrel, salt pork, rancid lard, and wormy apples, or with the meager, contaminated, and nutritionally inadequate diet that has to suffice for the majority of the world's population. The only really important problem with the diet of the United States is that people eat too much.

The history of our species shows that we have had always to walk a tightrope, as it were, between toxicity and adequacy of our daily diet until recent years, when the tightrope has become a fairly broad pathway. Among the many scientific advances are the discoveries of the essential vitamins, minerals, and essential amino acids. These discoveries have led to great reductions in many nutritional-deficiency diseases, such as rickets and beriberi, in underdeveloped countries.

From the *Archives of Internal Medicine,* May 1978, Vol. 138. Copyright 1978, American Medical Association. Reprinted by permission.

13. Format Fever (486 words)

ONE OF THE MOST POIGNANT MOMENTS IN radio history was May 10, 1982—the day the music died on WABC-AM, once the mightiest rock music station in the nation, as it surrendered to the creeping domination of FM music radio by switching to all-talk. To many in the industry, WABC's chin music sounded like nothing more than a funeral march for AM as we knew and loved it for half a century.

In a sense this was true. AM was in fact on its deathbed, the victim of poor fidelity and a stuffy image, but it has since exhibited encouraging signs of reviving, fighting back with new formats. At the same time, new formats have also been the salvation of FM stations, themselves feeling the pressure of new competition.

The history of radio is the history of formats. With the rise of FM in the mid-Sixties, the six or so standards—rock, adult, classical, beautiful, black, and country—were split into subcategories: rock broke up into adult contemporary, album-oriented-rock, contemporary hit, and oldie; country into hard-core and crossover. Talk stations divvied into news, news-talk, and telephone-talk. Even beautiful music, once just the sweet strains of the Longine Symphonette Society, split into young/old and vocal/instrumental variations in order to find specific new audiences.

These organisms are dividing yet again: The album-oriented-rock format alone is splitting into so many distinct subcategories—techno-pop, modern rock, eclectic, neoprogressive, and so on—that the umbrella term *AOR* is already obsolete. Two beautiful-music stations are playing only love songs; black-oriented stations now specialize in funk, rap, soul, and urban contemporary; and in the crowded area of adult-contemporary music, stations are experimenting with shades of "hard" and "soft" in an effort to capture the ever-elusive forty-year-old pop-music fan.

AM stations, now attracting fewer than 38 percent of all listeners, are converting rapidly to formats that do not necessarily demand high fidelity. That's the reason we're hearing, for instance, so many radio psychologists dispensing chipper advice. Meanwhile, at least two all-comedy stations have already premiered, one AM station in Texas is going with wall-to-wall Beatles, and sports play-by-play is growing impressively on AM stations all over.

Targeting a small segment of the audience is called narrowcasting. Listeners like it because highly specialized radio stations give them more control over what they hear, but the real reason it is so popular is that advertisers *love* it. With narrowcasting, advertising efficiency goes way up as overall costs go down. Diversification is the goal of cable too, but the costs of programs and delivery are comparatively so low in radio broadcasting that the audio medium ought to be able to beat out video by several years. We are approaching the unstated goal of all radio programmers: to create a station aimed so perfectly that the listener will no longer have to wait, ever, for the song that he wants to hear.

From Esquire Magazine, March 1984. Reprinted by permission.

14. Over-Generalizing (449 words)
STUART CHASE

One swallow does not make a summer, nor can two or three cases often support a dependable generalization. Yet all of us, including the most polished eggheads, are constantly falling into this mental mantrap. It is the commonest, probably the most seductive, and potentially the most dangerous, of all the fallacies.

You drive through a town and see a drunken man on the sidewalk. A few blocks further on you see another. You turn to your companion: "Nothing but drunks in this town!" Soon you are out in the country, bowling along at fifty. A car passes you as if you were parked. On a curve a second whizzes by. Your companion turns to you: "All the drivers in this state are crazy!" Two thumping generalizations, each built on two cases. If we stop to think, we usually recognize the exaggeration and the unfairness of such generalizations. Trouble comes when we do not stop to think—or when we build them on a prejudice.

This kind of reasoning has been around for a long time. Aristotle was aware of its dangers and called it "reasoning by example," meaning too few examples. What it boils down to is failing to count your swallows before announcing that summer is here. Driving from my home to New Haven the other day, a distance of about forty miles, I caught myself saying: "Every time I look around I see a new ranch-type house going up." So on the return trip I counted them; there were exactly five under construction. And how many times had I "looked around"? I suppose I had glanced to right and left—as one must at side roads and so forth in driving—several hundred times.

In this fallacy we do not make the error, developed in Chapter 4, of neglecting facts altogether and rushing immediately to the level of opinion. We start at the fact level properly enough, but *we do not stay there*. A case or two and up we go to a rousing over-simplification about drunks, speeders, ranch-style houses—or, more seriously, about foreigners, Negroes, labor leaders, teen-agers.

Over-generalizing takes many forms. It crops out in personal thinking and conversations as above. It is indispensable to those who compose epigrams and wisecracks, and most critics and reviewers find it very handy. It is standard for columnists and commentators who try to compress the complicated news stories of the day "into a nutshell." Newspaper headlines are a continuing exhibit of over-generalizing, but more from typographical necessity than deliberate intent. Cartoonists are under continual temptation. Those persons who go about scenting plots and conspiracies in the most innocent happenings are confirmed addicts, and so are those who follow esoteric cults of all varieties.

Woodrow Ohlsen and Frank L. Hammond, "Over Generalizing—Fallacy Number One" from *From Paragraph to Essay*. Copyright © 1963 Charles Scribner's Sons. Reprinted with the permission of Charles Scribner's Sons.

15. PRACTICAL MATTERS
What to Do About Soap Ends (277 words)

This is admittedly not a problem qualitatively on the order of what to do about the proliferation of nuclear weaponry, but quantitatively it disturbs a great deal of Mankind—all those millions, in fact, who've ever used a bar of soap—except, of course, me. I've solved the problem of what to do about those troublesome, wasteful, messy little soap ends, and I'm ready now to deliver my solution to a grateful world.

The solution depends on a fact not commonly known, which I discovered in the shower. Archimedes made his great discovery about displacement ("Eureka!" and all that) in the bathtub, but I made mine in the shower. It is not commonly known that if, when you soap yourself, you hold *the same side* of the bar of soap cupped in the palm of your hand, that side will, after a few days, become curved and rounded, while the side of the bar you're soaping yourself *with* will become flat. (In between showers or baths, leave the bar curved side down so it won't stick to whatever it's resting on.) When the bar diminishes sufficiently, the flat side can be pressed onto a new bar of soap and will adhere sufficiently overnight to become, with the next day's use, a just slightly oversize new bar, ready to be treated in the same way as the one that came before it, in perpetuity, one bar after another, down through the length of your days on earth, with never a nasty soap end to trouble you ever again. Eureka, and now on to those nuclear weapons. Man is at his best, I feel, when in his problem-solving mode.

—L. R. H.

BY BOB SPITZ

16. OVERDOING IT (363 words)

Sometimes too much exercise can be worse than none at all

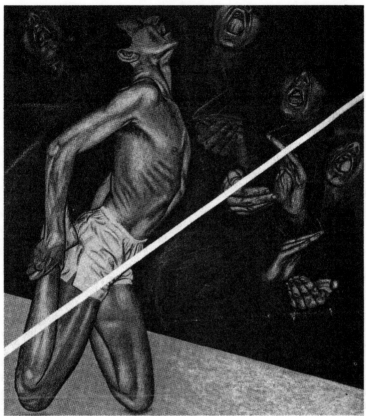

MY FRIENDS think that I am falling apart. It is an allegation I tend to deny, though from the physical evidence I'm forced to admit they have a pretty good case. First there was the hamstring I pulled a few years ago while beating out a grounder to third base. Then a pinched nerve in my foot kept me off skis and skates for two seasons. Daily squash matches exacerbated that injury, compounding it with the beginnings of a tremendous lower-back pain. And lately my foray into jogging has laden my ankles with crippling pain. Injuries aside, my doctor claims I'm in excellent health. "You're just overdoing it," he says.

Is he serious? Me?—prospective swimming ace, speed skater, and junk-ball pitcher—overdoing it? Just overdoing it? The pronouncement sounded too anemic to suit my self-image, too unathletic.

Still, my mirror betrays me as a beleaguered jock. A victim of great expectations, I push on past the rigors of a many-tiered exercise program, yearning to fulfill my promise. I keep driving a young man's body with the dauntless spirit of a teenager, and I'm grinding away at the gears.

No one warned me when I was a sports tyro that one day in the not-too-distant future I'd have to slacken the pace. And it seems that I'm not the only one who missed out on that advice.

Most people I know who work out regularly see themselves as an incarnation of some Olympic medalist hell-bent on immortality. Nightly, after work, they transform their bodies into human Veg-O-Matics: bending, stretching, chopping, slicing, dicing, and grinding what's left of themselves into a tortured mass of muscle. Not all that surprisingly, they constitute the same group whose bodies look like derelict lab specimens: their bones ache, arms bruise, feet swell, joints stiffen, knees dislocate, all while they contemplate tomorrow's grueling regimen.

Are our bodies worse for the wear? The answer is a resounding yes. Overdoing it not only wears out the parts, it also places us in direct violation of the Primary Law of Biofitness: Something's gotta give. And that something—our body—always does.

Reprinted from *Esquire*, March 1984.

17. Aspects of the Self: Names, Values, and Self-Concept (440 words)

ALICE:	Must a name mean something?
HUMPTY-DUMPTY:	Of course it must. . . . My name means the shape I am. . . . With a name like yours, you might be any shape, almost.

Lewis Carroll, Through the Looking Glass

What's in a name? Possibly a great deal. The voyages of the *Starship Enterprise* were more dynamic with Captain Kirk and Mr. Spock than they would have been with Captain Milquetoast and Mr. Anderson. The *Reggie* candybar seemed to provide more quick energy than the *Reginald* would have. Marilyn Monroe was sexier than Norma Jean Baker. "Dr. J" is a wizard on the basketball court; Julius Erving sounds more like a lawyer. Richard Starkey is a factory worker in Liverpool, but Ringo Starr is, well, a star.

What we label ourselves can reflect our attitudes about ourselves. Are you a Bob or a Robert? An Elizabeth or a Betty? Shakespeare wrote that a rose by any other name would smell as sweet, but perhaps a rose by the name of skunkweed would impress us as smelling just plain awful.

Names also influence our self-identities. Eric Berne (1976b) wrote that the names parents give us often reflect what they expect us to become:

> Charles and Frederick were kings and emperors. A boy who is steadfastly called Charles or Frederick by his mother, and insists that his associates call him that, lives a different life style from one who is commonly called Chuck or Fred, while Charlie and Freddie are likely to be horses of still another color. (p. 162)

Berne gives us another example, names of two famous neurologists, H. Head and W. R. Brain.

Psychologists have found that different names give rise to different expectations. In a British study, John received high ratings on kindness and trustworthiness. Tonys were sociable, Agneses old, and both Agneses and Matildas unattractive. Robins impressed raters as being bright and young.

Unusual names may create childhood problems but seem to be linked to success in adulthood. In an American study, men with names like David, John, Michael, and Robert were rated as better, stronger, and more active than men with names like Ian, Dale, and Raymond (Marcus, 1976). Children with common names tend to be more popular (McDavid & Harari, 1966). But college professors and upper-level army brass frequently have unusual names: *Omar* Bradley, *Dwight* Eisenhower. There are high frequencies of unique, even odd, names in *Who's Who*. In a survey of 11,000 North Carolina high school students (Zweigenhaft, 1977), boys and girls with unusual first names had more than their share of academic achievements. In a related study, no differences in personality were found between Wesleyan men with common or unusual names. But women with unusual names scored more optimally on several personality scales of the California Psychological Inventory (Zweigenhaft et al., 1980).

18. The Challenges of Life (448 words)

Long ago and far away our universe began with a "big bang" that sent countless atoms and other particles hurling into every corner of space. For 15 to 20 billion years, galaxies and solar systems have been condensing from immense gas clouds, sparkling for some aeons, then winking out. Human beings have evolved only recently, on an unremarkable rock, circling an average star in a typical, spiral-shaped galaxy.

Since the beginning of time, the universe has been in flux—changing. Early forms of life were challenged by a changing climate, the appearance of new species, eruptions, and earthquakes. Some creatures adapted to these challenges by evolution or by learning new patterns of behavior. Others have not met the challenges and have become extinct, falling back into the distant mists of time. Because of our unique capacity for adjustment, human beings have been most successful at meeting these challenges.

Still, at first our survival on planet Earth was far from guaranteed. We had to fight predators like the leopard. We had to forage across parched lands for food. We may have gone to war with other humanlike creatures in order to compete for land and food. Through all this, we prevailed. Only a few hundred years ago the Black Death plague wiped out many millions of us. But the human species survived. And prospered. Many millions of us still go to bed hungry at night, but most of us who live in the United States and other developed nations no longer need to worry about having enough to eat nor about clothing ourselves through the bleakest winters. Those of us who have prospered are more concerned about overeating than the prospect of starvation. In a sense, we have been so successful that many of us worry about whether we shall find self-fulfillment through our work, rather than whether we shall find and keep a job. Education and increased affluence have led many of us to become concerned with the meaning of life, rather than whether we shall manage to survive.

Still, the times change and do challenge us. While Americans once assumed that their children's standard of living would exceed their own, a recent poll (Watts, 1981) shows that the possibility of a lower standard of living is the most frequently mentioned concern of Americans today. But even though Americans are concerned about the economy, their general level of optimism is rebounding to that of the mid-1960s, when inflation was low, we were at peace, and energy was cheap and plentiful. In fact, younger Americans, aged 18 to 29, are as optimistic about the future as they were in the 1960s (Watts, 1981), suggesting that they see themselves capable of meeting contemporary challenges and growing from the encounter.

Many of today's challenges are familiar, including emotional problems like anxiety and interpersonal challenges like social shyness and the development of intimate relationships. But other challenges have a contemporary ring to them. These include the challenges of changing roles, technology, resources, and a changing society.

From ADJUSTMENT AND GROWTH, Second Edition by Spencer A. Tathus and Jeffrey S. Nevid. Copyright © 1983 by CBS College Publishing; copyright © 1980 by Holt, Rinehart and Winston. Reprinted by permission of CBS College Publishing.

19. A POLICE SHOOT FOR SCREEN CREDIT (426 words)

By WILLIAM OVEREND

Los Angeles Times Service

LOS ANGELES—A badge and a gun are all that's needed on most police departments. But on the Los Angeles Police Department, it helps to have a good agent too.

Over the years, LAPD officers have written best-selling novels and books, movies and television shows, and even some poetry. It's not always cops-and-robbers stuff, either. A former LAPD officer created *Star Trek*.

The result is that LAPD has what no other police department has had or possibly ever wanted to have—a literary tradition.

Many people are at least vaguely aware that Jack Webb's *Dragnet* helped make the LAPD famous, but they don't realize that hundreds of television police shows since have been written by LAPD officers who got their start with Webb.

They may know the story of how ex-cop Joseph Wambaugh wrote the first three of his books and novels while still a member of the LAPD, upsetting some of the department brass while he was at it.

But they're not so familiar with the story of how Gene Roddenberry, the creator of *Star Trek*, joined the LAPD before Wambaugh came along to get some street experience for his subsequent career as a television and movie writer.

It's been Roddenberry's secret over the years that the character of Spock, the pointy-eared Vulcan science officer on the USS Enterprise, was modeled in part on former LAPD Chief William H. Parker.

It was also Roddenberry, Parker's speech writer in the early 1950s, who wrote most of the chapters in *Parker on Police*, a book regarded as a classic text on police philosophy and credited to Parker without mention of Roddenberry's role.

Today there's a new generation of LAPD writers cranking out screenplays and toiling over novels. There are vice cops and narcotics officers and patrolmen writing for the movies and television, plus a flock of retired cop writers equally busy at work on everything from murder stories to their own autobiographies.

There's even an Academy Award winner working in the LAPD public affairs office. He's Sandy Barnett, 75, a civilian employee of the department and a former newspaper reporter who won his Oscar in 1964 for the best original story written directly for the screen. It was *Father Goose*, starring Cary Grant.

The lucrative financial rewards that have come for many of LAPD's writers—they earn a minimum of $13,000 for a one-hour television show often written in a week, small fortunes if they get anywhere close to Wambaugh and Roddenberry status—tempt officers regardless of rank.

Reading Rate Chart

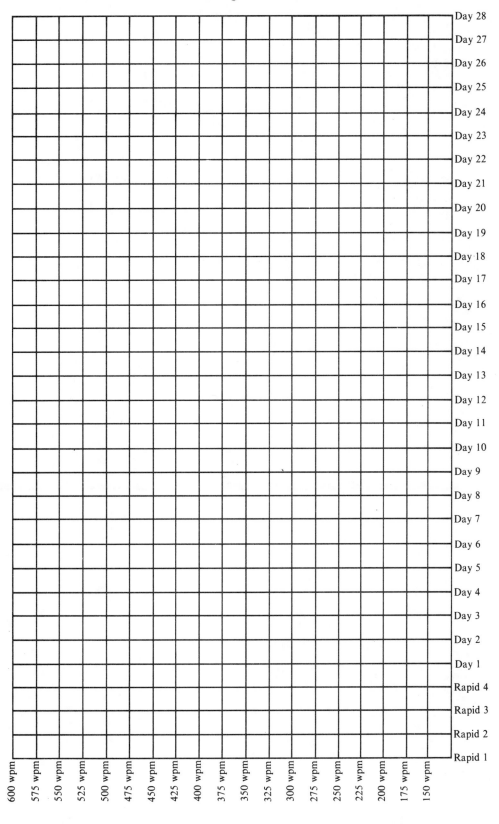

Day 28
Day 27
Day 26
Day 25
Day 24
Day 23
Day 22
Day 21
Day 20
Day 19
Day 18
Day 17
Day 16
Day 15
Day 14
Day 13
Day 12
Day 11
Day 10
Day 9
Day 8
Day 7
Day 6
Day 5
Day 4
Day 3
Day 2
Day 1
Rapid 4
Rapid 3
Rapid 2
Rapid 1

600 wpm 575 wpm 550 wpm 525 wpm 500 wpm 475 wpm 450 wpm 425 wpm 400 wpm 375 wpm 350 wpm 325 wpm 300 wpm 275 wpm 250 wpm 225 wpm 200 wpm 175 wpm 150 wpm

Appendix B
Mini-Dictionary

Using This Dictionary

A dictionary is one of the few books you use today that you will continue to find useful throughout your life. It is useful at school and at home. You might hear an unfamiliar word used on a television show. You might read a newspaper with articles, ads, and features similar to those used in the following lesson section, and need to look up certain words. Knowing how to find information about words in your dictionary is a skill you will always need.

The words in a dictionary are arranged systematically in a way that makes them easy to find. All words are in one alphabetical list. A dictionary tells you how to spell the word, how to pronounce it, and what it means. It may also tell you where the word came from.

Guide Words

Two guide words are printed at the top of every page in this dictionary. All the main entries that fall between these two words in alphabetical order are on the page.

Homographs

Sometimes two or more words have the same spelling, although their origins and meanings are different. Such words are called homographs. In this dictionary, each homograph is entered separately and is followed by a small raised number called a *superscript:*

van¹ (van), *n.* the front of an army, fleet, or other advancing group. [short for *vanguard*]
van² (van), *n.* **1** a large enclosed truck or wagon for moving furniture or household goods. **2** a small, enclosed truck designed for light hauling or for recreational use. **3** BRITISH. a railroad baggage car. [short for *caravan*]

Most homographs are pronounced alike. However, there are some with different pronunciations:

vi o la¹ (vē ō′lə), *n.* a stringed musical instrument like a violin, but somewhat larger and lower in pitch; a tenor or alto violin. [< Italian]
vi o la² (vī′ə lə, vī ō′lə), *n.* **1** any of several hybrid garden violets resembling the pansy but with a more delicate and uniform coloring of the flowers. **2** any violet. [< New Latin < Latin, violet]

Inflected Forms

A reviewer for the book section of a newspaper is writing about the plot of a historical novel set in the Middle Ages, and needs this information:

What is the plural form of *knight-errant*?
How do you spell the superlative of *dizzy*?
Is the past tense of *regret* spelled with one *t* or two *t's*?

Answers to these questions can be found in your dictionary, although the words you need are not main entries. They are inflected forms of words which are listed as main entries, and such forms are included in the entry for the root word.

Inflected forms are listed near the beginning of the entry, directly after the part-of-speech label. They are printed in boldface type.

knight-er rant (nīt′er′ənt), *n., pl.* **knights-er rant**. . . .
diz zy (diz′ē), *adj.,* **-zi er, -zi est,** *v.,* **-zied, -zy ing**. . . .
re gret (ri gret′), *v.,* **-gret ted, -gret ting,** *n.* . . . .

Inflected forms of verbs are regularly formed by adding *-ed* for the past tense and past participle and *-ing* for the present participle. Plural forms of nouns regularly add *-s* or *-es* to the root word. Comparative forms of adjectives and adverbs regularly add *-er,* and superlative forms add *-est,* to the root word. This dictionary does not list such regularly inflected forms.

Whenever there is any change from the regular, this dictionary includes the inflected forms. In addition, completely irregular forms are listed separately as main entries.

came (kām), *v.* pt. of **come.** *I came to school late this morning.*
ox en (ok′sən), *n.* pl. of **ox.**
slid (slid), *v.* pt. and a pp. of **slide.**

Variant inflected forms. Some nouns have more than one plural form, and some verbs have variant inflected forms. In such cases, the dictionary includes both forms. They are equally acceptable.

ap pen dix (ə pen′diks), *n., pl.* **-dix es** or **-di ces**. . . .
kid nap (kid′nap), *v.,* **-napped, -nap ping** or **-naped, -naping,** . . . .
kill deer (kil′dir′), *n., pl.* **-deers** or **-deer**. . . .
ser aph (ser′əf), *n., pl.* **-aphs** or **-a phim**. . . .

Run-on Entries

Many derivatives formed by adding suffixes to other words are found at the end of the entry for the root word. They are divided into syllables, and are printed in boldface type. Such a word is called a *run-on entry.*

can tan ker ous (kan tang′kər əs), *adj.* hard to get along with because of a nature that is ready to make trouble and oppose anything suggested; ill-natured; quarrelsome. [Middle English *contecker* contentious person < *conteck* strife, quarreling < Anglo-French] **—can tan′ker ous ly,** *adv.* **—can tan′ker ousness,** *n.*
-ness, *suffix added to adjectives to form nouns.* **1** quality or condition of being ___ : *Preparedness = condition of being prepared.* **2** ___ action; ___ behavior: *Carefulness = careful action; careful behavior.* [Old English *-ness, -niss*]

In order to get the meaning of a run-on entry, you combine the meaning of the entry word with the meaning of the suffix. Read the entries printed above, and you will see that the meaning of *cantankerousness* is "quality or condition of being hard to get along with" or "ill-natured behavior."

Idioms

Many phrases or expressions in English cannot be understood from the ordinary meanings of the words that form them.

"This job is right *up my alley,* and I love being able to *bring home the bacon,*" said Jim Dandy, guitarist with the new group, Birds of Passage.

Such expressions are called idioms. This dictionary lists them under the most important word. Here are the listings for the idioms above:

al ley[1] (al′ē), *n., pl.* **-leys. 1** a narrow back street in a city or town, especially one running between rows of buildings. **2** BRITISH. a narrow street. **3** path in a park or garden, bordered by trees, shrubbery, or bushes. **4** a long, narrow lane along which the ball is rolled in bowling; bowling alley. **5** Often, **alleys,** *pl.* building having a number of alleys for bowling. **6 up one's alley,** INFORMAL. fitting in with one's skills or interests: *Model airplanes are right up her alley.* [< Old French *alee* a going < *aler* go]

ba con (bā′kən), *n.* **1** salted and smoked meat from the back and sides of a hog. **2 bring home the bacon, a** succeed; win. **b** earn a living. [< Middle French < Germanic]

Sometimes an entry includes several part-of-speech listings. In such cases an idiom is placed with the part of speech used in the idiom.

plank (plangk), *n.* **1** a long, flat piece of sawed timber thicker than a board, especially one more than two inches (five centimeters) thick and four inches (ten centimeters) wide. **2** article or feature of the platform of a political party or other organization. **3 walk the plank,** be put to death by being forced to walk off a plank extending from a ship's side over the water. Pirates used to make their prisoners do this. —*v.t.* **1** cover or furnish with planks. **2** cook or serve on a board, often with a decorative border of vegetables and potatoes: *planked steak.* **3 plank down,** INFORMAL. put down or pay then and there: *plank down a package. She planked down her money.* [< Old North French < Latin *planca*]

When there are many idioms, they are placed in an alphabetical list at the end of the other definitions.

foot (fut), *n., pl.* **feet** (or **foot** for 7), *v.* —*n.* **1** the end part of a leg; part that a person, animal, or thing stands on. **2** an organ present in some invertebrates, especially the muscular, ventral protuberance of the mollusks, used for locomotion. **3** part opposite the head of something; end toward which the feet are put: *the foot of a bed.* **4** the lowest or underlying part; bottom; base: *the foot of a hill.* **5** part of a stocking that covers the foot. **6** infantrymen; infantry. **7** unit of length, equal to twelve inches: *six feet high, a six-foot log.* See **measure** for table. **8** one of the units of rhythm into which a line of poetry is divided. This line has four feet: "The boy | stood on | the burn | ing deck." **9** lower edge or bottom of a sail. **10** thing or part resembling an animal's foot: *the foot of a chair.*
on foot, standing or walking.
put one's best foot forward, INFORMAL. do one's best.
put one's foot down, make up one's mind and act firmly.
put one's foot in it, INFORMAL. be extremely tactless in words or actions; blunder.
under foot, in the way.
with one foot in the grave, almost dead; dying.
—*v.t.* **1** walk: *We footed the whole ten miles.* **2** add up: *Foot this column of numbers.* **3** INFORMAL. pay (a bill, etc.). **4** walk or dance on; set foot on; tread. **5** make or renew the foot of (a stocking, etc.). —*v.i.* Also, **foot it. a** go on foot; walk. **b** dance. **c** move fast; hurry.

How to Use and Understand the Pronunciations

Words would be easy to pronounce if each letter of the alphabet represented only one sound. However, that is not possible. The English language has more than 40 sounds, and its alphabet has only 26 letters.

Since the spelling of a word can mislead you as to how it is pronounced, the dictionary includes pronunciations for each word. The pronunciation is given in parentheses directly after the entry word.

gnat (nat) **kneel** (nēl) **run** (run)

Teach Yourself

1. Pronounce each of the words above. How many different sounds do you hear in each word?
2. Look at the pronunciation symbols in parentheses after each word. Is the number of symbols the same as the number of sounds you heard?
3. Is one of the symbols used in more than one word? What is that symbol?
4. The pronunciation symbol always stands for the same sound. Write the three words above. In each word, underline the letter or letters used to spell the sound that appears in all the words.

The Pronunciation Key

The 41 symbols used in this dictionary to represent the speech sounds of English appear in the full pronunciation key opposite the inside cover at the front and back of this book.

Each symbol represents a sound. The words printed after each symbol contain the sound it represents. More than half of the symbols are letters of the alphabet, printed in regular type. The five vowel letters (a, e, i, o, u) are used to represent the short vowel sounds. The consonant letters (except *c, q,* and *x*) are used to represent single consonant sounds.

For easy reference, the following short pronunciation key is placed at the top of each right-hand page.

a hat	i it	oi oil	ch child	a in about
ā age	ī ice	ou out	ng long	e in taken
ä far	o hot	u cup	sh she	ə = i in pencil
e let	ō open	u put	th thin	o in lemon
ē equal	ô order	ü rule	TH then	u in circus
er term			zh measure	< = derived from

A

ab do men (ab′də mən, ab dō′mən), *n.* **1** the lower part of the body of mammals between the thorax and the pelvis, containing the major digestive organs. **2** the posterior of the three parts of the body of an insect or a crustacean. [< Latin]

ab er ra tion (ab′ə rā′shən), *n.* **1** a deviating from the right path or usual course of action. **2** an abnormal structure or development. **3** a temporary mental disorder. **4** failure of a lens or mirror to bring to a single focus the rays of light coming from one point. Aberration causes a blurred image or an image with a colored rim. **5** a slight periodic variation in the apparent position of a heavenly body, caused by the movement of the earth while the light from the heavenly body travels through the telescope. [< Latin *aberrationem* < *ab-* away + *errare* wander]

a buse (*v.* ə byüz′; *n.* ə byüs′), *v.,* **a bused, a bus ing,** *n.* —*v.t.* **1** use wrongly; make improper use of; misuse; *to abuse a privilege.* **2** treat roughly or cruelly; mistreat: *to abuse a dog by beating it.* **3** use harsh and insulting language about or to; revile: *The candidates abused each other.* —*n.* **1** a wrong or improper use; misuse: *an abuse of civil rights.* **2** rough or cruel treatment: *abuse of a helpless prisoner.* **3** a bad practice or custom: *Slavery is an abuse.* **4** harsh and insulting language. [< Old French *abuser* < Latin *abusum* misused < *ab-* away + *uti* to use] **-a bus′er,** *n.*

ac ces si ble (ak ses′ə bəl), *adj.* **1** easy to reach, enter, or use; convenient or attainable: *A telephone should be put where it will be accessible.* **2** that can be entered or reached: *This rocky island is accessible only by helicopter.* **3** capable of being influenced; susceptible (*to*): *An open-minded person is accessible to reason.* **4** that can be obtained; available: *Not many facts about the case were accessible.* **-ac ces′si ble ness,** *n.* **-ac ces′si bly,** *adv.*

a cous tic (ə kü′stik), *adj.* **1** having to do with the sense or the organs of hearing. **2** having to do with the science of sound. **3** directed, controlled, or actuated by sound waves: *an acoustic mine.* **4** de-

From SCOTT, FORESMAN ADVANCED DICTIONARY by E. L. Thorndike and Clarence L. Barnhart. Copyright © 1983, 1979 by Scott, Foresman and Company. Reprinted by permission.

signed to absorb or reduce noise: *a ceiling of acoustic tile.* [< Greek *akoustikos* < *akouein* hear] —**a cous′ti cal ly,** *adv.*

ac ro nym (ak′rə nim), *n.* word formed from the first letters or syllables of other words, such as UNESCO (United Nations Educational, Scientific, and Cultural Organization). [< Greek *akros* tip + *onyma* name]

a dopt (ə dopt′), *v.t.* 1 take or use as one's own choice: *adopt an idea, adopt a new custom.* 2 accept, endorse, or approve formally or officially: *The committee adopted the resolution by a vote of 20 to 5.* 3 take (a child of other parents), as approved by law, and bring up as one's own child. 4 take (a word) from a foreign language into regular use without intentionally changing its form: *In English we have adopted the German words "Gneiss" and "Hamburger."* [< Latin *adoptare* < *ad-* to + *optar* choose —**a dopt′a ble,** *adj.* —**a dopt′er,** *n.*

ad journ (ə jėrn′), *v.t.* put off until a later time; postpone: *The members of club voted to adjourn the meeting until two o'clock tomorrow.* —*v.i.* 1 stop business or proceedings for a time; recess: *The court adjourned from Friday until Monday.* 2 transfer the place of meeting. 3. INFORMAL. go (*to* another place), especially for conversation. [< Old French *adjourner* < *a* to + *jorn* day]

a dul ter ant (ə dul′tər ənt), *n.* substance used to adulterate something, especially something that destroys purity or quality without greatly altering appearance.

ad vo cate (*v.* ad′və kāt; *n.* ad′və kit, ad′və kāt), *v.,* -**cat ed, -cat ing,** *n.* —*v.t.* speak or write in favor of; recommend publicly (a measure, policy, etc.); support. —*n.* 1 person who defends, maintains, or publicly recommends a proposal, belief, theory, etc.; supporter. 2 lawyer who pleads the cause of anyone in certain courts of law. [< Latin *advocatum* summoned < *ad-* to + *vocare* to call] —**ad′vo ca′tion, n.** —**ad′vo ca′tor,** *n.*

af flu ent (af′lü ənt), *adj.* 1 having an abundance of money, property, etc.; wealthy; rich. 2 abundant; plentiful. 3 flowing freely. —*n.* stream flowing into a larger stream or body of water; tributary. [< Latin *affluentem* flowing out < *ad-* + *fluere* to flow —**af′flu ent ly,** *adv.*

Af ghan i stan (af gan′ə stan), *n.* country in SW Asia, between Pakistan and Iran. 13,600,000 pop.; 250,000 sq. mi. *Capital:* Kabul.

ag gres sion (ə gresh′ən), *n.* 1 the first step in a quarrel or war; an unprovoked attack. 2 practice of making assaults or attacks on the rights or territory of others as a method or policy, 3 (in psychology) an act or attitude of hostility, usually arising from feelings of inferiority or frustration. [< Latin *aggressionem* < *ad-* up to + *gradi* to step]

al lied (ə līd′, al′īd), *adj.* 1 united by agreement or treaty; combined for some special purpose: *allied nations.* 2 associated; connected: *allied banks.* 3 related: *The dog and the wolf are allied animals.* 4 **Allied,** of or by the Allies.

al ien ate (ā′lyə nāt, ā′lē ə nāt), *v.t.,* -**at ed, -at ing.** 1 turn away the normal feelings, fondness, or devotion of anyone; make unfriendly; estrange: *The colonies were alienated from England by disputes over trade and taxation.* 2 transfer (property, a property right, etc.) to the ownership of another: *Enemy property was alienated during the war.* 3 turn away; transfer. —**al′ien a′tor,** *n.*

al li ance (ə lī′əns), *n.* 1 union formed by mutual agreement, especially to protect or further mutual interests. 2 a joining of independent nations by treaty. 3 a joining of family interests through marriage. 4 the nations, persons, etc., who are allied. 5 any joining of efforts or interests by persons, families, states, or organizations: *an alliance between church and state.* 6 similarity in structure or descent; relationship. [< Old French *aliance* < *alier* unite. SEE ALLY.]

al ma nac (ôl′mə nak), *n.* 1 an annual table or book of tables containing a calendar of days, weeks, and months and often including astronomical data, weather predictions, church days, dates of holidays, changes of the moon, hours of sunrise and sunset, and other miscellaneous information. 2 an annual reference book containing summaries of information on particular subjects. [< Medieval Latin *almanachus* < Arabic *almanakh*]

a mo ral (ā môr′əl, ā mor′əl; a môr′əl, a mor′əl), *adj.* 1 not classifiable as good or bad because not involving any question of morality; nonmoral. 2 unable to distinguish between right and wrong. —**a mo′ral ly,** *adv.*

an ti so cial (an′ti sō′shəl), *adj.* 1 opposed to the principles upon which society is based: *Murder and stealing are antisocial acts.* 2 against

a hat	**i** it	**oi** oil	**ch** child	**a** in about
ā age	**ī** ice	**ou** out	**ng** long	**e** in taken
ä far	**o** hot	**u** cup	**sh** she	**ə** = **i** in pencil
e let	**ō** open	**u** put	**th** thin	**o** in lemon
ē equal	**ô** order	**ü** rule	**TH** then	**u** in circus
er term			**zh** measure	**<** = derived from

the general welfare: *antisocial behavior.* 3 opposed to friendly relationship and normal companionship with others; not sociable.

ap a thy (ap′ə thē), *n., pl,* -**thies.** 1 lack of interest in or desire for activity; indifference. See **indifference** for synonym study. 2 lack of feeling. [< Greek *apatheia* < *a-* without + *pathos* feeling]

ap praise (ə prāz′), *v.t.,* -**praised, -prais ing.** 1 estimate the quality or merit of; judge: *Few can properly appraise the work of a new artist.* 2 estimate the value of; fix a price for; value: *The paintings were appraised at $100,000.* See **estimate** for synonym study. [< Middle French *aprisier* < Latin *appretiare* < *ad-* to + *pretium* price] —**ap prais′ing ly,** *adv.*

ar a ble (ar′ə bəl), *adj.* (of land) suitable for producing crops which require plowing and tillage. —*n.* arable land. [< Latin *arabilis* able to be plowed < *arare* to plow]

ar ray (ə rā′), *n.* 1 proper order; regular arrangement; formation: *The troops marched in battle array.* 2 display of persons or things; imposing group: *The array of good players on the other team made our side look weak.* 3 military force; soldiers. 4 clothes, especially for some special or festive occasion; dress; attire: *bridal array.* 5 (in mathematics) an orderly arrangement of objects or symbols in rows and columns. —*v.t.* 1 put in order for some purpose; marshal: *The general arrayed his troops for the battle.* 2 dress in fine clothes; adorn. [< Anglo-French *arayer* < Old French *a-* to + *rei* order] —**ar ray′er,** *n.*

ar tic u late (*adj.* är tik′yə lit; *v.* är tik′yə lāt), *adj., v.,* -**lat ed, -lat ing.** —*adj.* 1 uttered in distinct syllables of words: *A baby cries and gurgles, but does not use articulate sounds.* 2 able to put one's thoughts into words easily and clearly: *She is the most articulate of the sisters.* 3 consisting of sections united by joints; jointed. *The backbone is an articulate structure.* —*v.t.* 1 speak distinctly; express in clear sounds and words: *Be careful to articulate your words so that everyone in the room can understand you.* 2 unite by joints: *The two bones are articulated like a hinge.* —*v.i.* 1 express oneself in words: *I was so excited I could hardly articulate.* 2 fit together in a joint: *After his knee was injured, he was lame because the bones did not articulate well.* —**ar tic u late ly** (är tik′yə lit lē), *adv.* —**ar tic u late ness** (är tik′yə lit nis), *n.* —**ar tic′u la′tor,** *n.*

as cer tain (as′ər tān′), *v.t.* find out for certain by trial and research; make sure of; determine: *ascertain the facts about a robbery.* [< Old French *ascertener* < *a-* to + *certain* certain] —**as′cer tain′a ble,** *adj.* —**as′cer tain′ment,** *n.*

a skew (ə skyü′) *adv., adj.* out of the proper position; turned or twisted the wrong way; awry.

as sert (ə sert′) *v.t.* 1 state positively; declare firmly; affirm: *She asserts that she will go whether we do or not.* See **declare** for synonym study. 2 maintain (a right, a claim, etc.); insist upon: *Assert your independence.* 3 **assert oneself,** put oneself forward; make demands: *A leader must assert himself sometimes in order to be followed.* [< Latin *assertum* asserted < *ad-* to + *serere* join —**as sert′er, as ser′tor,** *n.*

as ter isk (as′tə risk′), *n.* a star-shaped mark (*) used in printing and writing to call attention to a footnote, indicate the omission of words or letters, etc. —*v.t.* mark with an asterisk. [< Greek *asteriskos,* diminutive of *aster* star]

at las (at′ləs), *n.* 1 book of maps. 2 book of plates or tables illustrating any subject. 3 **Atlas,** (in Greek myths) a Titan whose punishment for revolt against Zeus was to support the heavens on his shoulders. 4 the first cervical vertebra, which supports the skull. [< Latin < Greek]

auc tion eer (ôk′shə nir′), *n.* person whose business is conducting auctions. —*v.t.* sell at an auction.

av ar ice (av′ər is), *n.* too great a desire for money or property; greed for wealth. [< Old French < Latin *avaritia* < *avarus* greedy]

ax is (ak′sis), *n., pl.* **ax es.** 1 an imaginary or real line that passes through an object and about which an object turns or seems to turn. The earth's axis passes through the North and the South Poles. 2 a central or principal line around which parts are arranged symmetrically. The axis of a cone is the straight line joining its apex and the center of its base. 3 any line used for reference. 4 in anatomy: **a** a central or principal structure extending lengthwise and having the parts of the body arranged around it: *The axis of the skeleton is the spinal column.* **b** the second cervical vertebra. 5 in botany: **a** the central part or support on which parts are arranged. **b** the main stem and root. 6 any of three lines, one parallel to the axis of the propeller, and the other two perpendicular to this and to each other, about which an aircraft or spacecraft revolves. 7 (in art, design, etc.) an imaginary central line in a composition, referred to for balance of parts or the like. 8 one of the three or four imaginary lines assumed in defining the position of the plane faces of a crystal and classifying the crystal. 9 an important line of relation: *the Rome-Berlin axis.* 10 **the Axis,** Germany, Italy, Japan, and their allies, during World War II. [< Latin]

B

bar ba rism (bär′bə riz′əm), *n.* 1 condition of uncivilized people: *People who have no form of writing live in barbarism.* 2 a barbarous act, custom, or trait. 3 use of a word or expression not in accepted use. 4 a nonstandard word or expression. EXAMPLE: *his′n* for *his.*

bar ter (bär′tər), *v.i.* trade by exchanging one kind of goods or services for other goods or services without using money. —*v.t.* 1 exchange (goods or services of equivalent or supposed equivalent value): *The Indians bartered furs for beads and guns.* 2 **barter away,** give away without an equal return: *barter away one's soul for wealth.* —*n.* 1 act of bartering; trading by exchanging goods. 2 something bartered. [< Old French *barater* to exchange]—**bar′ter er,** *n.*

beam (bēm), *n.* 1 a large, long piece of timber, ready for use in building. 2 a similar piece of metal, stone, reinforced concrete, etc. 3 any of the main horizontal supports of a building or ship. 4 part of a plow by which it is pulled. 5 the crosswise bar of a balance, from the ends of which the scales or pans are suspended. 6 the balance itself. 7 ray or rays of light. See synonym study below. 8 a bright look or smile. 9 a radio signal directed in a straight line, used to guide aircraft, ships, etc. 10 side of a ship, or the sideward direction at right angles to the keel, with reference to wind, sea, etc. The weather beam is the side toward the wind. 11 the widest part of a ship. 12 **on the beam, a** (of a ship) at right angles to the keel. **b** (of an aircraft) on the right course, as indicated by the directing radio signals. **c** SLANG. just right.
—*v.t.* 1 throw out or radiate (beams or rays of light); emit in rays. 2 direct (a broadcast): *beam programs at Russia.* —*v.i.* 1 shine radiantly. 2 look or smile brightly.
[Old English *beam* tree, piece of wood, ray of light]
Syn. *n.* 7 **Beam, ray** means a line of light. **Beam** applies to a shaft, long and with some width, coming from something that gives out light: *The beam from the flashlight showed a kitten.* **Ray** applies to a thin line of light, usually thought of as radiating, or coming out like the spokes of a wheel, from something bright: *There was not a ray of moonlight in the forest.*

ben e fi cial (ben′ əfish′əl), *adj.* producing good; favorable; helpful: *Sunshine and moisture are beneficial to plants.* —**ben′e fi′cial ly,** *adv.*—**ben′e fi′cial ness,** *n.*

ber serk (ber′serk′, bər serk′) *adv.* **go berserk** or **run berserk,** be carried away by madness or wild fury; become violently angry. —*adj.* 1 of unsound mind; mad; insane. 2 violently angry. [< *berserker*]

bib li og ra phy (bib′lē og′rə fē), *n. pl.* **-phies.** 1 list of books, articles, etc., about a particular subject or person. 2 list of books, articles, etc., by a certain author, 3 study of the authorship, editions, dates, etc., of books, manuscripts, articles, etc. 4 list of the books, articles, etc., consulted or referred to by an author in the preparation of an article or book.

bi as (bī′əs), *n., adj., adv., v.,* **-ased, -assing,** or **-assed, -as sing,** —*n.* 1 a slanting or oblique line, especially across a woven fabric. 2 **on the bias,** diagonally across the weave: *cloth cut on the bias.* 3 tendency to favor one side too much; inclination or leaning based on prejudice. See **prejudice** for synonym study. 4 in the game of bowls: **a** the lopsided shape of a ball that makes it swerve when rolled. **b** the weight or force that makes it swerve. —*adj.* slanting across the threads of cloth; oblique, diagonal. —*adv.* obliquely. — *v.t.* give a bias to; influence, usually unfairly; prejudice. [< Middle French *biais* slant]

bi o de grad a ble (bī′ō di grā′də bəl), *adj.* capable of being broken down by the action of bacteria: *a biodegradable detergent.*

bois ter ous (boi′stər əs), *adj.* 1 noisily cheerful; exuberant: *a boisterous game.* 2 rough and stormy; turbulent: *a boisterous wind.* 3 rough and noisy; clamorous: *a boisterous child.* [Middle English *boistrous*] —**bois′ter ous ly,** *adv.* —**bois′ter our ness,** *n.*

bom bard (bom bärd′) *v.t.* 1 attack with heavy shellfire from artillery, rockets, or naval guns: *Tanks and howitzers bombarded enemy positions all morning.* 2 drop bombs on; bomb: *Aircraft bombarded the hydroelectric plant and destroyed it.* 3 keep attacking vigorously: *The lawyer bombarded the witness with question after question.* 4 strike (the nucleus of an atom) with a stream of fast-moving particles, radioactive rays, etc., to change the structure of the nucleus.

boon¹ (bün), *n.* 1 great benefit; blessing: *Those warm boots were a boon to me in the cold weather.* 2 ARCHAIC. something asked for or granted as a favor. [< Scandinavian (Old Icelandic) *bon* petition]

boon² (bün), *adj.* 1 full of cheer; jolly; merry: *a boon companion.* 2 kindly; pleasant [< Old French *bon* good < Latin *bonus*]

bra zen (brā′zn), *adj.* 1 having no shame; shameless; impudent. See **bold** for synonym study. 2 loud and harsh; brassy. 3 made of brass 4 like brass in color or strength —*v.t.* 1 make shameless or impudent. 2 **brazen it out** or **brazen it through,** act as if one did not feel ashamed of it: *Although he was caught lying, he tried to brazen it out by telling another lie.* [Old English *bræsen bræs* brass] — **bra′zen ly,** *adv.*—**bra′zen ness,** *n.*

bring (bring), *v.t.,* **brought, bring ing.** 1 come with or carry (some thing or person) from another place: *Bring me a clean plate.* See synonym study below. 2 cause to come: *What brings you into town today?* 3 win over to a belief or action; influence; persuade; convince: *She was brought to agree by our arguments.* 4 sell for: *Meat brings a high price this time of year.* 5 present before a court of law: *They brought a charge against me.* 6 cause (a ship, etc.) to come or go into a certain position or direction: *bring by the board.*
bring about, cause to happen; cause: *The flood was brought about by a heavy rain.*
bring around or **bring round, a** restore to consciousness: *When I fainted, they brought me around.* **b** convince; persuade: *At first my parents refused to let me go to the party, but soon I brought them around and they let me go.*
bring forth, a give birth to; bear. **b** reveal; show: *New evidence was brought forth by the lawyer.*
bring forward, a reveal; show: *the judge ordered the prisoner to be brought forward.*
b (in accounting or bookkeeping) carry over from one page to another.
bring off, carry out successfully.
bring on, cause to happen; cause: *My bad cold brought on pneumonia.*
bring out, a reveal; show: *The lawyer brought out new evidence at the trial.* **b** offer to the public.
bring over, convince; persuade: *Try to bring him over to our way of thinking.*
bring to, a restore to consciousness: *She fainted when she heard the news, but they finally brought her to.* **b** stop; check.
bring up, a care for in childhood. **b** educate or train, especially in behavior or manners. **c** suggest for action or discussion. **d** stop suddenly. **e** vomit. [Old English *bringan*] —**bring′er,** *n.*
Syn. 1 **Bring, fetch** mean to come to a person or place with or carrying something.
Bring means to come with someone or something from another place to the place where the speaker is: *I brought some cake home with me.* **Fetch** means to go and get someone or something: *Please take the car and fetch him.*

bris tle (bris′əl), *n., v.,* **-tled, -tling,** —*n.* 1 one of the short, stiff hairs of a hog or wild boar, used to make brushes. 2 any short, stiff hair of an animal or plant. 3 a synthetic substitute for a hog's bristles. —*v.t.* 1 provide with bristles. 2 cause (hair) to stand up straight. —*v.i.* 1 stand up straight: *The angry dog's hair bristled.* 2 have one's hair stand up straight: *The frightened kitten bristled when it saw the dog.* 3 show that one is aroused and ready to fight: *The whole country bristled with indignation.* 4 be thickly set: *Our path bristled with difficulties.* [Middle English *brustel,* Old English *byrst* bristle—**bris′tle like′,** *adj.*

brute (brüt), *n.* 1 mammal or reptile without power to reason. See **animal** for synonym study. 2 a cruel, coarse, or sensual person. —*adj.* 1 not possessing reason or understanding: *brute beasts.* 2 of or characteristic of animals as distinguished from man; dull; stupid. 3 cruel; coarse. 4 sensual. 5 lacking intelligence; not having sense or sensation: *the brute forces of nature* [< Old French *brut* < Latin *brutum* heavy, dull]

a hat	**i** it	**oi** oil	**ch** child	a in about
ā age	**ī** ice	**ou** out	**ng** long	e in taken
ä far	**o** hot	**u** cup	**sh** she	ə = i in pencil
e let	**ō** open	**u** put	**th** thin	o in lemon
ē equal	**ô** order	**ü** rule	**TH** then	u in circus
er term			**zh** measure	< = derived from

C

cal or ie (kal′ər ē), *n., pl.* **-or ies.** 1 either of two units for measuring the amount of heat: **a small carorie,** the quantity of heat necessary to raise the temperature of a gram of water one degree centigrade. **b large calorie,** the quantity of heat necessary to raise the temperature of a kilogram of water one degree centigrade. 2 unit of the energy supplied by food, corresponding to the large calorie. An ounce of sugar will produce about one hundred such calories. 3 quantity of food capable of producing such an amount of energy. Also, **calory.** [< French < Latin *calor* heat]

ca pac i ty (kə pas′ə tē), *n., pl.* **-ties.** 1 amount of room or space inside; largest amount that can be held by a container: *A gallon can has a capacity of 4 quarts.* 2 power of receiving and holding: *a theater with a seating capacity of 400.* 3 ability to learn or do; power or fitness: *a great capacity for learning.* 4 ability to withstand some force or perform some function: *the capacity of a metal to retain heat* 5 the physical power or ability to produce: *the maximum capacity of a machine.* 6 maximum output: *Steel factories worked at capacity during the war.* 7 capacitance. 8 position or relation. A person may act in the capacity of guardian, trustee, voter, friend, etc. 9 legal power or qualification [< Latin *capacitatem* < *capere* take]

ca pit u late (kə pich′ə lāt), *v.i.,* **-lat ed, -lat ing,** surrender on certain terms or conditions: *The men in the fort capitulated on condition that they be allowed to go away unharmed.* [< Medieval Latin *capitulatum* arranged under headings or chapters < Latin *capitulum* small head < *caput* head] —**ca pit′u la′tor,** *n.*

car bine (kär′bin, kär′bēn′) *n.* a short, light rifle or musket. [< French *carabine*]

car di ol o gist (kär′dē ol′ə jist), *n.* an expert in cardiology.

car ol (kar′əl), *n., v.,* **-oled, -ol ing,** or **-olled, -ol ling.** —*n.* 1 song of joy. 2 hymn of joy sung at Christmas. 3 (in the Middle Ages) a dance done in a ring with accompaniment of song —*v.i.* sing joyously; sing: *the birds were caroling in the trees.* —*v.t.* 1 sing joyously. 2 praise with carols. [< Old French *carole* < Latin *choraula* < Greek *choraules* flute player accompanying a choral dance < *choros* dance + *aulos* flute] —**car′ol er, car′ol ler,** *n.*

cen trif u gal (sen trif′yə gəl, sen trif′ə gəl), *adj.* 1 moving or tending to move away from a center. 2 making use of or acted upon by centrifugal force. [< Latin *centrum* center + *fugere* flee —**cen trif′u gal ly,** *adv.*

chart (chärt), *n.* 1 map used by sailors to show the coasts, rocks, and shallow places of the sea. *The course of a ship is marked on a chart.* See **map** for synonym study. 2 an outline map showing special conditions or facts: *a weather chart.* 3 sheet of information arranged in lists, pictures, tables, or diagrams. 4 such a list, table, picture, or diagram. 5 a graphic representation of any variable, such as temperature, pressure, production, or sales. —*v.t.* 1 make a chart of; show on a chart. 2 plan in detail: *She is now charting the course of her campaign.* [< Middle French *charte* < Latin *charta* leaf of paper < Greek *chartes.* Doublet of CARD¹.] —**chart′less,** *adj.*

chro mo some (krō′mə sōm), *n.* any of the rod-shaped bodies found in the nucleus of a cell that appear during cell division. Chromosomes are derived from the parents and carry the genes that determine heredity. See **cell** for diagram. [< Greek *chroma* color + *soma* body]

chron ic (kron′ik), *adj.* 1 lasting a long time: *Rheumatism is often a chronic disease.* 2 suffering long from an illness: *a chronic invalid.* 3 never stopping; constant; habitual: *a chronic liar.* [< Greek *chronikos* of time < *chronos* time] —**chron′i cal ly,** *adv.*

chron o graph (kron′ə graf), *n.* 1 instrument for measuring very short intervals of time accurately, such as a stopwatch. 2 instrument for recording the exact instant of an astronomical or other occurrence. [< Greek *chronos* time + English *-graph*]

cir cum spect (ser′kəm spekt), *adj.* watchful on all sides; cautious or prudent; careful. [< Latin *circumspectum* < *circum* around + *specere* look]—**cir′cum spect′ly,** *adv.*—**cir′cum spect′ness,** *n.*

ci vil i ty (sə vil′ə tē), *n., pl.,* **-ties.** 1 polite behavior; courtesy. 2 act or expression of politeness or courtesy.

clan des tine (klan des′tən), *adj.* arranged or made in a stealthy or underhanded manner; concealed; secret: *a clandestine plan.* See **secret** for synonym study. [< Latin *clandestinus* < *clam* secretly] —**clan des′tine ly,** *adv.* —**clan des′tine ness,** *n.*

co a li tion (kō′ə lish′ən), *n.* 1 union; combination. 2 alliance of statesmen, political parties, etc., for some special purpose. In wartime several countries may form a temporary coalition against a common enemy. [< Medieval Latin *coalitionem* < Latin *coalescere.* SEE COALESCE.]

cog ni tion (kog nish′ən), *n.* 1 act of knowing; perception; awareness. 2 thing known, perceived, or recognized. [< Latin *cognitionem* < *cognoscere* perceive < *co-* (intensive) + *gnoscere* known]

co hab it (kō hab′it), *v.i.* live together as husband and wife do. —**co hab′i ta′tion,** *n.*

col lo qui al ism (kə lo′kwē ə liz′əm), *n.* 1 a colloquial word or phrase. 2 a colloquial style or usage.

colo nel (ker′nl), *n.* a commissioned officer in the army, air force, or Marine Corps ranking next above a lieutenant colonel and next below a brigadier general. [< Middle French *coronel, colonel* < Italian *colonello* commander of a regiment < *colonna* military column < Latin *columna* column]
Colonel is an example of a word whose pronunciation has survived a change in spelling. The word, from the French, developed two parallel forms, *colonel, coronel,* each pronounced in three syllables. For 150 years the word has been pronounced (ker′nl), from the *coronel* form, but spelling has kept *colonel.*

com bat ant (kəm bat′nt, kom′bə tənt), *n.* one that takes part in combat; fighter. —*adj.* 1 fighting. 2 ready to right; fond of fighting.

com mend (kə mend′), *v.t.* 1 speak well of; praise. See **praise** for synonym study. 2 recommend. 3 hand over for safekeeping; entrust: *She commended the child to her aunt's care.* [< Latin *commendare* < *com-* + *mandare* commit, command]

com men sur ate (kə men′shər it, kə men′sər it), *adj.* 1 in the proper proportion; proportionate: *The pay should be commensurate with the work.* 2 of the same size or extent; equal. 3 commensurable [< Late Latin *commensuratum* < Latin *com-* together + *mensura* measure] —**com men′sur ate ly,** *adv.* —**com men′sur ate ness,** *n.* —**com men′sur a′tion,** *n.*

com pen sate (kom′pən sāt), *v.,* **-sat ed, -sat ing.** —*v.t.* 1 make an equal return to; give an equivalent to: *The hunters gave the farmer $100 to compensate him for their damage to his field.* See **pay** for synonym study. 2 pay: *The company compensated her for extra work.* —*v.i.* 1 balance by equal weight, power, etc.; make up (*for*): *Skill sometimes compensates for lack of strength.* 3 make amends. [< Latin *compensatum* balanced out < *com-* + *pensare* weigh < *pendere* weigh out]

com ple ment (*n.* kom′plə mənt; *v.* kom′plə ment), *n.* 1 something that completes or makes perfect. 2 number required to fill: *The ship now has its full complement of men, and no more can be taken on.* 3 word or group of words completing a predicate. In "The man is good," *good* is a complement. 4 amount needed to make an angle or an arc equal to 90 degrees. 5 (in mathematics) those members of a set that do not belong to a subset. 6 substance found in normal blood serum and protoplasm which combines with antibodies to destroy bacteria and other foreign bodies. —*v.t.* supply a lack of any kind; complete. See synonym study below. [< Latin *complementum* < *complere* to complete]
Syn. *v.t.* **Complement, supplement** mean to complete. **Complement**

means to complete by supplying something that is missing but necessary to make a perfect whole: *The two texts complement each other; what is sketchily dealt with in either one is treated fully in the other.* Supplement means to add something to make better or bigger or richer in some way: *Outside reading supplements a person's education.*

complement, compliment. *Complement* means something that completes or makes perfect, or a number required to fill (related to *complete*): *Education was the complement to her natural abilities.* *Compliment* has to do with politeness and praise: *Their progress deserved the principal's compliment.*

com po nent (kəm pō′nənt), *n.* one of the parts that make up a whole; necessary part: *Because alcohol is a solvent, it is a component of many liquid medicines.* See **element** for synonym study. —*adj.* that composes; constituent: *Blade and handle are the component parts of a knife.* [< Latin *componentem* put together < *com-* together + *ponere* put]

com press (*v.* kəm pres′; *n.* kom′pres), *v.t.* squeeze together; make smaller by pressure. —*n.* 1 pad of dry or wet cloth applied to some part of the body to create pressure or to reduce inflammation. 2 machine for compressing cotton into bales. [< Latin *compressare*, frequentative of *comprimere* < *com-* together + *premere* to press]

con cept (kon′sept), *n.* idea of a class of objects; general notion; idea: *the concept of equality.* [< Lain *conceptum* < *concipere*. SEE CONCEIVE.]

con fab u late (kən fab′yə lāt), *v.t.*, **-lat ed, -lat ing.** INFORMAL. talk together informally and intimately; chat. [ultimately < Latin < *com-* together + *fabulari* talk < *fabula* fable] —**con fab′u la′tion,** *n.*

con gen i tal (kən jen′ə təl), *adj.* 1 present at birth: *a congenital deformity.* 2 inborn; deep-seated: *congenital dislikes.* [< Latin *congenitus* born with < *com-* + *genitus* born] —**con gen′i tal ly,** *adv.*

con gest (kən jest′), *v.t.* 1 fill too full; over-crowd: *a street congested with traffic.* 2 cause too much blood or mucus to gather in (one part of the body). —*v.i.* 1 become over-crowded. 2 become too full of blood or mucus. [< Latin *congestum* brought together < *com-* + *genere* carry]

con note (kə nōt′), *v.t.*, **-not ed, -not ing.** suggest in addition to the literal meaning; imply. *Portly, corpulent,* and *obese* all mean fleshy; but *portly* connotes dignity; *corpulent,* bulk; and *obese,* and unpleasant excess of fat. [< Medieval Latin *connotare* < Latin *com-* with + *notare* to note]

con tin gent (kən tin′jənt), *n.* 1 share of soldiers, laborers, etc., furnished to a force from other sources: *The United States sent a large contingent of troops to Europe in World War II.* 2 group that is part of a larger group: *The New York contingent sat together at the national convention.* 3 an accidental or unexpected event. —*adj.* 1 depending on something not certain; conditional: *Our plans for a picnic are contingent upon fair weather.* 2 liable to happen or not to happen; possible; uncertain: *contingent expenses.* 3 happening by chance; accidental; unexpected. [< Latin *contingentem* touching closely < *com-* + *tangere* to touch] —**con tin′gent ly,** *adv.*

con text (kon′tekst), *n.* parts directly before and after a word, sentence, etc., that influence its meaning. You can often tell the meaning of a word from its context. [< Latin *contextus* < *contexere* weave together < *com-* + *texere* weave]

con viv i al (kən viv′ē əl), *adj.* 1 fond of eating and drinking with friends; jovial; sociable. 2 of or suitable for a feast or banquet; festive. [< Latin *convivium* feast < *com-* with + *vivere* to live] —**con viv′i al ly,** *adv.*

co ral (kôr′əl, kor′əl), *n.* 1 a stony substance, mainly calcium carbonate, consisting of the skeletons of polyps. Reefs and small islands consisting of coral are common in tropical seas and oceans. Red, pink, and white coral are often used for jewelry. 2 polyp that secretes a skeleton of coral and forms large branching or rounded colonies by budding. 3 a deep pink or red. —*adj.* 1 made of coral. 2 deep-pink or red. [< Latin *corallum* < Greek *korallion*]

cor ral (kə ral′), *n., v.,* **-ralled, -ral ling.** —*n.* 1 pen for keeping or for capturing horses, cattle, etc. 2 a circular camp formed by wagons for defense against attack. —*v.t.* 1 drive into or keep in a corral. 2 hem in; surround; capture: *The reporters corralled the candidate and asked him for a statement.* 3 form (wagons) into a circular camp. [< Spanish]

cor re late (kôr′ə lāt, kor′ə lāt), *v.,* **-lat ed, -lat ing.** —*v.t.* place in or bring into proper relation with one another; show the connection or relation between: *Try to correlate your knowledge of history with your knowledge of geography.* —*v.i.* be related one to the other; have a mutual relation: *The diameter and the circumference of a circle correlate.*

coun ter point (koun′tər point′), *n.* 1 melody added to another as an accompaniment. 2 act of adding melodies to a given melody according to fixed rules. 3 polyphony. [< Middle French *contrepoint*]

coup de grâce (kü′ də gräs′), *pl.* **coups de grâce** (kü′ də gräs′). 1 action that gives a merciful death to a suffering animal or person. 2 a finishing stoke. [< French, literally, stroke of grace]

cri ter i on (krī tir′ē ən), *n., pl.* **-ter i a** or **-ter i ons.** rule or standard for making a judgment; test: *Wealth is only one criterion of success.* See **standard** for synonym study. [< Greek *kriterion* < *krinein* decide, judge]

crouch (krouch), *v.i.* 1 stoop low with bent legs like an animal ready to spring. 2 shrink down in fear. 3 bow down in a timid or slavish manner; cover. —*v.t.* bend low. —*n.* 1 act or state of crouching. 2 a crouching position [perhaps blend of *couch* and *crook*]

crys tal lize (kris′tl īz), *v.,* **-lized, -liz ing,** —*v.i., v.t.* 1 form into crystals; solidify into crystals. *Water crystallizes to form snow.* 2 form into definite shape: *Our vague ideas crystallized into a clear plan.* 3 coat with sugar. **crys′tal liz′a ble,** *adj.* —**crys′tal li za′tion,** *n.*

cur sor y (ker′sər ē), *adj.* without attention to details; hasty and superficial: *Even a cursory reading of the letter showed many errors.* [< Latin *cursorius* of a race < *currere* to run —**cur′sor i ly,** *adv.* —**cur′sor i ness,** *n.*

cystic fibrosis, a hereditary disease of the pancreas characterized by excessive secretion from internal organs and accompanying respiratory infection.

D

das tard ly (das′tərd lē), *adj.* like a dastard; mean and cowardly; sneaking. —**das′tard li ness,** *n.*

da ta (dā′tə, dat′ə), *n.pl.* of **datum.** facts from which conclusions can be drawn; things known or admitted; information. [< Latin, plural of *datum* (thing) given. Doublet of DIE².]

Data is the plural of the seldom-used singular *datum.* When *data* refers to a group of facts as a unit, it is used with a singular verb in informal English: *The data we have collected is not enough to be convincing.* In formal English *data* is regarded as a plural: *The data we have collected are not enough to be convincing.*

de fec tive (di fek′tiv), *adj.* 1 having a defect or defects; not perfect or complete; faulty. 2 lacking one or more of the usual forms of grammatical infection. *Ought* is a defective verb. 3 below normal in behavior or intelligence. —*n.* person who has some defect. —**de fec′tive ly,** *adv.* —**de fec′tive ness,** *n.*

de hy drate (dē hī′drāt) *v.,* **-drat ed, -drat inig.** —*v.t.* take water or moisture from; dry: *dehydrate vegetables.* — *v.i.* lose water or moisture. [< *de-* remove + Greek *hydros* water —**de′hy dra′tion,** *n.*

del e gate (*n.* del′ə gāt, del′ə git; *v.* del′ə gāt), *n., v.,* **-gat ed, -gat ing.** —*n.* 1 person given power or authority to act for others; representative to a convention, meeting, etc. 2 representative of a territory in the United States House of Representatives. 3 member of the lower branch of the legislature in Maryland, Virginia, and West Virginia. —*v.t.* 1 appoint or send (a person) as a representative: *Each club delegated one member to attend the state meeting.* 2 give over to another so that he may act for one: *delegate responsibility to an employee.* [< Latin *delegatum* delegated < *de-* + *legare* send with a commission]

de prive (de prīv′), *v.t.* **-prived, -priv ing.** 1 take away from by force; divest: *deprive a dictator of his power.* 2 keep from having or doing: *Worrying deprived me of sleep.* [< Old French *depriver* < *de-* + *priver* deprive]

de tach (di tach′), *v.t.* 1 loosen and remove; unfasten; separate: *She detached the trailer from the car.* 2 send away on special duty: *One squad of soldiers was detached to guard the road.* [< French *detacher* < *de-* dis- + *(at)tacher* attach] —**de tach′a ble,** *adj.*

dev as tate (dev′ə stāt), *v.t.* **-tat ed, -tat ing.** make desolate; lay waste; destroy; ravage: *A long war devastated the country.* [< Latin *devastatum* laid waste *de-* + *vastus* waste] —**dev′as tat′ing ly,** *adv.* —**dev′as ta′tion,** *n.* —**dev′as ta′tor,** *n.*

di a gram (dī′ə gram), *n.v.*, **-gramed, -gram ing** or **-grammed, -gram ming.** —*n.* 1 drawing or sketch which gives an outline or general scheme of something and shows the relations of its various parts. 2 (in mathematics) figure used to aid in the proof of a geometrical proposition or as a mathematical representation. —*v.t.* put on paper, a blackboard, etc., in the form of a drawing or sketch; make a diagram of. [< Greek *diagramma* < *dia-* apart, out + *gramma* lines (of a drawing, etc.)]

di a met ri cal ly (dī′ə met′rik lē) *adv.* 1 as a diameter. 2 directly; exactly; entirely: *diametrically opposed views.*

di lem ma (də lem′ ə), *n.* situation requiring a choice between two alternatives, which are or appear equally unfavorable: difficult choice. See *predicament* for synonym study. [< Greek *dilemma* < *di-* two + *lemma* premise]

din (din), *n.*, *v.*, **dinned, din ning.** —*n.* a continuing loud, confused noise. See *noise* for synonym study. *v.i.* make a din. —*v.t.* 1 strike with a din. 2 say over and over again; repeat in a tiresome way. [Old English *dynn*]

dir ec tive (də rek′tiv, dī rek′tiv), *n.* a general instruction on how to proceed or act, —*adj.* directing: serving to direct.

dis crim i nate (*v.* dis krim′ə nāt; *adj.* dis krim′ə nit), *v.*, **-nat ed, -nat ing,** *adj.* —*v.i.* 1 make or see a difference; make a distinction: *discriminate between a mere exaggeration and a deliberate falsehood.* 2 accord a particular person, class, etc., distinctive (and usually unfair) treatment: *discriminate against people because of their race or beliefs.* —*v.t.* make or see a difference between; distinguish; differentiate: *discriminate good books from poor ones.* See **distinguish** for synonym study. —*adj.* having discrimination; making careful distinctions. [< Latin *discriminatum* separated < *discrimen* separation < *discernere.* See DISCERN.] —**dis crim′i nate ly,** *adv.* —**dis crim′i na tor,** *n.*

dis si dent (dis′ə dənt), *adj.* disagreeing in opinion, character, etc.; dissenting. —*n.* person who disagrees or dissents. [< Latin *dissidentem* < *dis-* apart + *sedere* sit]

dis par ate (dis′pər it), *adj.* distinct in kind; essentially different; unlike. [< Latin *disparatum* < *dis-* apart + *parare* get] —**dis′par ate ly,** *adv.* —**dis′par ate ness,** *n.*

dis place ment (dis plās′mənt), *n.* 1 a displacing. 2 a being displaced. 3 weight of the volume of water displaced by a ship or other floating object. This weight is equal to that of the floating object.

Down's syndrome (dounz), form of mental retardation, caused by an extra chromosome which also produces abnormal body characteristics such as eyes that appear to be slanted and a broad, flattened face; mongolism. [<John L. H. *Down*, 1828–1896, English physician who first described it]

dregs (dregz), *no. pl.* 1 the solid bits of matter that settle to the bottom of a liquid: *the dregs of a coffee pot.* 2 the least desirable part. [< Scandinavian Old Icelandic) *dregg,* singular]

dump (dump), *v.t.* 1 empty out; throw down in a heap; unload in a mass: *The truck backed up to the hole and dumped the dirt in it.* 2 INFORMAL. get rid of; reject: *dump an unpopular candidate.* 3 sell in large quantities at a very low price or below cost, especially to do this in a foreign country at a price below that in the home country. —*v.i.* unload rubbish. —*n.* 1 place for throwing rubbish. 2 heap of rubbish. 3 SLANG. a dirty, shabby, or untidy place. 4 place for storing military supplies: *an ammunition dump.* [perhaps < Scandinavian (Danish) *dumpe* fall with a thud] —**dump′er,** *n.*

E

e col o gy (ē kol′ə jē), *n.* 1 branch of biology that studies the effect of environment upon the form, habits, and range of animals and plants and of their relation to each other. 2 branch of sociology that deals with the relations between human beings and their environment. [< German *Okologie* < Greek *oikos* house + *-logia* study of]

e go (ē′gō, eg′ō), *n.*, *pl.* **e gos.** 1 the individual as a whole in his capacity to think, feel, and act; self. 2 INFORMAL. conceit. 3 part of the personality that is conscious of the environment and adapts itself to it. [< Latin, I]

e gre gious (i grē′jəs), *adj.* 1 remarkably or extraordinarily bad; outrageous; flagrant: *an egregious blunder.* 2 remarkable; extraordinary. [< Latin *egregius* < *ex-* out + *gregem* herd, flock] —**e gre′gious ly,** *adv.* —**e gre′gious ness,** *n.*

a hat	i it	oi oil	ch child	a in about
ā age	ī ice	ou out	ng long	e in taken
ä far	o hot	u cup	sh she	ə = i in pencil
e let	ō open	u put	th thin	o in lemon
ē equal	ô order	ü rule	TH then	u in circus
er term			zh measure	< = derived from

e lab or ate (*adj.* i lab′ər it, i lab′rit; *v.* i lab′ə rāt′), *adj.*, *v.*, **at ed, -at ing.** —*adj.* worked out with great care; having many details; complicated. See synonym study below. —*v.t.* 1 work out with great care; add details to: *She is elaborating her plans for the new addition to the house.* 2 make with labor; produce. —*v.i.* talk, write, etc., in great detail; give added details: *The witness was asked to elaborate upon one of his statements.* [< Latin *elaboratum* worked out < *ex-* out + *labor* work] —**e lab′or ate ly,** *adv.* —**e lab′or ate ness,** *n.* —**e lab′o ra tor,** *n.*

Syn. *adj.* **Elaborate, studied, labored** mean worked out in detail. **Elaborate** emphasizes the idea of many details worked out with great care and exactness: *The elaborate decorations were perfect in every detail.* **Studied** emphasizes care in planning and working out details beforehand: *Her studied unconcern offended me.* **Labored** emphasizes great and unnatural effort to work out details: *The boy gave a labored excuse for arriving late at school.*

el e ment (el′ə mənt), *n.* 1 substance composed of atoms that are chemically alike and which cannot be separated into simpler parts by chemical means. Gold, iron, carbon, sulfur, oxygen, and hydrogen are among the 103 known elements. All matter is composed of either single elements or groups of elements. See pages 326 and 327 for table. 2 one of the basic parts of which anything is made up. See synonym study below. 3 a simple or necessary part to be learned first; first principle; rudiment: *teach the elements of grammar.* 4 one of the four substances—earth, water, air, and fire—that were once thought to be the fundamental constituents of matter. 5 **the elements,** the forces of the atmosphere, especially in bad weather: *The raging storm seemed to be a war of the elements.* 6 environment, sphere, or activity in which a particular person feels at home and able to do his best work or live to the full: *She was out of her element on the farm.* 7 the part that does the work in an electrical device. 8 (in military use) any unit or part of a larger group, formation, or maneuver. 9 in mathematics: **a** member of a set. **b** a very small part of a given magnitude similar in nature to the whole magnitude. **c** one of the lines, planes, points, etc., that make up a geometrical figure. 10 Often, **elements,** *pl.* bread and wine used in the Eucharist. [< Latin *elementum* rudiment, first principle] **Syn.** 2 **Element, component, constituent, ingredient** mean one of the parts of which something is made up. **Element,** the general word, applies to any essential or basic part of something: *The Latin element in English is surprisingly large.* **Component** means a part of something that joins together with other parts to form a unit: *Quartz and fledspar are the chief components of granite.* **Constituent,** often used interchangeably with *component,* differs in suggesting active helping to form the whole instead of just being an inactive part: *The colors of the rainbow are the constituents of white light.* **Ingredient** suggests that the helping parts lose individual identity in a mixture or combination: *Milk, eggs, and flour are basic ingredients in making a cake.*

em bla zon (em blā′zn), *v.t.* 1 display conspicuously; picture in bright colors. 2 decorate; adorn: *The knight's shield was emblazoned with his coat of arms.* 3 praise highly; honor publicly. —**em bla′zon er,** *n.* —**em bla′zon ment,** *n.*

em bry o (em′brē ō), *n.*, *pl.* —**bry os,** *adj.* —*n.* 1 animal during the period of its growth from the fertilized egg until its organs have developed so that it can live independently. The embryo of a mammal is usually called a fetus in its later stages (in human beings, more than three months after conception). 2 an undeveloped plant within a seed. 3 **in embryo,** in an undeveloped stage. —*adj.* undeveloped; embryonic. [< Medieval Latin < Greek *embryon* < *en-* in + *bryein* to swell]

en dorse (en dôrs′), *vt.*, **-dorsed, -dors ing.** 1 write one's name on the back of (a check, note, or other document) as evidence of its transfer or assuring its payment. 2 approve; support: *Parents heartily endorsed the plan for a school playground.* Also, **indorse.** [alteration of Middle English *endorsen* < Old French *endosser* < *en-* on + *dos* back] —**en dors′er,** *n.*

177

en gage (en gāj′), v., **-gaged, -gag ing.** —v.i. 1 keep oneself busy; be occupied; be active; take part: *He engages in politics. They engaged in conversation.* 2 bind oneself; promise; pledge: *I will engage to be there on time.* 3 lock together; mesh: *The teeth of one gear engage with the teeth of the other.* —v.t. 1 keep busy; occupy: *Work engages much of my time.* 2 take for use or work; hire: *We engaged two rooms in the hotel. I engaged a carpenter to repair the porch.* 3 promise or pledge to marry: *He is engaged to my sister.* 4 catch and hold; attract: *Bright colors engage a baby's attention.* 5 bind by a promise or contract; pledge: *He engaged himself as an apprentice to a printer.* 6 fit into; lock together: *The teeth of geared wheels engage each other.* 7 start a battle with; attack: *The troops engaged their enemy.* [< Old French *engagier* < *en gage* under pledge]

en gen der (en jen′dər), v.t. 1 bring into existence; produce; cause: *Filth engenders disease.* 2 beget: *Violence engenders violence.* [< Old French *engendrer* < Latin *ingenerare* < *in-* in + *generare* create]

en hance (en hans′), v.t. **-hanced, -hanc ing.** make greater in quality, value, or importance; add to; heighten: *The gardens enhanced the beauty of the house.* [< Anglo-French *enhauncer,* variant of Old French *enhaucier* < *en-* on, up + *haucier* raise] —**en hance′ment,** n.

en tre pre neur (än′trə prə ner′), n. person who organizes and manages a business or industrial enterprise, attempting to make a profit but taking the risk of a loss. [< French < *entreprendre* undertake]

e nu me rate (i nü′mə rāt′, i nyü′mə rāt′), v.t., **-rat ed, -rat ing.** 1 name one by one; list: *He enumerated the capitals of the 50 states.* 2 find out the number of; count. [< Latin *enumeratum* counted < *ex-* out + *numerus* number] —**e n u′me ra′tion,** n. —**e nu′me ra′tor,** n.

e pit o me (i pit′ə mē), n. 1 a condensed account; summary. An epitome contains only the most important points of a literary work, subject, etc. 2 person or thing that is typical or representative of something: *Solomon is often spoken of as the epitome of wisdom.* [< Greek *epitome* < *epitemnein* cut short < *epi-* + *temnein* to cut]

e rot ic (i rot′ik), adj. of or having to do with sexual passion or love. [< Greek *erotikos* of Eros] —**e rot′i cal ly,** adv.

er ro ne ous (ə rō′nē əs), adj. containing error; wrong; mistaken; incorrect: *the erroneous belief that the earth is flat.* —**er ro′ne ous ly,** adv. **er ro′ne ous ness,** n.

et y mol o gy (et′ə mol′ə jē), n., pl. **-gies.** 1 the derivation of a word. 2 account or explanation of the origin and history of a word. 3 study dealing with linguistic changes, especially with individual word origins. [< Greek *etymologia* < *etymon* the original sense or form of a word (neuter of *etymos* true, real) + *-logos* treating of].

e vap o ra tion (i vap′ə rā′shən), n. 1 a changing of a liquid into vapor. 2 a being changed into vapor. 3 removal of water or other liquid. 4 disappearance.

ex cerpt (n. ek′serpt; v. ek serpt′), n. passage taken out of a book, etc.; quotation; extract. —v.t. take out (passages) from a book, etc.; quote. [< Latin *excerptum* plucked out < *ex-* + *carpere* to pluck]

ex pend i ture (ek spen′də chür, ek spen′də chər), n. 1 a using up; spending: *To keep such a large house in good repair requires the expenditure of much money, time and effort.* 2 amount of money, etc., spent; expense: *Limit your expenditures to what is necessary.*

ex plic it (ek splis′it), adj. 1 clearly expressed; distinctly stated; definite: *He gave such explicit directions that everyone understood them.* 2 not reserved; frank; outspoken. [< Latin *explicitum* unfoled, explained < *ex-* out + *plicare* to fold] —**ex plic′it ly,** adv. —**ex plic′it ness,** n.

ex tant (ek′stənt, ek stant′), adj. still existing; not destroyed or lost: *Some of Washington's letters are extant.* [< Latin *exstantem* standing out, existing < *ex-* out + *stare* to stand]

ex ten sion (ek sten′shən), n. 1 an extending; stretching. 2 a being extended. 3 an extended part; addition. 4 range; extent. 5 telephone connected with the main telephone or with a switchboard but in a different location. 6 the provision of courses of study by a university or college to people unable to take courses in the regular session. 7 (in physics) that property of a body by which it occupies a portion of space.

ex ter nal (ek ster′nl), adj. 1 on the outside; outer. 2 entirely outside; coming from without: *the external air.* 3 to be used only on the outside of the body: *Liniment and rubbing alcohol are external*

remedies. 4 having existence outside one's mind. 5 easily seen but not essential; superficial: *Going to church is an external act of worship.* 6 having to do with international affairs; foreign: *War affects a nation's external trade.* —n. 1 an outer surface or part; outside. 2 **externals,** pl. clothing, manners, or other outward acts or appearances: *He judges people by mere externals.* [< Latin *externus* outside < *ex* out of] —**ex ter′nal ly,** adv.

F

fact (fakt), n. 1 thing known to be true or to have really happened: *Many scientific facts are based on actual observation.* 2 what has really happened or is the case; reality: *The fact of the matter is, I did not go.* 3 something said or supposed to be true or to have really happened: *We doubted his facts.* 4 crime or offense: *an accessory after the fact.* 5 OBSOLETE. deed; act. 6 **as a matter of fact,** in fact. 7 **in fact,** truly; really. [< Latin *factum* (thing) done < *facere* do. Doublet of FEAT.]

fal la cious (fə lā′shəs), adj. 1 that causes disappointment; deceptive; misleading: *a fallacious peace.* 2 logically unsound; erroneous: *fallacious reasoning.* —**fal la′cious ly,** adv. —**fal la′cious ness,** n.

fan ta sy (fan′tə sē, fan′tə zē), n., pl., **-sies.** 1 play of the mind; product of the imagination; fancy. 2 picture existing only in the mind; any strange mental image or illusion. Fantasies seem real to a delirious person. 3 a wild, strange fancy. 4 caprice; whim. 5 (in music) fantasia. Also, **phantasy.** [< Old French *fantasie* < Latin *phantasia* < Greek, appearance, image, ultimately < *phainein* to show]

fa nat ic (fə nat′ik), n. person who is carried away beyond reason by his feelings or beliefs, especially in religion or politics. —adj. unreasonably enthusiastic or zealous, especially in religion or politics. [< Latin *fanaticus* inspired by divinity < *fanum* temple]

fea si ble (fē′zə bəl), adj. 1 that can be done or carried out easily; possible without difficulty or damage; practicable: *The committee selected the plan that seemed most feasible.* See **possible** for synonym study. 2 likely; probable: *The witness's explanation of the accident sounded feasible.* 3 suitable; convenient: *The road was too rough to be feasible for travel by automobile.* [< Old French *faisable,* ultimately < Latin *facere* do] —**fea′si ble ness,** n. —**fea′si bly,** adv.

fea ture (fē′chər), n., v., **-tured, -tur ing.** —n. 1 part of the face. The eyes, nose, mouth, chin, and forehead are features. 2 **features,** pl. the face. 3 form or cast of the face. 4 a distinct part or quality; thing that stands out and attracts attention: *The main features of southern California are the climate and the scenery.* See synonym study below. 5 a main attraction, especially a full-length motion picture. 6 a special article, comic strip, etc., in a newspaper. —v.t. 1 be a feature of. 2 make a feature of: *The local newspapers featured the President's visit.* 3 INFORMAL. be like in features; favor. [< Old French *feture* < Latin *factura* a doing, making < *facere* do, make]

fe lo ni ous (fə lō′nē əs), adj. 1 having to do with a felony; criminal. 2 very wicked; villainous. —**fe lo′ni ous ly,** adv. —**fe lo′ni ous ness,** n.

fem i nist (fem′ə nist), n. person who believes in or favors feminism. —adj. believing in or favoring feminism.

fe tus (fē′təs), n. an animal embryo during the later stages of its development in the womb or in the egg, especially a human embryo more than three months old. Also, **foetus.** [< Latin]

fick le (fik′əl), adj. 1 likely to change or give up a loyalty, attachments, etc., without reason; inconstant: *a fickle friend.* 2 likely to change in nature; uncertain: *fickle weather.* [Old English *ficol* deceitful] —**fick′le ness,** n.

fix ate (fik′sāt), v., **-at ed, -at ing.** —v.t. 1 make fixed so as to establish a habit. 2 concentrate (one's attention) on something. —v.i. 1 become fixed or fixated. 2 have or develop an abnormal attachment or prejudice.

flank (flangk), n. 1 the fleshy or muscular part of the side of an animal or person between the ribs and the hip. 2 piece of beef cut from this part. See **beef** for diagram. 3 side of a mountain, building, etc. 4 the far right or the far left side of an army, fleet, or fort. —v.t. 1 be at the side of: *A garage flanked the house.* 2 get around the far right or the far left side of. 3 attack from or on the side. —v.i. 1 occupy a position on a flank or side. 2 present the flank or side. [< Old French *flanc* < Germanic]

flex i ble (flek′sə bəl), *adj.* 1 easily bent; not stiff; bending without breaking: *Leather, rubber, and wire are flexible.* 2 easily adapted to fit various conditions: *The actor's flexible voice accommodated itself to every emotion.* 3 easily managed; willing to yield to influence or persuasion. See synonym study below. —**flex′i bly,** *adv.*

Syn. 3 **Flexible, pliant, limber** mean bent or bending easily. **Flexible** means capable of being bent or twisted easily and without breaking, or, used figuratively, of being adaptable: *Great thinkers have flexible minds.* **Pliant** means inherently tending to bend or, figuratively, to yield easily to an influence: *He was too weak and pliant to make up his own mind.* **Limber,** used chiefly of the body, means having flexible muscles and joints and suggests easy movement: *A dancer has limber legs.*

fluc tu ate (fluk′chü āt), *v.i.* **-at ed, -at ing.** 1 rise and fall; change continually; vary irregularly; waver; vacillate: *The temperature fluctuates from day to day. His emotions fluctuated between hopefulness and despair.* 2 move in waves. [< Latin *fluctuatum* moving as a wave < *fluctus* wave < *fluere* to flow]

fun da men tal (fun′də men′tl), *adj.* 1 of or forming a foundation or basis; essential; basic: *Reading is a fundamental skill.* 2 in music: **a** having to do with the lowest note of a chord. **b** designating a chord of which the root is the lowest note. —*n.* 1 something fundamental; essential part: *the fundamentals of grammar.* 2 (in music) the lowest note of a chord. 3 (in physics) that component of a wave which has the greatest wave length or lowest frequency. —**fun′da men′tal ly,** *adv.*

fo cus (fō′kəs), *n., pl.* **-cus es** or **-ci,** *v.,* **-cused, -cus ing** or **-cussed, -cus sing.** —*n.* 1 point at which rays of light, heat, etc., meet, diverge, or seem to diverge after being reflected from a mirror, bent by a lens, etc. 2 focal length. 3 the correct adjustment of a lens, the eye, etc., to make a clear image: *If my camera is not brought into focus, the photograph will be blurred.* 4 the central point of attraction, attention, activity, etc.: *The new baby was the focus of attention.* 5 (in geometry) a fixed point used in determining a conic section. A parabola has one focus while an ellipse or a hyperbola has two foci. —*v.t.* 1 bring (rays of light, heat, etc.) to a focus. 2 adjust (a lens, the eye, etc.) to make a clear image. 3 make (an image, etc.) clear by adjusting a lens, the eye, etc. 4 concentrate or direct: *When studying, he focused his mind on his lessons.* —*v.i.* 1 converge to a focus. 2 adjust the eye or an optical instrument for clear vision: *Focus upon some distant object.* [< Latin, hearth]

for mal ism (fôr′mə liz′əm), *n.* strict observance of outward forms and ceremonies, especially in religious worship.

for mat (fôr′mat), *n.* 1 shape, size, and general arrangement of a book, magazine, etc. 2 the design, plan, or arrangement of anything: *the format of a television show.* [< French < Latin *(liber) formatus* (book) formed (in a special way)]

for ti fy (fôr′tə fī), *v.,* **-fied, -fy ing.** —*v.t.* 1 strengthen against attack; provide with forts, walls, etc. 2 give support to; strengthen. 3 enrich with vitamins and minerals: *fortify bread.* —*v.i.* build forts, walls, etc.; protect a place against attack. [< Middle French *fortifier* < Late Latin *fortificare* < Latin *fortis* strong + *facere* to make] —**for′ti fi er,** *n.*

frus tra tion (fru strā′shən), *n.* 1 a frustrating. 2 a being frustrated.

fu tile (fyü′tl, fyü′tīl), *adj.* 1 not successful; useless; ineffectual: *He fell down after making futile attempts to keep his balance.* See **vain** for synonym study. 2 not important; trifling. [< Latin *futilis* pouring easily, worthless < *fundere* pour] —**fu′tile ly,** *adv.*

G

ge net ic (jə net′ik), *adj.* 1 having to do with origin and natural growth. 2 of or having to do with genetics. 3 or or having to do with genes. —**ge net′i cal ly,** *adv.*

gen ial[1] (jē′nyəl), *adj.* 1 smiling and pleasant; cheerful and friendly; kindly: *a genial welcome.* 2 helping growth; pleasantly warming; comforting: *a genial climate.* [< Latin *genialis,* literally, belonging to the genius < *genius*] —**gen′ial ly,** *adv.* —**gen′ial ness,** *n.*

gen i tal (jen′ə təl), *adj.* having to do with reproduction or the sex organs. —*n.* **genitals,** *pl.* the external sex organs. [< Latin *genitalis,* ultimately < *gignere* beget]

a hat	i it	oi oil	ch child	a in about
ā age	ī ice	ou out	ng long	e in taken
ä far	o hot	u cup	sh she	ə = i in pencil
e let	ō open	u put	th thin	o in lemon
ē equal	ô order	ü rule	TH then	u in circus
er term			zh measure	< = derived from

glad i a tor (glad′ē ā′tər), *n.* 1 slave, captive, or paid fighter who fought at the public shows in the arenas in ancient Rome. 2 a skilled contender in any fight or struggle. [< Latin < *gladius* sword]

glob al (glō′bəl), *adj.* 1 of the earth as a whole; worldwide. 2 shaped like a globe; spherical. —**glob′al ly,** *adv.*

graph (graf), *n.* 1 a symbolic diagram, used in mathematics, chemistry, etc., in which a system of one or more curves, lines, etc., shows how one quantity depends on or changes with another. 2 (in mathematics) a curve or other line representing the mathematical relations of the elements in an equation or function. —*v.t.* make a graph of. [short for *graphic formula*]

grat i fy (grat′ə fī), *v.t.,* **-fied, -fy ing.** 1 give pleasure to; please: *Flattery gratifies a vain person.* 2 give satisfaction to; satisfy; indulge: *gratify one's hunger with a large meal.* See **humor** for synonym study. [< Latin *gratificari* < *gratus* pleasing + *facere* make, do] —**grat′i fi er,** *n.* —**grat′i fy′ing ly,** *adv.*

grat is (grat′is, grāt′is), *adv., adj.* for nothing; free of charge. [< Latin, ablative plural of *gratia* favor]

grave[1] (grāv), *n.* 1 hole dug in the ground where a dead body is to be buried. 2 mount or monument over it. 3 any place of burial: *a watery grave.* 4 death. [Old English *græf.* Related to GRAVE[3].]

grave[2] (grāv), *adj., grav er, grav est, n.* —*adj.* 1 earnest; thoughtful; serious: *People are grave in church.* 2 not gay; dignified; solemn: *grave music, a grave ceremony.* 3 important; weighty; momentous: *a grave decision.* 4 somber: *grave colors.* 5 having a grave accent. 6 (in phonetics) low in pitch; not acute. —*n.* grave accent. [< Middle French < Latin *gravis* heavy, serious] —**grave′ly,** *adv.,* —**grave′ness,** *n.*

grave[3] (grāv), *v.t.* **graved, grav en** or **graved, grav ing.** 1 engrave; carve. 2 impress deeply; fix firmly. [Old English *grafan*]

grave[4] (grāv), *v.t.* **graved, grav ing.** clean (a ship's bottom) and cover with tar. [origin uncertain]

grave[5] (grä′vā), in music: —*adj.* slow and solemn in tempo. —*adv.* slowly and solemnly. [< Italian < Latin *gravis* serious, heavy]

guer ril la (gə ril′ə), *n.* member of a band of fighters who harass the enemy by sudden raids, ambushes, the plundering of supply trains, etc. Guerrillas are not part of a regular army. —*adj.* of or by guerrillas: *a guerrilla attack.* Also, **guerilla.** [< Spanish, diminutive of *guerra* war; of Germanic origin]

H

he ret i cal (hə ret′ə kəl), *adj.* 1 of or having to do with heresy or heretics. 2 containing heresy; characterized by heresy. —**he ret′i cal ly,** *adv.*

hi e rar chy (hī′ə rär′kē), *n., pl.* **-chies.** 1 organization of persons or things arranged one above the other according to rank, class, or grade. 2 government by priests or church officials. 3 group of church officials of different ranks. In the hierarchy of the church, archbishops have more authority than bishops. [< Medieval Latin *hierarchia* < Greek *hieros* sacred + *archos* ruler]

hi er o glyph ic (hī′ər o glif′ik), *n.* 1 picture, character, or symbol standing for a word, idea, or sound; hieroglyph. The ancient Egyptians used hieroglyphics instead of an alphabet like ours. 2 letter or word that is hard to read. 3 **hieroglyphics,** *pl.* **a** system of writing that uses hieroglyphics. **b** writing that is hard to read. 4 a secret symbol. —*adj.* 1 or or written in hieroglyphics. 2 hard to read. [< Late Latin *hieroglyphicus* < Greek *hieroglyphikos* < *hieros* sacred + *glyphe* a carving] —**hi′er o glyph′i cal ly,** *adv.*

hor ren dous (hô ren′dəs, ho ren′dəs), *adj.* causing horror; horrible. —**hor ren′dous ly,** *adv.*

hy poth e size (hī poth′ə sīz), *v.,* **sized, -siz ing.** —*v.i.* make a hypothesis. —*v.t.* assume; suppose.

I

im bibe (im bīb′), v., **-bibed, -bib ing,** —v.t. 1 drink in; drink. See **drink** for synonym study. 2 absorb: *The roots of a plant imbibe moisture from the earth.* 3 take into one's mind: *A child often imbibes superstitions that last all his life.* —v.i. drink. [< Latin *imbibere* < *in-* in + *bibere* to drink] —**im bib′er,** n.

im ma ture (im′ə chur′, im′ə tur′, im′ə tyur′), adj. not mature; undeveloped. —**im′ma ture′ly,** adv. —**im′ma ture′ness,** n.

im pact (im′pakt), n. 1 a striking (of one thing against another); collision. 2 a forceful or dramatic effect: *the impact of automation on society.* —v.t. 1 drive or press closely or firmly into something; pack in. 2 come upon; hit; reach: *The capsule impacted the moon.* [< Latin *impactum* struck against < *in-* on + *pangere* to strike] —**im pac′tion,** n.

im pede (im pēd′), v.t. **-ped ed, -ped ing.** stand in the way of; hinder; obstruct: *Our progress was impeded by the deep snow.* See **prevent** for synonym study. [< Latin *impedire* < *in-* on + *pedem* foot] —**im ped′er,** n.

im per a tive (im per′ə tiv), adj. not to be avoided; that must be done; urgent: *It is imperative that this very sick child should stay in bed.* 2 expressing a command or request: *an imperative statement.* 3 (in grammar) having to do with a verb form which expresses a command, request, or advice. "Go!" and "Stop, look, listen!" are in the imperative mood. —n. 1 something imperative; command: *The great imperative is "Love thy neighbor as thyself."* 2 a verb form in the imperative mood. 3 the imperative mood. [< Latin *imperativus* <*imperare* to command] —**im per′a tive ly,** adv. —**im per′a tive ness,** n.

im ple ment (n. im′plə mənt; v. im′plə ment), n. a useful article of equipment; tool; instrument; utensil. A plow, an ax, a shovel, and a broom are implements. See **tool** for synonym study. —v.t. 1 provide with implements or other means. 2 provide the power and authority necessary to accomplish or put (something) into effect: *implement an order.* 3 carry out; get done: *Do not undertake a project unless you can implement it.* [< Late Latin *implementum* that which fills a need < Latin *implere* to fill < *in-* in + *plere* to fill] —**im′ple men ta′tion,** n.

im ply (im plī′), v.t., **-plied, ply ing.** 1 mean without saying so; express indirectly; suggest: *Her smile implied that she had forgiven us.* 2 involve as a necessary part or condition: *Speech implies a speaker.* 3 signify; mean. [< Old French *emplier* involve; put (in) < Latin *implicare* < *in-* in + *plicare* to fold. Doublet of EMPLOY, IMPLICATE.] See **infer** for usage note.

im pulse (im′puls), n. 1 a sudden, driving force or influence; thrust; push: *the impulse of a wave, the impulse of hunger, the impulse of curiosity.* 2 the effect of a sudden, driving force or influence. 3 a sudden inclination or tendency to act: *The angry crowd was influenced more by impulse than by reason.* 4 stimulus that is transmitted, especially by nerve cells, and influences action in the muscle, gland, or other nerve cells that it reaches. 5 surge of electrical current in one direction. [< Latin *impulsus* < *impellere*. See IMPEL.]

in ac ces si ble (in′ək ses′ə bəl), adj. 1 hard to get at; hard to reach or enter: *The house on top of the steep hill is inaccessible.* 2 not accessible; that cannot be reached or entered at all. —**in′ac ces′si bly,** adv.

in can ta tion (in′kan tā′shən), n. 1 set of words spoken as a magic charm or to cast a magic spell. 2 the use of such words. [< Latin *incantationem* < *incantare* enchant < *in-* against + *cantare* to chant]

in ci dence (in′sə dəns), n. 1 range of occurrence or influence; extent of effects: *the incidence of a disease.* 2 a falling on or affecting. 3 the falling or striking of a projectile, ray of light, etc., on a surface. 4 angle of incidence.

in gest (in jest′), v.t. take (food, etc.) into the body for digestion. [< Latin *ingestum* carried in < *in-* in + *gerere* carry]

in hib it (in hib′it), v.t. 1 hold back; hinder or restrain; check: *Some drugs can inhibit normal bodily activity.* 2 prohibit; forbid. [< Latin *inhibitum* held in < *in-* in + *habere* to hold —**in hib′it er,** n.

i ni tial (i nish′əl), adj., n., v., **-tialed, -tial ing** or **-tialled, -tail ling.** —adj. 1 of, having to do with, or occurring at the beginning; first; earliest: *My initial effort at skating was a failure.* 2 standing at the beginning: *the initial letter of a word.* —n. 1 the first letter of a word or name. 2 an extra large letter, often decorated, at the beginning of a chapter or other division of a book or illuminated manuscript. —v.t. mark or sign with initials: *John Allen Smith initialed the note J.A.S.* [< Latin *initialis* < *initium* beginning < *inire* begin < *in-* in + *ire* go] —**i ni′tial ly,** adv.

in sol u ble (in sol′yə bel), adj. 1 that canot be dissolved; not soluble: *Fats are insoluble in water.* 2 that canot be solved; unsolvable. —**in sol′u ble ness,** n.—**in sol′u bly,** adv.

in tan gi ble (in tan′jə bəl), adj. 1 not capable of being touched or felt: *Sound and light are intangible.* 2 not easily grasped by the mind; vague: *The very popular girl had that intangible quality called charm.* —n. something intangible. —**in tan′gi ble ness,** n. —**in tan′gi bly,** adv.

in ter act (in′tər akt′), v.i. act on each other.

in ter re late (in′tər ri lāt′), v.t. **-lat ed, -lat ing,** bring into relation to each other.

in ti mate¹ (in′tə mit), adj. 1 very familiar; known very well; closely acquainted: *intimate friends.* See **familiar** for synonym study. 2 resulting from close familiarity; close: *an intimate connection, intimate knowledge of a matter.* 3 personal; private: *A diary is a very intimate book.* 4 far within; deepest; inmost: *the intimate recesses of the heart.* —n. a close friend. [earlier *intime* < French < Latin *intimus* inmost. See INTIMATE².] —**in′ti mate ly,** adv. —**in′ti mate ness,** n.

in ti mate² (in′tə māt), v.t., **-mat ed, -mat ing.** 1 suggest indirectly; hint. See **hint** for synonym study. 2 make known; announce; notify. [< Latin *intimatum* made known, brought in < *intimus* inmost, superlative of *in* in] —**in′ti mat′er,** n.

in trigue (n. in trēg′, in′trēg; v in trēg′), n., v., **-trigued, -tri guing.** —n. 1 secret scheming; underhand planning to accomplish some purpose; plotting. 2 a crafty plot; secret scheme. 3 a secret love affair. —v.i. 1 form and carry out plots; plan in a secret or underhand way. 2 have a secret love affair. —v.t. excite the curiosity and interest of: *The book's unusual title intrigued me.* [< French < Italian *intrigo* < *intrigare* entangle < Latin *intricare* —**in tri′guer,** n.

in tu i tive (in tü′ ə tiv, in tyü′ tiv), adj. 1 perceiving or understanding by intuition: *an intuitive mind.* 2 acquired by intuition; instinctive; natural: *an artist's intuitive understanding of color.* —**in tu′i tive ly,** adv.

J

jack al (jak′ôl, jakəl), n. 1 any of several species of wild dogs of Asia, Africa, and eastern Europe, which hunt in packs at night and feed on small animals and carrion left by large animals. 2 person who does menial work for another. [< Turkish *cakāl* < Persian *shaghāl*]

jar gon (jär′gən, jär′gon), n. 1 confused, meaningless talk or writing. 2 language that is not understood. 3 language or dialect composed of a mixture of two or more languages, such as pidgin English. 4 language of a special group, profession, etc. Doctors, actors, and sailors have jargons. —v.i talk jargon. [< Old French]

jour nal (jer′ nl), n. 1 a daily record of events or occurrences. 2 record or account of what a person thinks, feels, notices, etc., such as a diary. 3 a ship's log. 4 record of the daily proceedings of a legislative or other public body. 5 newspaper, magazine, or other periodical. 6 (in bookkeeping) a book in which every item of business is written down, so that the item can be entered under the proper account. 7 the part of a shaft or axle that turns in a bearing. [< Old French < Late Latin *diurnalis.* Doublet of DIURNAL.]

L

lack a dai si cal (lak′ə dā′zə kəl), adj. lacking interest or enthusiasm; languid; listless; dreamy. [< *lackaday* alas, variant of *alack a day!*] —**lack′a dai′si cal ly,** adv.

lei sure (lē′zhər, lezh′ər), n. 1 time free from required work in which a person may rest, amuse himself, and do the things he likes to do. 2 condition of having time free from required work. 3 **at leisure, a** free; not busy. **b** without hurry; taking plenty of time. 4 **at one's leisure,** when one has leisure; at one's convenience. —adj. 1 free; not busy: *leisure hours.* 2 leisured: *the leisure class.* [< Old French *leisir* < Latin *licere* be allowed]

les bi an or **Les bi an** (lez′bē ən), n. a homosexual female. —adj. having to do with homosexuality in females. [<*Lesbos*]

lin e ar (lin′ē ər), *adj.* 1 of, in, or like a line, especially a straight line. 2 made of lines; making use of lines. 3 of length. 4 long and narrow, as a leaf. **—lin′e ar ly,** *adv.*

lin guis tics (ling gwis′tiks), *n.* the science of language, including the study of speech sounds, language structures, and the history and historical relationship of languages and linguistic forms.

lu bri cate (lü′brə kāt), *v.,* **-cat ed, -cat ing.** *—v.t.* 1 apply oil, grease, or other substance to (a machine, etc.) to make it run smoothly and easily. 2 make slippery or smooth; expedite. *v.i.* act as a lubricant. [< Latin *lubricatum* made slippery < *lubricus* slippery] **—lu′bri ca′tion,** *n.* **—lu′bri ca′tor,** *n.*

M

mag ni tude (mag′nə tüd, mag′nə tyüd), *n.* 1 greatness of size. 2 great importance, effect, or consequence. 3 size, whether great or small. 4 degree of brightness of a star. The brightest stars are of the first magnitude. Those just visible to the naked eye are of the sixth magnitude. Each degree is 2.512 times brighter than the next degree. 5 number expressing this. 6 (in mathematics) a number given to a quantity so that it may be compared with similar quantities. [< Latin *magnitudo* < *magnus* large]

ma nip u late (mə nip′yə lāt), *v.t.* **-lated, -lat ing.** 1 handle or treat, especially skillfully: *manipulate the controls of an airplane.* 2 manage cleverly, sometimes using personal influence, especially unfair influence: *He so manipulated the ball team that he was elected captain.* 3 change for one's own purpose or advantage; treat unfairly or dishonestly: *manipulate a company's accounts to conceal embezzlement.* [< Latin *manipulus* handful < *manus* hand + root of *plere* to fill] **—ma nip′u la′tor,** *n.*

map (map), *n., v.,* **mapped, map ping.** *—n.* 1 drawing representing the earth's surface or part of it, usually showing countries, cities, rivers, seas, lakes, and mountains. See synonym study below. 2 drawing representing the sky or part of it, showing the position of the stars, etc. 3 **put on the map,** make well-known. *—v.t.* 1 make a map of; show on a map. 2 arrange in detail; plan: *map out the week's work.* 3 (in mathematics) to cause an element in (one set) to correspond to an element in the same or another set. [< Medieval Latin *mappa* < Latin, napkin, cloth (on which maps were once drawn)] **—map′like′,** *adj.* **—map′per,** *n.* **Syn.** *n.* 1 **Map, chart** mean a drawing representing a surface or area. **Map** applies particularly to a representation of some part of the earth's surface showing relative geographical positions, shape, size, etc.: *A map of a city shows streets and parks.* **Chart** applies particularly to a map used in navigation, showing deep and shallow places, islands, channels, etc., in a body of water, or altitudes, radio beacons, air currents, airplanes, etc., for flying: *The reef that the ship struck is on the chart.*

mat i nee or **mat i née** (mat′n ā′), *n.* a dramatic or musical performance held in the afternoon. [< French *matinee* < Old French *matin* morning]

ma trix (mā′triks), *n., pl.* **-tri ces** or **-trix es.** 1 that which gives origin or form to something enclosed within it, such as the mold for a casting or the rock in which gems, fossils, etc., are embedded. 2 womb. 3 the formative part of a tooth or fingernail. 4 the intercellular nonliving substance of a tissue. 5 (in mathematics) a set of quantities in a rectangular array, subject to operations such as multiplication or inversion according to specified rules. [< Latin, womb < *mater* mother]

may hem (mā′hem), *n.* 1 crime of intentionally maiming a person or injuring him so that he is less able to defend himelf. 2 any crime of violence which causes permanent physical injury. [< Anglo-French *mahem* < Old French *mahaignier* to maim]

mes mer ize (mez′mə rīz′, mes′mə rīz′), *v.t. v.i.* **-ized, iz ing.** hypnotize. [< Franz A. *Mesmer,* 1734–1815, Austrian physician who made hypnotism popular] **—mes′mer iz′er,** *n.*

met a bol ic (met′ə bol′ik), *adj.* of or having to do with metabolism. **—met′a bol′i cal ly,** *adv.*

me tab o lism (mə tab′ə liz′əm), *n.* the sum of the physiological processes by which an organism maintains life. In metabolism protoplasm is broken down to produce energy, which is then used by the body to build up new cells and tissues, provide heat, and engage in physical activity. Growth and action depend on metabolism. [< Greek *metabole* change < *meta-* after + *bole* a throwing]

a hat	i it	oi oil	ch child	a in about
ā age	ī ice	ou out	ng long	e in taken
ä far	o hot	u cup	sh she	ə = i in pencil
e let	ō open	u put	th thin	o in lemon
ē equal	ô order	ü rule	TH then	u in circus
er term			zh measure	< = derived from

met ro nome (met′rə nōm), *n.* device that can be adjusted to make loud ticking sounds at different speeds. Metronomes are used especially to mark time for persons practicing on musical instruments. [< Greek *metron* measure + *-nomos* regulating < *nemein* regulate]

mi grate (mī′grāt), *v.i.,* **-grat ed, -grat ing.** 1 move from one place to settle in another. 2 go from one region to another with the change in the seasons. Most birds migrate to warmer countries in the winter. [< Latin *migratum* moved]

mi crom e ter (mī krom′ə tər), *n.* 1 instrument for measuring very small distances, angles, objects, etc. Certain kinds are used with a microscope or telescope. 2 micrometer caliper.

mis con cep tion (mis′kən sep′shən), *n.* a mistaken idea or notion; wrong conception.

mo bi lize (mō′bə līz), *v.,* **-lized, -liz ing.** *—v.t.* 1 call (troops, ships, etc.) into active military service; organize for war. 2 organize or call to take part, usually during an emergency: *mobilize Red Cross units for rescue work in a flood.* 3 put into motion or active use: *mobilize the wealth of a country.* *—v.i.* 1 assemble and prepare for war: *The troops mobilized quickly.* 2 organize or assemble in an emergency. [< French *mobiliser* < *mobile* mobile]

mode¹ (mōd), *n.* 1 manner or way in which a thing is done; method: *Riding a donkey is a slow mode of travel.* 2 manner or state of existence of a thing: *Heat is a mode of motion.* 3 (in grammar) mood. 4 in music: **a** any of various arrangements of the tones of an octave. **b** either of the two classes (major and minor) of keys. **c** any of the various scales used in ancient Greek and medieval music, having the intervals differently arranged. 5 (in statistics) the value of the variable with the highest frequency in a set of data. [< Latin *modus* measure, manner]

mode² (mōd), *n.* style, fashion, or custom that prevails; the way most people are behaving, talking, dressing, etc. [< French < Latin *modus* mode¹]

mon i tor (mon′ə tər), *n.* 1 pupil in school with special duties, such as helping to keep order and taking attendance. 2 person who gives advice or warning. 3 something that reminds or gives warning. 4 a low, armored warship, chiefly of the late 1800's, having a low freeboard and one or more revolving turrets, each with one or two heavy guns. 5 **Monitor,** the first warship of this type designed for the Union Navy in the Civil War. It engaged in a famous battle with the Merrimac on July 9, 1862. 6 any of a family of large, carnivorous lizards of Africa, southern Asia, Australia, and the East Indies. 7 receiver or other device used for checking and listening to radio or television transmissions, telephone messages, etc., as they are being recorded or broadcast. *—v.t., v.i.* 1 check the quality, wave frequency, etc., of (radio or television transmissions, telephone messages, etc.) by means of a monitor. 2 listen to (broadcasts, telephone messages, etc.) for censorship, military significance, etc. 3 (in physics) test the intensity of radiations, especially of radiations produced by radioactivity. 4 check in order to control something. [< Latin, admonisher < *monere* admonish, warn]

mu ti late (myü′tl āt), *v.t.,* **-lat ed, -lat ing.** 1 cut, tear, or break off a limb or other important part of; injure seriously by cutting, tearing, or breaking off some part; maim. 2 make (a book, story, song, etc.) imperfect by removing parts. [< Latin *mutilatum* maimed] **—mu′ti la′tor,** *n.*

muck rake (muk′rāk′), *v.i.,* **-raked, -rak ing.** hunt for and expose real or alleged corruption in government, big business, etc.

myr i ad (mir′ē əd), *n.* 1 ten thousand. 2 a very great number: *There are myriads of stars.* *adj.* 1 ten thousand. 2 countless; innumerable. [< Greek *myriados* ten thousand; countless]

N

neg a tiv ism (neg′ə tə viz′əm), *n.* tendency to say or do the opposite of what is suggested.

niche (nich), *n., v.,* **niched, nich ing.** —*n.* 1 recess or hollow in a wall for a statue, vase, etc.; nook. 2 a suitable place or position; place for which a person is suited. —*v.t.* place in a niche or similar recess. [< Middle French, ultimately < Latin *nidus* nest]

O

ob sess (ob ses′), *v.t.* fill the mind of; keep the attention of to an unreasonable or unhealthy extent; haunt: *Fear that someone might steal his money obsessed him.* [< Latin *obsessum* possessed; < *ob-* on + *sedere* sit]

o paque (ō pāk′), *adj.* 1 not letting light through; not transparent or translucent. 2 not conducting heat, sound, electricity, etc. 3 not shining; dark; dull. 4 hard to understand; obscure. 5 stupid. —*n.* something opaque. [< Latin *opacus* dark, shady] —**o paque′ly,** *adv.* —**o paque′ness,** *n.*

op press (ə pres′), *v.t.* 1 govern harshly; keep down unjustly or by cruelty: *A good government will not oppress the poor.* 2 weigh down; lie heavily on; burden: *A sense of trouble ahead oppressed my spirits.* [< Medieval Latin *oppressare* < Latin *opprimere* press against < *ob-* against + *premere* to press]

op tion (op′shən), *n.* 1 right or freedom of choice: *Pupils in our school have the option of taking Spanish, French, or German.* 2 act of choosing: *Where to travel should be left to each person's option.* 3 thing that is or can be chosen. See **choice** for synonym study. 4 right to buy something at a certain price within a certain time: *We paid $500 for an option on the land.* 5 (in insurance) the right of an insured person to decide how he shall receive the money due him on a policy. [< Latin *optionem,* related to *optare* opt]

o ra to ry[1] (ôr′ə tôr′ē, ôr′ə tōr′ē; or′ə tôr′ē, or′ə tōr′ē), *n.* 1 skill in public speaking; eloquent speaking or language. 2 the art of public speaking. [< Latin (*ars*) *oratoria* oratorical (art) < *orare* speak formally, pray]

o ra to ry[2] (ôr′ə tôr′ē, ôr′ə tōr′ē; or′ə tôr′ē, or′ə tōr′ē), *n., pl.* **-ries.** a small chapel, room or other place set apart for private prayer. [< Late Latin *oratorium* < Latin *orare* plead, pray. Doublet of ORATORIO.]

or gan (ôr′gən), *n.* 1 a musical instrument consisting of one or more sets of pipes of different lengths, sounded by compressed air supplied by a bellows, and played by means of keys arranged in one or more keyboards; pipe organ. Organs are used especially in church. 2 any of certain similar instruments somewhat like the pipe organ but sounded by electronic devices. 3 any of various other musical instruments, such as a hand organ, reed organ, or mouth organ. 4 any part of an animal or plant that is composed of various tissues organized to perform some particular function. The eyes, stomach, heart, and lungs are organs of the body. Stamens and pistils are organs of flowers. 5 means of action; instrument: *A court is an organ of government.* 6 newspaper or magazine that speaks for and gives the views of a political party or some other group or organization. [< Latin *organum* < Greek *organon* instrument, related to *ergon* work]

o ri ent (*n., adj.* ôr′ē ənt; ōr′ē ənt; *v.* ôr′ē ent, ōr′ē ent), *n.* 1 the east. 2 **the Orient,** countries in Asia as distinguished from those in Europe and America; the East. —*adj.* 1 **Orient,** of the Orient; Oriental. 2 bright; shining: *an orient pearl.* 3 ARCHAIC. rising: *the orient sun.* —*v.t.* 1 put facing east. 2 place or build (a church) with the chief altar at the eastern end of its longer axis. 3 place so that it faces in any indicated direction: *The building is oriented north and south.* 4 find the direction or position of; determine the compass bearings of. 5 bring into the right relationship with surroundings; adjust to a new situation, condition of affairs, etc. [< Latin *orientem* the East, literally, rising (with reference to the rising sun)]

or gan ic (ôr gan′ik), *adj.* 1 of the bodily organs; affecting an organ: *an organic disease.* 2 of or obtained from plants or animals: *organic fertilizer.* 3 grown by using decaying plant and animal matter instead of artificial fertilizers: *organic foods.* 4 (in chemistry) of compounds containing carbon; containing carbon. Starch is an organic compound. 5 having organs or an organized physical structure 6 made up of related parts, but being a unit; coordinated; organized: *The United States is an organic whole made up of 50 states.* 7 being part of the structure or constitution of a person or thing; fundamental: *The Constitution is the organic law of the United States.* —**or gan′i cal ly,** *adv.*

os ten si ble (o sten′sə bəl), *adj.* according to appearances; declared as genuine; apparent; pretended; professed: *Her ostensible purpose was borrowing sugar, but she really wanted to see the new furniture.* [< Latin *ostensum* shown, ultimately < *ob-* toward + *tendere* to stretch] —**os ten′si bly,** *adv.*

o vum (ō′vəm), *n., pl.* **o va.** a female germ cell, produced in the ovary; egg. After the ovum is fertilized, a new organism or embryo develops. [< Latin, egg]

P

pal try (pôl′trē), *adj.* **-tri er, -tri est.** 1 almost worthless; trifling; petty; mean. 2 of no worth; despicable; contemptible. [probably related to Low German *paltrig* ragged, torn] —**pal′tri ly,** *adv.* —**pal′tri ness,** *n.*

pam per (pam′pər), *v.t.* indulge too much; allow too many privileges; spoil: *pamper a child, pamper one's appetite.* [Middle English *pamperen*] —**pam′per er,** *n.*

par a lyze (par′ə līz), *v.t.* **-lyzed, -lyz ing.** 1 affect with a lessening or loss of the power of motion or feeling: *His left arm was paralyzed.* 2 make powerless or helplessly inactive; cripple: *Fear paralyzed my mind.* Also, BRITISH **paralyze.** —**par′a lyz′er,** *n.*

par a noi a (par′ə noi′ə), *n.* 1 form of psychosis characterized by continuing, elaborate delusions of persecution or grandeur. 2 an irrational distrust of others; complex of persecution. [< Greek, mental derangement < *paranous* out of one's mind < *para-*[1] + *nous* mind]

pe nal ize (pē′nl īz, pen′l īz), *v.t.,* **-ized, -iz ing.** 1 declare punishable by law or by rule; set a penalty for: *Speeding on city streets is penalized. Fouls are penalized in many sports and games.* 2 inflict a penalty on; punish: *The football team was penalized five yards.* 3 subject to a disadvantage; handicap: *His deafness penalizes him in public life.*

per cap i ta (pər kap′ə tə), for each person: *$40 for eight men is $5 per capita.* [< Latin]

per ceive (pər sēv′), *v.t.,* **-ceived, -ceiv ing.** 1 be aware of through the senses; see, hear, taste, smell, or feel. See **see** for synonym study. 2 take in with the mind; observe; understand: *I soon perceived that I could not make him change his mind.* [< Old French *perceivre* < Latin *percipere* < *per-* thoroughly + *capere* to grasp] —**per ceiv′a ble,** *adj.* —**per ceiv′a bly,** *adv.*

per cept (per′sept), *n.* 1 that which is perceived. 2 understanding that is the result of perceiving.

per cep tion (pər sep′shən), *n.* 1 act of perceiving: *His perception of the change came in a flash.* 2 power of perceiving: *a keen perception.* 3 understanding that is the result of perceiving: *I now have a clear perception of what went wrong.* [< Latin *perceptionem* < *percipere* perceive. See PERCEIVE.]

per cip i ent (pər sip′ē ənt), *adj.* 1 that perceives or is capable of perceiving; conscious. 2 having keen perception; discerning. —*n.* person or thing that perceives. [< Latin *percipientem* perceiving]

per tain (pər tān′), *v.i.* 1 belong or be connected as a part, possession, etc.: *We own the house and the land pertaining to it.* 2 have to do with; be related; refer: *documents pertaining to the case.* 3 be appropriate: *We had turkey and everything else that pertains to Thanksgiving.* [< Old French *partenir* < Latin *pertinere* reach through, connect < *per-* through + *tenere* to hold]

phe nom e non (fə nom′ə non), *n., pl.,* **-na** (or **-nons** for 4). 1 fact, event, or circumstance that can be observed: *Lightning is an electrical phenomenon.* 2 any sign, symptom, or manifestation: *Fever and inflammation are phenomena of disease.* 3 any exceptional fact or occurrence: *historical phenomena.* 4 an extraordinary or remarkable person or thing. A genius or prodigy is sometimes called a phenomenon. [< Greek *phainomenon* < *phainesthai* appear]

phys i o log i cal (fiz′ē ə loj′ə kəl), *adj.* 1 having to do with physiology: *Digestion is a physiological process.* 2 having to do with the normal or healthy functioning of an organism: *Food and sleep are physiological needs.* —**phys′i o log′i cal ly,** *adv.*

piv ot al (piv′ə təl), *adj.* 1 of, having to do with, or serving as a pivot. 2 being that on which something turns, hinges, or depends; very important. —**piv′ot al ly,** *adv.*

piz za (pēt′sə), *n.* a spicy, pielike Italian dish made by baking a large flat layer of bread dough covered with cheese, tomato sauce, herbs, etc. [< Italian]

plague (plāg), *n., v.,* **plagued, pla guing.** —*n.* 1 highly contagious, epidemic, and often fatal bacterial disease that occurs in several forms, one of which is bubonic plague. The plague is common in Asia and has several times swept through Europe. 2 any epidemic disease; pestilence. 3 punishment thought to be sent from God. 4 thing or person that torments, annoys, troubles, or is disagreeable. —*v.t.* 1 cause to suffer from a plague. 2 vex; annoy; bother. See **tease** for synonym study. [< Late Latin *plaga* pestilence < Latin, blow, wound] —**pla′guer,** *n.*

plum met (plum′it), *n.* plumb, —*v.i.* plunge; drop. [< Old French *plommet* < *plomb* lead < Latin *plumbum*]

po di um (pō′dē əm), *n., pl.* **-di ums, -di a** (-dē ə). 1 a raised platform, especially one used by a public speaker or an orchestra conductor. 2 a raised platform surrounding the arena in an ancient amphitheater. 3 a continuous projecting base or pedestal. [< Latin < Greek *podion* < *podos* foot]

pop u lace (pop′yə lis), *n.* the common people; the masses.

po tas si um (pə tas′ē əm), *n.* a soft, silver-white metallic element that occurs in nature only in compounds, is essential for the growth of plants, and oxidizes rapidly when exposed to the air. Potassium is one of the most abundant elements in the earth's crust. *Symbol:* K; *atomic number* 19. See pages 326 and 327 for table. [< New Latin < English *potash*]

pos tu late (*n.* pos′chə lit; *v.* pos′chə lāt), *n., v.,* **-lat ed, -lat ing.** —*n.* something taken for granted or assumed as a basis for reasoning; fundamental principle; necessary condition: *One postulate of plane geometry is that a straight line may be drawn between any two points.* —*v.t.* 1 assume as a postulate; take for granted. 2 require; demand; claim. [< Latin *postulatum* a demand < *postulare* to demand] —**pos′tu la′tion,** *n.*

pre cip i ta tion (pri sip′ə tā′shən), *n.* 1 act or state of precipitating; throwing down or falling headlong. 2 a hastening or hurrying. 3 a sudden bringing on: *the precipitation of war without warning.* 4 unwise or rash rapidity; sudden haste. 5 the separating out of a substance from a solution as a solid. 6 the depositing of moisture in the form of rain, dew, snow, etc. 7 something that is precipitated, such as rain, dew, or snow. 8 amount that is precipitated.

pre de ter mine (prē′di ter′mən), *v.t.,* **-mined, -min ing.** 1 determine or decide beforehand: *We met at the predetermined time.* 2 direct or impel beforehand (to something). —**pre′de ter′mi na′tion,** *n.*

pre na tal (prē nā′tl) *adj.* 1 before childbirth: *A woman soon to have a baby requires prenatal care.* 2 occurring before birth: *prenatal injury to the skull.* —**pre na′tal ly,** *adv.*

pre req ui site (prē rek′wə zit), *n.* something required beforehand: *That high school course is usually a prerequisite to college work.* —*adj.* required beforehand.

pre sci ent (prē′shē ənt, presh′ē ənt; prē′shənt, presh′ənt), *adj.* knowing beforehand; foreseeing. —**pre′sci ent ly,** *adv.*

prime¹ (prīm), *adj.* 1 first in rank or importance; chief; principal: *The community's prime need is a new school.* 2 first in time or order; primary: *the prime causes of war.* 3 first in quality; first-rate; excellent: *prime ribs of beef.* 4 in mathematics: **a** having no common integral divisor but 1 and the number itself. **b** having no common integral divisor but 1: *2 is prime to 9.* 5 ranking high or highest in some scale or rating system: *prime borrowers, prime time on television.* —*n.* prime number. [< Latin *primus* first] —**prime′ness,** *n.*

prime² (prīm), *n.,* 1 the best time, stage, or state: *be in the prime of life.* 2 the best part. 3 the first part; beginning. 4 springtime. 5 Also, **Prime.** the second of the seven canonical hours, or the service for it. 6 prime number. 7 one of the sixty minutes in a degree. 8 the mark (′) indicating this. B′ is read ″B prime.″ [Old English *prim* the first period (of the day) < Latin *prima* (*hora*) first (hour of the Roman day)] —**prime′ly,** *adv.* —**prime′ness,** *n.*

prime³ (prīm), *v.t.,* **primed, prim ing.** 1 prepare by putting something in or on. 2 supply (a gun) with powder. 3 cover (a surface) with a first coat of paint or oil so that the finishing coat of paint will not soak in. 4 equip (a person) with information, words, etc. 5 pour water into (a pump) to start action. [origin uncertain]

pro cras ti nate (prō kras′tə nāt), *v.i., v.t.,* **-nat ed, -nat ing.** put things off until later; delay, especially repeatedly. [< Latin *procrastinatum* postponed, ultimately < *pro-* forward + *cras* tomorrow] —**pro cras′ti na′tion,** *n.* —**pro cras′ti na′tor,** *n.*

a hat	i it	oi oil	ch child	a in about
ā age	ī ice	ou out	ng long	e in taken
ä far	o hot	u cup	sh she	ə = i in pencil
e let	ō open	u put	th thin	o in lemon
ē equal	ô order	ü rule	TH then	u in circus
er term			zh measure	< = derived from

prim i tive (prim′ə tiv), *adj.* 1 of early times; of long ago: *Primitive people often lived in caves.* 2 first of the kind: *primitive Christians.* 3 very simple; such as people had early in human history: *A primitive way of making fire is by rubbing two sticks together.* 4 original; primary. —*n.* 1 artist belonging to an early period, especially before the Renaissance. 2 artist who does not use the techniques of perspective, shading, or the like in painting. 3 painting or other work of art produced by a primitive. 4 person living in a primitive society or in primitive times. [< Latin *primitivus* < *primus* first] —**prim′i tive ly,** *adv.* —**prim′i tive ness,** *n.*

pro for ma (prō fôr′mə), LATIN. for the sake of form; as a matter of form.

pro gres sive (prə gres′iv), *adj.* 1 making progress; advancing to something better; improving: *a progressive nation.* 2 favoring progress; wanting improvement or reform in government, business, etc. 3 moving forward; developing: *a progressive disease.* 4 going from one to the next; passing on successively from one member of a series to the next. 5 of, following, or based on the theories and practices of progressive education: *a progressive school.* 6 (in grammar) showing the action as going on. *Is reading, was reading,* and *has been reading* are progressive forms of *read.* 7 **Progressive,** of a Progressive Party. 8 increasing in proportion to the increase of something else: *A progressive income tax is one whose rate goes up as a person's earnings increase.* —*n.* 1 **a** person who favors improvement and reform in government, religion, or business, etc. **b** progressivist. 2 **Progressive,** member of a Progressive Party. —**pro gres′sive ly,** *adv.* —**pro gres′sive ness,** *n.*

prop a gan da (prop′ə gan′də), *n.* 1 systematic effort to spread opinions or beliefs; any plan or method for spreading opinions or beliefs: *The life insurance companies engaged in health propaganda. Clever propaganda misled the enemy into believing it could not win the war.* 2 opinions or beliefs thus spread. 3 **Propaganda,** committee of cardinals established in 1622 to supervise foreign missions. [< New Latin (*congregatio de*) *propaganda* (*fide*) (congregation for) propagating (the faith)]

pro po nent (prə pō′nənt), *n.* 1 person who makes a proposal or proposition. 2 person who supports something; advocate. [< Latin *proponentem* propounding]

pro ton (prō′ton), *n.* an elementary particle charged with one unit of positive electricity, found in the nuclei of atoms and having a mass about 1,836 times that of an electron. [< Greek *proton* first]

psy cho a nal y sis (sī′kō ə nal′ə sis), *n.* 1 examination of a person's mind to discover the unconscious desires, fears, anxieties, etc., which produce mental and emotional disorders. 2 method of psychotherapy based on such examination.

psy chol o gy (sī kol′ə jē), *n., pl.* **-gies.** 1 science or study of the mind; branch of science dealing with the actions, feelings, thoughts, and other mental or behavioral processes of people and animals. 2 the mental states and processes of a person or persons; mental nature and behavior.

pur port (*v.* pər pôrt′, pər pōrt′; per′pôrt, per′pōrt; *n.* per′pôrt, per′pōrt), *v.t.* 1 claim or profess: *The document purported to be official.* 2 have as its main idea; mean. —*n.* meaning; main idea: *The purport of her letter was that she could not come.* See **meaning** for synonym study. [< Anglo-French *purporter* < Old french *purforth* + *porter* carry] —**pur port′ed ly,** *adv.*

Q

ques tion naire (kwes′chə ner′, kwes′ chə nar′), *n.* a written or printed list of questions, used to gather information, obtain a sampling of opinion, etc. [<French]

R

rat i fy (rat′ə fī), *v.t.*, **-fied, -fy ing**. confirm formally to make valid; give sanction or approval to: *The Senate ratified the treaty.* See **approve** for synonym study. [< Old French *ratifier* < Medieval Latin *ratificare*, ultimately < Latin *ratum* fixed + *facere* to make]—**rat′i fi′er**, *n.*

re ca pit u late (rē′kə pich′ə lāt), *v.t., v.i.*, **-lat ed, -lat ing**. repeat or recite the main points of; tell briefly; sum up. ′ < Latin *recapitulatum* summarized < *re-* again + *capitulum* chapter, section, diminutive of *caput* head] —**re′ca pit′u la′tor**, *n.*

re cruit (ri krüt′), *n.* 1 a newly enlisted soldier, sailor, etc. 2 a new member of any group or class. —*v.t.* 1 get (men) to join an army, navy, etc. 2 strengthen or supply (an army, navy, etc.) with new men. 3 get (new members) by enrolling, hiring, etc. 4 increase or maintain the number of. 5 get a sufficient number or amount of; renew; replenish. —*v.i.* 1 get new men for an army, navy, etc. 2 renew health, strength, or spirits; recuperate. [< French *recrute, recrue* recruit(ing), new growth, ultimately < *re-* again + *croître* to grow] —**re cruit′er**, *n.* —**re cruit′ ment**, *n.*

re dun dant (ri dun′dənt), *adj.* 1 not needed; extra; superfluous. 2 that says the same thing again; using too many words for the same idea; wordy: *The use of "two" in the phrase "the two twins" is redundant.* [< Latin *redundantem* overflowing < *re-* back + *unda* wave] —**re dun′dant ly**, *adv.*

rel e vant (rel′ə vənt), *adj.* bearing upon or connected with the matter in hand; to the point. See **pertinent** for synonym study. [< Latin *relevantem* relieving, refreshing < *re-* back + *levis* light²]—**rel′e vant ly**, *adv.*

re me di al (ri mē′dē əl), *adj.* tending to relieve or cure; remedying; helping. —**re me′di al ly**, *adv.*

ren dez vous (rän′də vü), *n., pl.* **-vous** (-vüz), *v.*, **-voused** (-vüd), **-vous ing** (-vü′ing). —*n.* 1 an appointment or engagement to meet at a fixed place or time; meeting by agreement. 2 a meeting place; gathering place: *The family had two favorite rendezvous, the library and the garden.* 3 place agreed on for a meeting at a certain time, especially of troops or ships. 4 a meeting at a fixed place or time: *the rendezvous of a lunar module and the command ship.* —*v.i.* meet at a rendezvous.—*v.t.* bring together (troops, ships, space capsules, etc.) at a fixed place. [< Middle French < *rendez-vous* present yourself!]

re plen ish (ri plen′ish), *v.t.* fill again; provide a new supply for; renew: *replenish one's wardrobe. You had better replenish the fire.* [< Old French *repleniss-*, a form of *replenir*, fill again, ultimately < Latin *re-* again + *plenus* full] —**re plen′ish er**, *n.* —**re plen′ish ment**, *n.*

res o lu tion (rez′ə lü′shən), *n.* 1 thing decided on; thing determined: *I made a resolution to get up early.* 2 act of resolving or determining. 3 power of holding firmly to a purpose; determination. 4 a formal expression of the opinion or will of a deliberative or legislative body or other group: *a joint resolution of the Congress.* 5 a breaking into parts or components. 6 act or result of resolving a question, difficulty, etc.; answer or solution: *the resolution of a plot in a novel.* 7 (in medicine) the reduction or disappearance of inflammation without the formation of pus. 8 (in music) the progression of a voice part or of the harmony as a whole from a dissonance to a consonance. 9 (in optics) resolving power.

res pite (res′pit), *n., v.*, **-pit ed, -pit ing**. —*n.* 1 time of relief and rest; lull: *a respite from the heat.* 2 a putting off; delay, especially in carrying out a sentence of death; reprieve. —*v.t.* 1 give a respite to. 2 put off; postpone. [< Old French *respit* < Late Latin *respectus* expectation < Latin, regard. See RESPECT.]

re tal i ate (ri tal′ē āt), *v.i.*, **-at ed, -at ing**. pay back wrong, injury, etc.; return like for like, usually to return evil for evil: *If we insult them, they will retaliate.* [< Latin *retaliatum* paid back] —**re tal′i a′tion**, *n.*

rhet or ic (ret′ər ik), *n.* 1 art of using words effectively in speaking or writing. 2 book about this art. 3 mere display in language. [< Latin *rhetorica* < Greek *rhetorike (techne) (art)* of an orator < *rhetor* orator]

rick (rik), *n.* an outdoor stack of hay, straw, etc., especially one which is covered to protect it from rain. —*v.t.* form into a rick or ricks. [Old English *hreac*]

rit u al (rich′ü əl), *n.* 1 form or system of rites. The rites of baptism, marriage, and burial are parts of the ritual of most churches. 2 a prescribed order of performing a ceremony or rite. Secret societies have a ritual for initiating new members. 3 book containing rites or ceremonies. 4 the carrying out of rites. —*adj.* of or having to do with rites or rituals; done as a rite: *a ritual dance, ritual laws.* —**rit′u al ly**, *adv.*

S

sa dis tic (sə dis′tik), *adj.* of sadism or sadists. —**sa dis′ti cal ly**, *adv.*

sav vy (sav′ē), *v.*, **-vied, -vy ing**, *n.* SLANG. —*v.t., v.i.* know; understand. —*n.* understanding; intelligence; sense. [partly < French *savez-(vous)?* do you know?, partly < Spanish *sabe* or *sabes* you know; both ultimately < Latin *sapere* be wise]

sche ma (skē′mə), *n., pl.* **-ma ta** (-mə tə). 1 draft or outline of a plan, project, etc. 2 plan; scheme. [< Latin]

scho las tic (skə las′tik), *adj.* 1 of schools, scholars, or education; academic: *scholastic achievements, scholastic life.* 2 of or like scholasticism. 3 pedantic or formal. —*n.* 1 Often, **Scholastic**, person who favors scholasticism. 2 theologian and philosopher in the Middle Ages. —**scho las′ti cal ly**, *adv.*

scuff (skuf), *v.i.* walk without lifting the feet; shuffle. —*v.t.* wear or injure the surface of by hard use: *scuff one's shoes.* —*n.* 1 a scuffing. 2 kind of heelless slipper. [variant of *scuffle*]

sickle cell anemia, a hereditary form of anemia in which the normally round red blood cells become sickle cells, ineffective in carrying oxygen.

sig nif i cant (sig nif′ə kənt), *adj.* 1 full of meaning; important; of consequence: *July 4, 1776, is a significant date for Americans.* 2 having a meaning; expressive: *Smiles are significant of pleasure.* 3 having or expressing a hidden meaning: *A significant nod from my friend warned me to stop talking.* [< Latin *significantem* signifying] —**sig nif′i cant ly**, *adv.*

si mul ta ne ous (sī′məl tā′nē əs, sim′əl tā′nē əs), *adj.* 1 existing, done, or happening at the same time: *The two simultaneous shots sounded like one.* 2 indicating two or more equations or inequalities, with two or more unknowns, for which a set of values of the unknowns is sought that is a solution of all the equations or inequalities. [< Medieval Latin *simultaneus* simulated < Latin *similis* like; confused in sense with Latin *simul* at the same time] —**si′mul ta′ne ous ly**, *adv.* —**si′mul ta′ne ous ness**, *n.*

si ne die (sī′nē dī′ē), without a day specified for another meeting, trial, etc.; indefinitely: *The committee adjourned sine die.* [< Latin, without a day]

Soc ra tes (sok′rə tēz′), *n.* 469?–399 B.C., Athenian philosopher whose teachings were written down by his disciple Plato.

sole¹ (sōl), *adj.* 1 one and only; single: *the sole heir.* See **single** for synonym study. 2 only: *We three were the sole survivors.* 3 of or for only one person or group and not others; exclusive: *the sole right of use.* 4 without help; alone: *a sole undertaking.* [<Old French *soul* < Latin *solus*]

sole² (sōl), *n., v.*, **soled, sol ing**, —*n.* 1 the bottom or undersurface of the foot. 2 bottom of a shoe, slipper, boot, etc. 3 piece of leather, rubber, etc., cut in the same shape. 4 the undersurface; under part; bottom. *v.t.* put a sole on: *sole shoes.* [< Old French < Latin *solea* kind of sandal]

sole³ (sōl), *n., pl,* **soles** or **sole**. 1 any of a family of flatfishes having a small mouth and small, close-set eyes. European sole is valued highly as food. 2 any of certain related fishes. [< Old French, sole² (because of the flatness of the fish)]

som no lent (som′nə lənt), *adj.* 1 sleepy; drowsy. 2 tending to produce sleep. [< Latin *somnolentus* < *somnus* sleep] —**som′no lent ly**, *adv.*

so ci ol o gy (sō′sē ol′ə jē), *n.* study of the nature, origin, and development of human society and community life; science of social facts. Sociology deals with the facts of crime, poverty, marriage, the church, the school, etc. [< Latin *socius* companion + English *-logy*]

so lil o quy (sə lil′ə kwē), *n., pl.* **-quies**. 1 a talking to oneself. 2 speech made by an actor to himself when alone on the stage. It reveals his thoughts and feelings to the audience, but not to the other characters in the play. [< Late Latin *soliloquium* < Latin *solus* alone + *loqui* speak]

sor did (sôr′did), *adj.* 1 dirty; filthy: *live in a sordid hut.* 2 caring too much for money; meanly selfish; greedy. 3 mean; low; base; contemptible. 4 of a dull or dirty color. [< Latin *sordidus* dirty < *sordere* be dirty < *sordes* dirt] —**sor′did ly,** *adv.* —**sor′did ness,** *n.*

sov er eign (sov′rən), *n.* 1 supreme ruler; king or queen; monarch. 2 person, group, or nation having supreme control or dominion; master: *sovereign of the seas.* 3 a British gold coin, worth 20 shillings, or one pound. —*adj.* 1 having the rank or power of a sovereign. 2 greatest in rank or power. 3 independent of the control of other governments; supreme. 4 above all others; greatest: *Character is of sovereign importance.* 5 very excellent or powerful. [< Old French *soverain,* ultimately < Latin *super* over] —**sov′er eign ly,** *adv.*

sparse (spärs), *adj.,* **spars er, spars est.** 1 occurring here and there; thinly scattered: *a sparse population, sparse hair.* See **scanty** for synonym study. 2 scanty; meager. [< Latin *sparsum* scattered] —**sparse′ly,** *adv.* —**sparse′ness,** *n.*

spec i fy (spes′ə fī), *v.t.,* **-fied, -fy ing.** 1 mention or name definitely; state or describe in detail: *Did you specify any particular time for us to call?* 2 include in the specifications: *He delivered the paper as specified.* [< Late Latin *specificare* < *specificus.* See SPECIFIC.] —**spec′i fi′er,** *n.*

spec ta tor (spek′tā tər, spek tā′tər), *n.* person who looks on without taking part; observer; onlooker. [< Latin < *spectare* to watch < *specere* to view]

stag ger (stag′ər), *v.i.* 1 sway or reel (from weakness, a heavy load, or drunkenness); totter: *stagger under a heavy load of books.* See **reel**[2] for synonym study. 2 become unsteady; waver: *The troops staggered under the severe gunfire.* 3 hesitate. —*v.t.* 1 make sway or reel: *The blow staggered me for a moment.* 2 cause to doubt, hesitate, or falter. 3 confuse or astonish greatly; overshelm: *The difficulty of the examination staggered her.* 4 make helpless. 5 arrange in a zigzag order or way. 6 arrange at intervals or at other than the normal times: *stagger vacations in an office.* —*n.* 1 a swaying or reeling. 2 **staggers,** *pl.* nervous disease of horses, cattle, etc., that makes them stagger or fall suddenly. [< Scandinavian (Old Icelandic) *stakra*] —**stag′ger er,** *n.*

sta tus (stā′təs, stat′əs), *n.* 1 social or professional standing; position; rank: *lose status. What is her status in the government?* 2 state; condition: *Diplomats are interested in the status of world affairs.* [< Latin < *stare* to stand. Doublet of STATE.]

ster e o type (ster′ē ə tīp′, stir′ē ə tīp′), *n., v.,* **-typed, -typ ing.** —*n.* 1 method or process of making metal printing plates from a mold of composed type. 2 a printing plate cast from a mold. 3 a fixed form, character, image, etc.; conventional type. —*v.t.* 1 make a stereotype of. 2 print from stereotypes. 3 give a fixed or settled form to. —**ster′e o typ′er,** *n.*

ster ile (ster′əl), *adj.* 1 free from living germs or microorganisms: *keep surgical instruments sterile.* 2 not producing seed, offspring, crops, etc.: *sterile land, a sterile cow.* 3 not producing results: *sterile hopes.* 4 mentally or spiritually barren. [< Latin *sterilis*] —**ster′ile ly,** *adv.*

stra te gic (strə tē′jik), *adj.* 1 of strategy; based on strategy; useful in strategy: *a strategic retreat.* 2 important in strategy: *The Panama Canal is a strategic link in our national defense.* 3 of or having to do with raw material necessary for warfare which must be obtained, at least partially, from an outside country. 4 specially made or trained for destroying key enemy bases, industry, or communications behind the lines of battle: *a strategic bomber.* —**stra te′gi cal ly,** *adv.*

strat e gy (strat′ə jē), *n., pl.* **-gies.** 1 science or art of war; the planning and directing of military movements and operations. 2 the skillful planning and management of anything. 3 plan based on strategy. [< Greek *strategia* < *strategos* general < *stratos* army + *agein* to lead]

Strategy differs from **tactics.** *Strategy* refers to the overall plans of a nation at war. *Tactics* refers to the disposition of armed forces in combat.

sub con scious (sub kin′shəs), *adj.* not wholly conscious; existing in the mind but not fully perceived or recognized: *a subconscious fear.* —*n.* thoughts, feelings, etc., that are present in the mind but not fully perceived or recognized. —**sub con′scious ly,** *adv.*

a hat	i it	oi oil	ch child	a in about
ā age	ī ice	ou out	ng long	e in taken
ä far	o hot	u cup	sh she	ə = i in pencil
e let	ō open	u put	th thin	o in lemon
ē equal	ô order	ü rule	TH then	u in circus
er term			zh measure	< = derived from

sub se quent (sub′sə kwənt), *adj.* 1 coming after; following; later: *subsequent events.* 2 **subsequent to,** after; following; later than: *on the day subsequent to your call.* [< Latin *subsequentem* < *sub-* up to, near + *sequi* follow] —**sub′se quent ly,** *adv.* —**sub′se quent ness,** *n.*

suc cinct (sək singkt′), *adj.* expressed briefly and clearly; expressing much in few words; concise. See **concise** for synonym study. [< Latin *succinctum* girded up <*sub-* up + *cingere* to gird] —**suc cinct′ly,** *adv.* —**suc cinct′ness,** *n.*

suf fice (sə fīs′), *v.,* **-ficed, -fic ing,** —*v.i.* be enough; be sufficient: *The money will suffice for one year.* —*v.t.* make content; satisfy: *A small amount of cake sufficed the baby.* [< Latin *sufficere* < *sub-* near + *facere* to make]

su i cid al (sü′ə sī′dl), *adj.* 1 having to do with suicide; leading to suicide; causing suicide. 2 ruinous to one's own interests; disastrous to oneself: *It would be suicidal for a store to sell many things below cost.* —**su′i cid′al ly,** *adv.*

sul len (sul′ən), *adj.* 1 silent because of bad humor or anger: *The sullen child refused to answer my question.* See synonym study below. 2 showing bad humor or anger. 3 gloomy; dismal: *The sullen skies threatened rain.* [Middle English *soleine,* ultimately < Latin *solus* alone] —**sul′len ly,** *adv.* —**sul′len ness,** *n.* **Syn.** 1 **Sullen, sulky, glum** mean silent and bad-humored or gloomy. **Sullen** suggests an ill-natured refusal to talk or be cooperative because of anger or bad humor or disposition: *It is disagreeable to have to sit at the breakfast table with a sullen person.* **Sulky** suggests moody or childish sullenness because of resentment or discontent: *Dogs sometimes become sulky because they are jealous.* **Glum** emphasizes silence and low spirits because of some depressing condition or happening: *He is glum about the results of the election.*

sun dry (sun′drē), *adj.* several; various: *From sundry hints, I guessed I was to be given a bicycle for my birthday.* [Old English *syndrig* separate < *sundor* apart]

sup pli cant (sup′lə kənt), *adj., n.* suppliant. —**sup′pli cant ly,** *adv.*

su prem a cy (sə prem′ə sē, su preme′ə sē), *n.* 1 condition or quality of being supreme. 2 supreme authority or power.

sus cep ti ble (sə sep′tə bəl), *adj.* 1 easily influenced by feelings or emotions; very sensitive: *Poetry appealed to his susceptible nature.* See **sensitive** for synonym study. 2 **susceptible of, a** capable of receiving, undergoing, or being affected by: *Oak is susceptible of a high polish.* **b** sensitive to. 3 **susceptible to,** easily affected by; liable to; open to: *Vain people are susceptible to flattery.* [< Late Latin *susceptibilis,* ultimately < Latin *sub-* up + *capere* to take] —**sus cep′ti ble ness,** *n.* —**sus cep′ti bly,** *adv.*

syn drome (sin′drōm), *n.* group of signs and symptoms considered together as characteristic of a particular disease. [< Greek *syndrome* < *syndromos* running together < *syn-* together + *dramein* to run]

syn the size (sin′thə sīz), *v.t.,* **-sized, -siz ing.** 1 combine into a complex whole. 2 make up by combining parts or elements. 3 treat synthetically. —**syn′the siz′er,** *n.*

sy ringe (sə rinj′, sir′inj), *n., v.,* **-ringed, -ring ing.** —*n.* 1 a narrow tube fitted with a plunger or rubber bulb for drawing in a quantity of fluid and then forcing it out in a stream. Syringes are used for cleaning wounds, injecting fluids into the body, etc. 2 hypodermic syringe. —*v.t.* clean, wash, inject, etc., by means of a syringe. [< Greek *syrinx, syringos* shepherd's pipe]

T

tab loid (tab′loid), *n.* a newspaper, usually having half the ordinary size newspaper page, that has many pictures, short articles, and large, often sensational, headlines. —*adj.* in the form of a summary, capsule, or digest; condensed. [< *Tabloid,* trademark for drugs concentrated in tablets]

tam per (tam′pər), *v.i.* 1 meddle improperly; meddle: *Do not tamper with the lock.* See **meddle** for synonym study. 2 **tamper with, a** influence improperly; bribe, corrupt: *Crooked politicians had tampered with the jury.* **b** change so as to damage or falsify. [ultimately variant of *temper* —**tam′per er,** *n.*

tech ni cal (tek′nə kəl), *adj.* 1 of or having to do with a mechanical or industrial art or applied science: *This technical school trains engineers, chemists, and architects.* 2 of or having to do with the special facts of a science or art: *"Electrolysis," "tarsus," and "proteid" are technical words.* 3 treating a subject technically; using technical terms: *a technical lecture.* 4 of or having to do with technique: *Her singing shows technical skill, but her voice is weak.* 5 judged strictly by the rules; strictly interpreted. [< Greek *technikos* < *techne* art, skill, craft] —**tech′ni cal ly,** *adv.*

ten ta tive (ten′tə tiv), *adj.* 1 done as a trial or experiment; experimental: *a tentative plan.* 2 hesitating: *a tentative laugh.* [< Medieval Latin *tentativus* < Latin *tentare* to try] —**ten′ta tive ly,** *adv.* **ten′ta tive ness,** *n.*

the or ist (thē′ər ist), *n.* person who theorizes.

thwart (thwôrt), *v.t.* prevent from doing something, particularly by blocking the way; oppose and defeat: *Lack of money thwarted the boy's plans for college.* See **frustrate** for synonym study. —*n.* 1 seat across a boat, on which a rower sits. 2 brace between the gunwales of a canoe. —*adj.* lying or passing across. —*adv.* across; crosswise; athwart. [< Scandinavian (Old Icelandic) *thvert* across] —**thwart′er,** *n.*

toil¹ (toil), *n.* hard work; labor: *succeed after years of toil.* See **work** for synonym study. —*v.i.* 1 work hard. 2 move with difficulty, pain, or weariness: *They toiled up the steep mountain.* [< Old French *toeillier* drag about < Latin *tudiculare* stir up < *tudicula* olive press < *tudes* mallet] —**toil′er,** *n.*

toil² (toil), *n.* Often, **toils,** *pl.* net or snare: *The thief was caught in the toils of the law.* [< Middle French *toile* < Latin *tela* web < *texere* to weave]

tol e rate (tol′ə rāt′), *v.t.,* **-rat ed, -rat ing.** 1 allow or permit: *The teacher would not tolerate any disorder.* 2 bear; endure; put up with: *They tolerated the grouchy old man only out of kindness.* 3 endure or resist the action of (a drug, poison, etc.): *a person who cannot tolerate penicillin.* [< Latin *toleratum* tolerated]

trans form (tran sfôrm′), *v.t.* 1 change in form or appearance. 2 change in condition, nature, or character. See synonym study below. 3 change (one form of energy) into another. A dynamo transforms mechanical energy into electricity. 4 change (an electric current) to a higher or lower voltage, from alternating to direct current, or from direct to alternating current. 5 (in mathematics) to change (a figure, term, etc.) to another differing in form but having the same value or quantity. —*v.t.* be transformed; change. —**trans form′a ble,** *adj.* **Syn.** *v.t.* 2 **Transform, transmute, convert** mean to change the form, nature, substance, or state of something. **Transform** suggests a thoroughgoing or fundamental change in the appearance, shape, or nature of a thing or person: *Responsibility transformed him from a careless boy into a capable leader.* **Transmute** suggests a complete change in nature or substance, especially to a higher kind: *He thus transmuted disapproval into admiration.* **Convert** suggests a change from one state or condition to another, especially for a new use or purpose: *convert boxes into furniture.*

tran sient (tran′shənt), *adj.* 1 passing soon; fleeting; not lasting: *Joy and sorrow are often transient.* See **temporary** for synonym study. 2 passing through and not staying long: *a transient guest in a hotel.* —*n.* visitor or boarder who stays for a short time. [< Latin *transientem* going through < *trans-* + *ire* go] —**tran′sient ly,** *adv.*

trite (trīt), *adj.* **trit er, trit est,** worn out by use; no longer new or interesting; commonplace; hackneyed: *"Cheeks like roses" is a trite expression.* See **commonplace** for synonym study. [< Latin *tritum* rubbed away] —**trite′ly,** *adv.* —**trite′ness,** *n.*

triv i al (triv′ē əl), *adj.* 1 not important; trifling; insignificant. 2 ARCHAIC. not new or interesting; ordinary. [< Latin *trivialis,* originally, of the crossroads, ultimately < *tri-* three + *via* road] —**triv′i al ly,** *adv.*

U

u ter us (yü′tər əs), *n., pl.* **u ter i** (yü′tə rī′). 1 the organ of the body in most female mammals that holds and nourishes the young till birth; womb. 21 a corresponding part in lower animals. [< Latin]

V

va gar y (və ger′ē, vā′gər ē), *n., pl.* **—gar ies.** 1 an odd fancy; extravagant notion: *the vagaries of a dream.* 2 odd action; caprice; freak: *the vagaries of women's fashions.* [probably < Latin *vagari* wander < *vagus* rambling]

va gran cy (vā′grən sē), *n., pl.* **-cies.** 1 wandering idly from place to place without proper means or ability to earn a living: *The beggar was arrested for vagrancy.* 2 a wandering. 3 a vagrant act or idea.

va por (vā′pər), *n.* 1 moisture in the air that can be seen, such as steam, fog, mist, etc., usually due to the effect of heat upon a liquid. 2 gas formed from a substance that is usually a liquid or a solid; the gaseous form of a liquid or solid. 3 something without substance; empty fancy. 4 **the vapors,** ARCHAIC, low spirits. —*v.t.* 1 cause to rise or ascend in the form of vapor. 2 boast; swagger; brag. —*v.i.* 1 rise, ascend, or pass off as vapor. 2 give or send out vapor. 3 boast; swagger; brag. [< Latin] —**va′por er,** *n.*

var i a ble (ver′ē ə bəl, var′ē ə bəl), *adj.* 1 apt to change; changeable; uncertain: *variable winds.* 2 likely to shift from one opinion or course of action to another; inconsistent. 3 that can be varied: *curtain rods of variable length.* 4 deviating from the normal or recognized species, variety, structure, etc. 5 likely to increase or decrease in size, number, amount, degree, etc.; not remaining the same or uniform: *a constant or variable ratio.* —*n.* 1 thing or quality that varies. 2 in mathematics: **a** a quantity that can assume any of the values in a given set of values. **b** symbol representing this quantity. 3 a shifting wind. —**var′i a ble ness,** *n.* —**var′i a bly,** *adv.*

ver bal (ver′bəl), *adj.* 1 in words; of words: *A description is a verbal picture.* 2 expressed in spoken words; oral: *a verbal promise, a verbal message.* 3 word for word; literal: *a verbal translation from the French.* 4 having to do with a verb. Two common verbal endings are *-ed* and *-ing.* 5 derived from a verb: *a verbal adjective.* —*n.* noun, adjective, or other word derived from a verb. —**ver′bal ly,** *adv.* See **oral** for usage note.

ves tige (ves′tij), *n.* 1 a slight remnant; trace; mark: *Ghost stories are vestiges of a former widespread belief in ghosts.* See **trace¹** for synonym study. 2 (in biology) a part, organ, etc., that is no longer fully developed or useful but performed a definite function in an earlier stage of the existence of the same organism or in lower preceding organisms. 3 RARE. footprint or track. [< French < Latin *vestigium* footprint]

vi cis si tude (və sis′ə tüd, və sis′ə tyüd), *n.* 1 change in circumstances, fortune, etc.: *The vicissitudes of life may suddenly make a rich man very poor.* 2 change; variation. 3 regular change: *the vicissitude of day and night.* [< Latin *vicissitudo* < *vicis* turn, change]

vic tim ize (vik′tə mīz), *v.t.,* **-ized, iz ing.** 1 make a victim of; cause to suffer. 2 cheat; swindle. —**vic′tim i za′tion,** *n.* —**vic′tim iz′er,** *n.*

vig il (vij′əl), *n.* 1 a staying awake for some purpose; a watching; watch: *All night the mother kept vigil over the sick child.* 2 a night spent in prayer. 3 **vigils,** *pl.* devotions, prayers, services, etc., on the night before a religious festival. 4 the day and night before a solemn religious festival. [< Latin *vigilia* < *vigil* watchful]

vig or ous (vig′ər əs), *adj.* full of vigor; strong and active; energetic; forceful: *wage a vigorous war against disease.* —**vig′or ous ly,** *adv.* —**vig′or ous ness,** *n.*

vo ca tion al (vō kā′shə nəl), *adj.* 1 of or having to do with some occupation, business, profession, or trade. 2 of or having to do with studies or training for some occupation, etc.: *vocational guidance.* —**vo ca′tion al ly,** *adv.*

Glossary

abstract: A listing of books and articles that gives brief descriptions or summaries of the materials and tells where to find them.

acoustic segment: A portion of sound that can be identified by listeners.

affixes: Word prefixes and suffixes.

amniocentesis: The procedure in which amniotic fluid is extracted from the amniotic sac and then checked to learn if the fetus is genetically abnormal.

amnion: The sac in which the embryo is suspended.

amniotic fluid: The fluid that fills the amnion and surrounds the child before birth.

articulatory features: Properties of speech sounds.

bandwagon approach: A propaganda technique that attempts to convince people to do something by implying that everyone else is doing it.

bar graph: A graph that uses rectangular bars of different lengths to show relationships of size or quantity.

basal metabolism: The least amount of energy required to maintain the life of an organism at rest.

bronc: Short for *bronco*, a wild horse of North America.

capacity limitation: The ability of humans to attend consciously to only one thing at a time.

card-stacking: A propaganda technique that presents only those facts that support the argument in question.

careful reading: The slowest kind of reading; used to master difficult material at rates of 50 to 350 words per minute.

caveat emptor: A Latin phrase meaning "let the buyer beware."

context: The general background or situation of something. In reading, *context* refers to the letters, words, and longer units of written language surrounding a letter, word, or sentence.

context clue: The surrounding words and sentences that help the reader to determine the pronunciation or meaning of a word.

decision symbol: The symbol in a flow chart that asks a question that is answered by a "yes" or a "no."

direct aggression: An attack against the true source of one's frustration.

displaced aggression: An attack against something other than the true source of one's frustration; an example of this exists when an adult hits a child out of frustration over problems at his or her place of work.

entry word: The words one looks up in the dictionary; they are usually in bold print.

Fallopian tube: Either of two slender tubes that carry ova from the ovaries to the uterus.

feedback loop: In a model or diagram a loop that recycles part of the output of the model as additional input.

fetologist: An expert on fetuses.

fetus: The unborn child after about three months of development.

flattery: A propaganda technique that appeals to an individual's desire to be special or important by implying that the individual is superior.

flowchart: A graphic representation of information that shows the steps to follow to solve a problem or attain a goal.

flowlines: The lines on a flowchart that indicate the order in which steps or processes occur.

gazetteer: A geographical dictionary.

genetic therapy: A form of therapy that attempts to prevent birth defects or cure diseases by the manipulation or removal of defective genes.

glittering generality: A propaganda technique that uses vague, nice-sounding words to praise a person, idea, or product.

graphic comprehension: The ability to understand maps, charts, graphs, and other pictorial presentations of information.

hierarchical chart: A chart that shows the relationships among a group of related things which differ in importance. For example, in a hierarchial chart of animal intelligence, monkeys and dogs would be higher than roaches and rats.

hydrologic cycle: The process by which water falls to the earth's surface, accumulates, is converted into vapor, and is absorbed by the atmosphere until it returns again as precipitation.

humidifier: A machine used to add moisture to dry air.

input/output symbol: The symbol on a flowchart that shows what information is needed to solve a problem.

interest group: A group of people who try to get other people to serve their own special needs.

Library of Congress Classification System: The system used by most colleges and universities to classify, shelve, and locate books, periodicals, and other materials.

life change units: A way of estimating the stress placed on an individual by life changes such as divorce, vacation, and taking out a loan.

main idea: The general meaning of something. In reading it can be thought of as: 1) the topic of a passage, 2) a good title for a passage, 3) the most important statement in a passage, or 4) an important generalization that summarizes the major significance of a passage.

metabolic: Refers to body metabolism, the combined processes that convert food into heat, energy, growth, and activity.

microcards: Opaque 3″ × 5″ cards which may have printing on both sides and required magnification for reading.

microfiche: Transparent 4″ × 6″ cards containing print that has been reduced in size 24 times.

microfilm: 16-mm or 35-mm filmstrips that contain printed material.

mitosis: The process of cell division.

mnemonics: Techniques used to aid memory.

mortuary science: The methods and techniques used in preparing the dead for burial.

name calling: A propaganda technique which uses emotionally charged "bad names" to arouse feelings of fear and hate.

negative reinforcement: The removal of an unpleasant stimulus in order to strengthen or encourage a desired behavior. For example, if the behavior to be strengthened is pushing a lever, a rat in a cage with an electrified-wire floor will come to engage in more lever pushing if the pushing of the lever turns off the electric shock.

oligopoletic competition: In business, competition that occurs when there are only a few sellers.

ontogeny: The development of a single organism.

overlearning: The continued study of material which an individual has already mastered.

PARR: A notetaking system consisting of the following steps: Prepare, Abbreviate, Revise, and Review.

phenylketonuria: A hereditary disease that results in mental and physical disability if not treated by a special diet during infancy.

phoneme: A unit of sound in a language.

phonological: Having to do with speech sounds.

phylogeny: The evolutionary development of a species of animals or plants.

physical map: A map that shows the natural features of a region, such as mountains and rivers.

pie chart: A chart that uses a circle to present information with the whole circle equaling 100% and each part representing a portion of the whole.

plain folks: A propaganda technique that attempts to gain people's confidence by making them feel that the person seeking support is similar to them.

political map: A map that shows governmental borders, cities, and only the most important physical features.

polyphasic thought: Thinking about two or more things at the same time.

pneumonoultramicroscopicsilicovolcanoconiosis: A lung disease caused by the inhalation of silicon dust.

positive reinforcement: The application of a pleasant stimulus in order to strengthen or encourage a desired behavior. For example, if an instructor praises students for attempting to give creative answers in class, an increase in the number of creative attempts by students should result.

PQMR: A strategy for studying textbooks; it consists of: Previewing, Questioning, Marking, and Reviewing.

primitivation: Regression to a primitive behavior such as thumb-sucking.

process chart: A drawing that shows the steps of a particular procedure.

process symbol: The symbol in a flowchart that tells what action must be taken to get a desired result.

punishment: The application of an unpleasant stimulus to discourage a particular behavior.

pursuit eye movement: The smooth movement of the eyes as they follow a moving target.

rapid reading: The continuous reading of simple material at a rate of 300 to 600 words per minute.

regression: The temporary return to an earlier, more primitive behavior. For example, under severe stress adults may throw temper tantrums or bite their nails.

Reconstruction: The period in American history after the Civil War.

repression: The unconscious blotting out of thoughts or desires.

retroactive inhibition: A form of negative transfer in which information already in the memory is blocked by more recently acquired information.

retrogressive behavior: Behavior that is characteristic of an earlier period in an individual's life; for example, thumb-sucking in an adult.

rhesus monkey: An Indian monkey commonly used in medical research.

Roberts Rules of Order: A standard set of rules for conducting meetings according to parliamentary procedure.

saccadic eye movements: The jerky motions of the eyes as they move from one stationary target to another.

scanning: The fastest type of reading in which the eyes search for a single word or phrase at rates of up to 3000 words per minute but without comprehension of the text.

selective attention: The process of blocking out all other external stimuli so that attention can be focused on one thing.

sexual response cycle: The pattern of sexual response in humans, consisting of four phases: excitement, plateau, orgasm, and resolution.

sexuality: According to Freud, the entire love life of the individual and all the gratifications that are necessary to his or her well-being.

skimming: A form of rapid reading in which the objective is to pick up main ideas and a few details while skipping most of the material.

social readjustment rating scale: A questionnaire devised by Holmes and Rahe to assess the amount of coping required to adjust to various events.

special feature map: A map that shows a particular feature of an area, for example, rivers.

stereotypy: A fixed, repetitive form of behavior.

stimulus: Something that excites the senses or brings about a behavior. For example, the smell of food (the *stimulus*) will cause a hungry college student to salivate (the behavior).

study sense: Common sense applied to study habits.

sublimation: 1. The process by which ice is changed into water vapor. 2. The expression of unacceptable impulses in acceptable ways, often unconsciously.

suboptimization: A procedure that sacrifices the attainment of one goal so that another goal may be achieved. For example, a child genius may intentionally perform poorly on exams in order to appear more like other children.

suppression: The conscious, deliberate attempt to control thoughts or behaviors.

surface structure: The grammatical relationships among words, phrases, and clauses in spoken or written language.

terminal symbol: The symbol in a flow chart that indicates the starting point and the end point.

testimonial: A propaganda technique in which a well-known person promotes a person, cause, or product outside his or her area of expertise.

testwiseness: The ability to maximize test performance by using organization principles and common sense.

topic sentence: The most important statement in a passage.

transfer: A propaganda technique in which characteristics of one person or object are conveyed to another.

transpiration: The process by which plants release water vapor into the air through their pores.

tree diagram: A hierarchial chart that has branches like a tree.

zygote: The cell produced by the union of two gametes or germ cells. In humans the zygote results when the sperm cell penetrates the egg cell.

Index

Notes

Notes

Notes

Notes